Stories and Stone

Stories and Stone

Writing the Ancestral Pueblo Homeland

edited by Reuben Ellis

The University of Arizona Press
Tucson

To my dear wife and friend, Linda Dove, with whom ancient places seem new.

The University of Arizona Press
© 1997 by Reuben Ellis
First University of Arizona Press paperbound edition 2004
All rights reserved
∞ This book printed on acid-free, archival-quality paper.
Manufactured in the United States of America.

09 08 07 06 05 04   6 5 4 3 2 1

Library of Congress Cataloging-in-Publication data

Stories and stone : writing the ancestral Pueblo homeland / edited by Reuben Ellis.
p. cm.
Originally published : Stories and Stone : Writing the Anasazi Homeland / edited and
with an introduction by Reuben Ellis. Boulder, CO.: Pruett Publishing Co.
Includes bibliographical references.
ISBN 0-8165-2366-5 (Paper : alk. paper)
1. American literature—Southwestern States. 2. Southwestern States—Literary collections. 3. Prehistoric peoples—Literary collections. 4. Southwestern States—Literary collections. 5. Pueblo Indians—Literary collections. 6. Landscape—Literary collections.
I. Ellis, Reuben J., 1955–
PS566.S86 2003
810.8'03278—dc22
2003024934
CIP

A Note on the Term *Anasazi*

Anasazi is the Navajo name for a farming people who lived in the Four Corners region between A.D. 1 and A.D. 1300. Their descendants, the Pueblo Indians of New Mexico and
Arizona, prefer the name *Ancestral Pueblo* rather than *Anasazi* in reference to their ancestors. Due to its extensive use throughout the book, however, it was not practical to revise
the term in this reprint edition.

Contents

Acknowledgments

For making possible this reissue of *Stories and Stone,* I would like to thank Patti Hartmann and the University of Arizona Press and Jim Pruett at Pruett Publishing Company. I would also like to express my appreciation to all the many students at Prescott College, in the classroom and in the field, who have helped inspire my ongoing interest in this book and who have convinced me to keep it alive. Thanks to my dad and to my mom, who by the way is my best publicist, and to Linda for her love, companionship, and spirited, good-humored conversation.

Key to sites on map

(1) Bandelier National Monument

(2) Barrier Canyon

(3) Bright Angel Pueblo

(4) Canyon de Chelly National Monument

(5) Casa Grande Ruins National Monument
      (Arizona)

(6) Casas Grandes (Mexico)

(7) Chaco Culture National Historical Park

(8) Chinle Wash

(9) Grand Gulch Primitive Area

(10) Fitzmaurice Ruin

(11) Hopi Mesa Area

(12) Hovenweep National Monument

(13) Mesa Verde National Park

(14) Montezuma Castle National Monument

(15) Navajo National Monument

(16) Quarai Ruins

(17) Ute Mountain Tribal Park

(18) Village of the Great Kivas

(19) Walnut Canyon National Monument

Introduction: Stories and Stone

The eastern rimrock was only barely visible against the sky when I awoke in a canyon deep within the desert of New Mexico. I climbed out of my sleeping bag and dressed in the bed of the pickup. There was no time for coffee this morning. By noon the bottom of the wash would be 104 degrees. This was the good time, and I wanted to get moving before the temperature started to rise. I filled my water bottles from the five-gallon can, checked the pressure of the tires, and rode out of camp. At the trailhead I turned off the pavement and rode up the double-track dirt road. I remember the silence of those mornings, the low hum of the mountain bike tires, the revolutions of the chain around the rings as I pedaled, the sound of my own breathing. I had been alone in the canyon for a couple of days, avoiding the few other visitors, riding early and late to stay out of the heat, holing up in the deep shade of the ruins during the middle of the day. I was becoming the only one there, and the sound of my own voice was growing steadily quieter but more surprising to my ear.

From the grayness, the soft haze of light above the fringe of sagebrush, the rock-and-adobe walls became visible as I approached. As the first thin line of sun washed over the ruins, the windows and entryways in the mortared rock opened to an ancient way of life. Although sage and cactus now grew where walls once stood, for me this was still a living place, a place where past and present meet and coexist. If T. S. Eliot in the *The Waste Land* saw London as the "Unreal City," surely this on the other hand was *real*—overgrown, eroded, with the dark colors and textures of this near, local place. I stopped the bicycle and let it fall over into the sand as I walked the last few yards into the complex of walls that make up the abandoned townscape of the pueblo. These were the walls I would walk beside, the rooms I would enter and sit within. As I had yesterday, and the day before, I would take the time to be in this place, to be quiet and alone. I walked into a small square room. The walls were shoulder-high. The roof, once of Douglas fir or piñon, was gone.

In the Park Service pamphlets and the coffeetable books, the masonry walls of the ancient pueblos of the Anasazi, spread throughout the Four Corners region of the American Southwest, are places to explore and protect—beautiful, stirring, a little

mysterious. In the scientific literature, they are richly important data. To the human-
ist, they are thematically suggestive and intellectually challenging. To the New Age
spiritual seeker, they are power spots. In my AAA guidebook they are vacation desti-
nations, recreational sites. When a Hopi elder speaks of them, they are mythically
present, historical because the story of their past continues to be told and told again.
At their tallest, they rise four stories; at their lowest, they barely protrude from rubble
and talus. The solidity and mass of stone, its participation in the substance of earth,
the articulated and detailed designs of the masonry facings, the scope and preconcep-
tion of the construction, the human events of occupation and abandonment implied
in the buildings—all these create the presence and integrity of the ruins.

The silence here is not really silence but rather part of the intricate language of
the people we have come to call *Anasazi*. They built this place and lived whole lives
here—noisy, complicated, unresolved human lives. But what they left us is a quiet language of what anthropologists call "material culture"—masonry walls, ceramic bowls,
burial sites, as well as intricate petroglyphs and pictographs, complex and beautiful
images carved or painted on rock depicting animals, plants, and headdressed humans.

I call this a language because the material culture of the ancients continues to
speak to us. In the rock art we find on the sandstone walls at ancient sites, for example, we intuitively look for story, the moments in time the images seem to record. We
imagine the events the ancient artist represented while standing high on an earthen
wall, carving with a sharpened stone or applying pigments to the rock. Though it may
seem a little less obvious to think of ruined walls as story, they too speak the quiet language of the ancients. A couple of years ago I heard Zuni artist Alex Seowtewa speak
at a conference in Sault Sainte Marie, in Michigan. In a talk that was mostly about
Zuni mural painting and the restoration of the mission church at the pueblo, Seowtewa seemed to digress when he told a brief story about an abandoned pueblo at Zuni.
He explained how four small dark stones had been set in the masonry of one of the
walls. The builder, he concluded, had wanted to remember four things that had happened to him. I've thought a lot about that remark and have come to see its insight.
For Seowtewa, the connection between building, memory, and storytelling was clear
and necessary. The reminder of the stones might have prompted the builders to keep
alive important events. Small children living in the pueblo a thousand years ago may
have asked their parents to tell again the stories of the stones.

For most of us today the ruins themselves take the place of that storytelling. The
four stones tell us that once there were four cherished memories, but they do not spin
the tales in the voice of someone we know. Perhaps for this reason Benjamin Wetherill

called the ancient ruins of the Southwest "symbols of the past," evidence that can only represent what might have been and prompt our own careful imagining. Buildings, after all, are made like good stories. I see this in the masonry of ancient ruins. Like a good story, the construction of stone walls too is a matter of field and line, relation and connection—courses of blocks, linear and temporal in their authorship, form, and reception, one stone following another horizontally, one course going up on top of another, just as a writer builds on events, character, and plot to create layers of meaning within a story. Terry Tempest Williams, in her essay reprinted here, even sees ancient potsherds and flaked stone within the context of language. "Stories. More stories," she writes. "If these artifacts are lifted from their birthplace they cease to speak." Rock art, ruins, flaked obsidian—stories and stone.

In trying to understand in some personal, felt, but honest terms the stories left behind by the Anasazi, we find ourselves in interesting company. From the 1870s, when the first geological surveys began sending photographs of Anasazi ruins back to American newspapers in the East, explorers, archaeologists, and tourists alike have marveled at the ruins, burial sites, artifacts, and rock art left behind by the Anasazi, appropriating them variously as scientific evidence, commercial resource, art, and touchstone to an imagined, romantic, and maybe simpler time. Indeed, the stories lodged in the stone of Anasazi culture have inspired other stories, a relatively old (by Euro-American standards) and growing body of writing that has been informed by the experience of the ruins. John Wesley Powell, Adolf Bandelier, Ernest Ingersoll, Charles F. Lummis, Willa Cather, Mary Austin, D. H. Lawrence, Frank Cushing, D'Arcy McNickle, Gerald Vizenor, Gary Snyder, Barry Lopez, Louis L'Amour, Tony Hillerman—these are writers we mostly think of in terms of other subjects: nature writing, modernism, contemporary Native Americans, poetry, cowboy novels, even detective fiction. But each of them has spent time walking among ruins, scanning the images of petroglyphs, and thinking about the Anasazi. There are others too. In fact, dozens of writers, mostly American, have recorded their perceptions, their best guesses, their refective experiences of the Anasazi in their work. The scope of this small, striking body of literature is wide: the novel, the personal essay, the short story, memoir, poetry, pieces that can't really be labeled at all.

Stories and Stone is a survey of this canon. A collection of stories about stories, the book's eight sections give shape to the varied ways that writers have experienced and described the ancient sites of the Southwest: Imagining in human terms how the ancients lived, exploring and traveling through new terrain, excavating ruin sites for scientific knowledge, reflecting on the broad meaning of the ruins, dealing with the contemporary social and political issues the ruins suggest, seeking a meaningful and ethical way of life in the homeland of the Anasazi, and appreciating the rugged desert landscape the Anasazi called home. The final section provides readers with a guide to visiting the ancient places mentioned by the authors assembled here, suggestions for "reading in place"—for exploring the wonderful relationship between words on a page and the more personal experience with the places they reveal.

Stories and Stone illustrates the profound and various influence of Anasazi culture on the men and women who stumbled across and later sought out the remnants of this ancient way of life. At best, the Anasazi have inspired and admonished visitors to try to understand a culture different from their own, to learn how humans developed successful ways of living within the environment of the American Southwest long before the arrival of Europeans. For many Native Americans, understanding the Anasazi has provided a meaningful link to their ancestry, traditions, and indigenousness.

The reactions of some non–Native Americans, however, to the ruins and rock art sites of the Southwest have been in some cases less than admirable or enduring. Mystified, some visitors have recoiled from the perceived strangeness of the ancients to the comfort of the values and present moment of their own experiences. Some have looked at the creations of ancient culture and wondered what was in it for them. Reading the many and varied ways that writers have responded to the Anasazi suggests in a larger sense the full complexity of human response to the American experience, the ways in which we can or cannot make connections to the past, to place and landscape, and to other peoples.

Archaeologist Alfred Kidder used to tell the story that one day, early in the century, he and Jesse Nusbaum made a harrowing climb to a cliff dwelling on a narrow ledge below the mesa top. Thinking they might have been the first in centuries to stand on the ledge, they were surprised to find an inscription on a sandstone slab. "What fools these mortals be," the letters spelled. The incription was signed "R. Wetherill," the name of the rancher and pioneer excavator of Mesa Verde. Appropriately enough, Wetherill had borrowed from Shakespeare to make meaning of his discovery. Richard Wetherill also left behind a series of newspaper articles and letters while his brother Benjamin A. ("Al") Wetherill fancied himself something of a poet. One of Al's more vivid but perhaps happily unpublished quatrains on the subject of the ancients reads:

Mud balls on the arching roof still show where children played.
Hand prints in the plaster soft, a thousand years have stayed.

Mother catches soon the youngster and we can almost hear him squall
As she paddles with her sandal where there are no pants at all.

The sense of comic history that Al Wetherill infuses into the mysterious ruins was a long time in coming. The first accounts we have of the Anasazi, early sixteenth-century exploration narratives, record mainly European disappointment that only ruins remained where fabled golden cities were expected. Later, ruins and rock art often appear in American literature detailing the uniqueness of the American setting, recalling Emerson's injunction that American writers draw upon their own native materials in composing a specifically national literature. In nineteenth- and early twentieth-century exploration literature they are markers of scientific inquiry and inventory. Sometimes the Anasazi were (as they continue to be) signs of a romantic, idealized past, sometimes elements of a specifically regional landscape, sometimes background to "local color" settings or objects of personal ambition. In this century, as in the works of Willa Cather, writing about the Anasazi and the ruins they left behind suggests both a philosophical continuity and a profound disjunction between modern and ancient life. Within the twentieth century's extension of the tradition of nineteenth-century transcendental nature writing, the ancients have figured prominently in the natural and historical landscape in the works of Mary Austin, John Van Dyke, and more recently Edward Abbey, Barry Lopez, and Ann Zwinger.

Most of the authors included in *Stories and Stone* are Euro-American, but since the 1950s a growing number of Native American writers, including D'Arcy McNickle, Leslie Marmon Silko, Simon Ortiz, and Wendy Rose, have drawn upon the Anasazi in their work as well, looking with a careful, respectful eye into the traditions of their own cultures. In recent years, the volume of writings about the Anasazi has increased noticeably, reflecting the growing number of people who have learned about the Southwest and its indigenous inhabitants. In general, the minor renaissance in western writing we see today continues the development of a more sensitive and accurate awareness of the Anasazi in the context of Native American traditions as well as in the broader context of American experience. I see this, for example, in the work of Reg Saner, Terry Tempest Williams, Dick Fleck, Ann Weiler Walka, and in the writing and photography of Bruce Hucko.

Representations of the Anasazi span all genres, appearing in autobiography, nonfiction narrative, the familiar essay, poetry, drama, and fiction. Some of the selections in *Stories and Stone* are more "literary" than others. Some of them are written by established authors, while others are written by men and women whose authority resides in other areas. For those familiar with writing about the Anasazi, there may seem to be egregious omissions here, and unlikely inclusions. We all make our own lists, I guess.

So who were the Anasazi? They were a particular people at a particular time in a wonderful place. The term *Anasazi* refers to a sophisticated Native American agrarian cultural continuum that developed in what today is known as the Four Corners region through several distinguishable stages, from at least 200 B.C. to the modern era. Early in the fourteenth century the Anasazi dispersed to become the Pueblo cultures we know today. When drought and erosion forced the Anasazi to migrate to the south and east, they left behind extensive rock art and masonry pueblo villages, some including over eight hundred rooms and suggesting populations of hundreds, or even thousands, of individuals.

While Christian Europe was pursuing its Crusades in the Holy Land, Anasazi farmers were raising corn, beans, and squash in mesa-top and canyon-bottom fields and maintaining elaborate social and religious practices that survive today among the Puebloans of the Southwest. Anasazi women were constructing extensive multistoried pueblo village complexes, and Anasazi engineers were building networks of roads extending for hundreds of miles within a trading system that reached as far as the Valley of Mexico. Today the ruins of this once extensive cultural continuum are found in four western states. San Juan County in southern Utah alone has thousands of identified Anasazi sites.

The ancestors of the Anasazi and other early southwestern peoples are thought to have come into the region sometime after 9000 B.C. They are known as paleohunters. They were nomads and wanderers and left behind Clovis-style projectile points embedded in the bones of the animals they killed, mammoths and bison. Although early peoples in the Southwest continued to rely on hunting and gathering to survive, domesticated corn reached the region from the Valley of Mexico sometime after 1500 B.C., and agriculture developed as a way of life. People began to stay put for part of the year, waiting for the corn to grow.

Several overlapping cultural groups developed: the Anasazi on the high desert, mesas, and canyons of the Colorado Plateau of northern New Mexico, Utah, Arizona, and southern Colorado; the Mogollon in the mountains of eastern Arizona and southwestern New Mexico; the Hohokam in the Sonoran Desert west of the Mogollon; the Sinagua east of the Verde River in central Arizona; and the Salado in the upper Salt River Valley east of Phoenix. Never self-contained or fully distinct, these peoples lived and developed in parallel, adapting in comparable ways to the demands of their specific environments, sharing technology and other cultural traits and trading commodities and what they knew. Later, the *Na-Dene*–speaking peoples, who would be called the Apaches and the Navajo by Europeans, arrived from the north, coexisting uneasily with the more settled Anasazi, sometimes raiding and sometimes trading with them.

Of these five cultural groups, the Anasazi was the most geographically extensive, inhabiting the full range of the Four Corners area. Moreover, it is this early culture that has entered most prominently into our twentieth-century awareness and popular imagination. When most of us think of the prehistoric people of the Southwest, images of the "cliff dwellers"—the Anasazi—come first to mind.

When novelist Henry Miller describes the rugged and primal landscape of the California coast in his *Big Sur and the Oranges of Hieronymus Bosch*, he dismisses Native Americans as late and largely inconsequential arrivals. "There are no ruins or relics to speak of," he writes. Miller's remark does not hold true of the Anasazi. In fact, the evidence the Anasazi left behind of their material culture is extensive. To survive as an agricultural people in the harsh arid climate of the Southwest, the Anasazi crafted digging sticks from the horns of mountain sheep and excavated check dams and catchment basins to trap the water that ran off the slickrock of the mesas. Anasazi artists recorded their cultural values in rock art panels hundreds of feet in length. The Anasazi pueblos at Chaco, Aztec, and Salmon, among others, were preplanned masonry structures, faced with or built entirely of dressed stones. Many of the walls have survived for eight hundred years and still rise precisely and vertically from the desert floor. Most pueblos include several distinctive chambers built partially underground, usually round in shape, and often with mural-decorated walls. Like those in use today in the pueblos of New Mexico and Arizona, these structures were *kivas,* or ceremonial chambers, the centers of Anasazi religious and community life. It was in the kiva that clan or sacred society members would gather for ritual observations around a central fire pit. The *sipapu,* a small hole in the floor of the kiva, represented the "earth navel," or point of human emergence into the world. The limited insights we have into Anasazi culture are mere glimpses of the depth and richness of its experience.

The common use of the generalized term *Anasazi* to describe this culture and its material remains tends to overlook diversity and chronological development. Archaeologists have developed a complex classification system over the years to help them understand this diversity. This system, known as the Pecos Classification, identifies eight stages of development: Basketmaker I–III and Pueblo I–V. During the Basketmaker stages I–III (200 B.C. to A.D. 700), named for the tightly woven baskets found in cave dwellings, the Anasazi lived first in relatively small groups mostly as hunters and gatherers. Cave dwellings gave way to partially underground pit houses, and agriculture increased. Life became more stationary, and utilitarian pottery slowly replaced basketry for many everyday functions.

Pit houses gradually were abandoned for above ground housing blocks, or *pueblos,* during the Pueblo stages I–V (A.D. 700 to the present) as the Anasazi became increasingly dependent on agriculture and as the social organization farming required resulted in larger village populations. Anasazi potters made an increasing variety of pottery types. Sometimes called the "classic" period of the Anasazi, the Pueblo III stage (A.D. 1100 to 1300) best represents the Anasazi as we most often think of them—living in large masonry pueblos of several stories, some built in cliff alcoves like Betatakin or Balcony House, some built on open ground like Lowry, Aztec, or Pueblo Bonito. Trade increased, and polychrome pottery appeared during this period.

Climate change, erosion of agricultural land, and possibly the hostility of neighboring nomadic peoples marked the end of the classic period of Anasazi culture, and by the end of the thirteenth century large areas of Anasazi territory had been abandoned. From about 1150 a prolonged drought began to change Anasazi culture forever. The Anasazi built fewer but larger pueblos, some housing over a thousand persons. Many were constructed seemingly with defense from attack in mind, often in natural rock alcoves beneath sheer cliffs. During this late Pueblo period, the Anasazi began to move south and east, abandoning their former dwellings, possibly searching for more stable environmental conditions and water sources that would more readily and predictably sustain agriculture. The period after 1300 until the time of first European contact is often regarded as an era of general cultural decline and regression among the Anasazi, although it may be just as useful to see it as yet another period of development and adaptation during which the Anasazi gradually dispersed into smaller culturally distinct communities. When the Spanish came to the Southwest, they found the less numerous Apache and Navajo living on lands left behind by the Anasazi and the probable descendents of the Anasazi thriving at Zuni, Acoma, the Hopi Mesas and along the Rio Grande in central New Mexico.

In addition to this chronological analysis, anthropologists classify Anasazi culture geographically as well, today distinguishing six principal divisions identified by cultural traits and area: Chaco, Mesa Verde, Rio Grande, Little Colorado, Kayenta, and Fremont. In addition to the Anasazi are the related Hohokam, Mogollon, Sinagua, and Salado cultures, also distinguished by the regions of their habitation. At some sites these subcultural distinctions are expressed chronologically, as at Salmon Ruins in New Mexico, where Chacoan structures supplant earlier Mesa Verdean ones within single building complexes. Today, the ruins of this once extensive cultural continuum are found in four states, throughout an area of 100,000 square miles. Chaco Canyon in northwest New Mexico contains nine "Great House" pueblos and hundreds of smaller structures, totaling thousands of individual rooms. Archaeologists have estimated that 200,000 logs brought by the Anasazi without benefit of draft animals or the wheel from as far as twenty-five miles away, were used in the construction of the buildings at Chaco.

The first European visitors to the ancient sites of the Southwest were Spanish explorers in the sixteenth century. The expedition of Francisco Vasquez de Coronado left Mexico City in 1540 and followed the legend of the golden cities of Cibola north to Zuni and the pueblos of the Rio Grande Valley. The Spaniards discovered no fewer than seventy inhabited pueblos, each housing between four hundred and one thousand persons. None of them were the fabled cities of gold studded with turquoise. Instead, they were modest villages of sun-baked adobe bricks or volcanic tuff, some of quarried sandstone. Along the way, the Spaniards passed the ruins of abandoned cities, first of the Mogollon culture, later of the Anasazi and Hohokam. Some of these ruins seemed far larger than the inhabited pueblos they encountered. The Spanish explorers showed only passing interest in the Anasazi sites they discovered along their way to anticipated wealth and glory. Expecting flourishing golden cities, the ruins of abandoned pueblos must have suggested to them the irony of deferred or defeated dreams.

Following the Spanish conquistadores of the seventeenth and eighteenth centuries were the explorer-missionary priests, men like Velez de Escalante, Francisco Atanasio Dominguez, and later Eusebio Kino, whose discoveries confirmed their predecessors' reports that the canyons and mesas of the Spanish northern frontier had once been inhabited for what seemed to be, well, a very long time. In the mid–nineteenth century the opening of the Santa Fe Trail and the acquisition in 1848 of nearly the entire present-day Southwest in the aftermath of the war with Mexico brought in growing numbers of Americans—soldiers, traders, and settlers. The spirit of Manifest Destiny that animated the American takeover of the Southwest largely overshadowed the antiquity of the region's indigenous inhabitation. Surviving commentary on the mysterious ruins and rock inscriptions of seemingly departed peoples is sketchy. In the late 1840s, references to the ruins of Chaco Canyon appear in reports by William

H. Emory and James Simpson, members of military reconnaissance parties sent out to discover what exactly America had won in its war with Mexico.

The years following the Civil War saw increased scientific exploration of the West. The Hayden Survey of 1874–77 marked the beginning of what would come to be the archaeological investigation of the Southwest: W. H. Holmes of the National Museum noted ruin sites discovered in the area south of the Dolores River in today's south-western Colorado, and photographer William H. Jackson recorded the images of ruins on the Mancos River in Colorado and in Chaco Canyon and Canyon de Chelly, in New Mexico and Arizona. Accompanying the Hayden Survey was *New York Tribune* journalist Ernest Ingersoll, and Ingersoll's feature stories about an ancient civilization in Colorado's Mancos Canyon fascinated East Coast readers and sent archaeologists packing for the trip west. At about the same time, Bureau of Ethnology crews under Victor and Cosmos Mindeleff undertook the first architectural studies of the pueblo ruins, and in the 1880s Jesse Walter Fewkes and Adolf Bandelier combined their interests in archaeology with their curiosity about the living indigenous peoples of the Southwest.

In spite of the fact that they were not the first to come across ancient ruins, ranchers Richard Wetherill and Charlie Mason occupy a pivotal place in the history of southwestern archaeology. After stumbling upon cliff dwellings on Colorado's Mesa Verde in the mid-1880s, Wetherill and Mason found the spectacular ruins of Cliff Palace in 1888 while searching for stray cattle. Digging through the ruins, not always with great care, the men unearthed remarkable objects—pottery, stonework, basketry, articles of clothing, storerooms of corn and squash, and the carefully prepared bodies of the dead, wrapped in woven feather robes and matting. This amateur excavation yielded a collection of artifacts exhibited in Denver in 1888 and 1889, which in turn inspired more-organized expeditions to cart away the mesa's artifacts to eastern museums and private collections as far away as Europe. The passage of the 1906 Antiquities Act encouraged scientific exploration on public lands, and the next year Edgar L. Hewlett established the Archaeological Institute of America and the School of American Research in Santa Fe. There followed the historic work of Alfred Kidder, Earl Morris, Byron Cummings, Neil Judd, Nels C. Nelson, Sylvanus Morley, Emil Haury, and A. E. Douglass—the men whose excavations and laboratory work through the 1930s established them as the founders of true scientific archaeology in the Southwest.

Of course, there was a world of things going on beyond the digs. The region continued to fill with settlers, towns were incorporated, and river bottomlands were put under the plow. The same prime land that had attracted the ancients became the cultivated fields of nineteenth century farmers, and the new inhabitants exposed a wealth of ancient tools, bones, and potsherds. Many farmers became at least inadvertent "pot hunters." Some were more methodical. It might have seemed innocent enough at the time, an entertainment, perhaps profitable. In the mid-1880s, on a school outing in the Animas Valley of northern New Mexico, a young student named Sherman Howe was sent by his teacher into an opening in a mound of rubble at what is today Aztec Ruin and discovered a burial chamber containing thirteen skeletons. The place became a local sensation.

The sensation was catching. Henry Ford changed the Southwest forever when he introduced the affordable automobile, and Fred Harvey did more than any other single man to open the region to organized tourism, including ruin sites like Chaco Canyon by conducting "detours" from the La Fonda Hotel in Santa Fe. A sense of what Richard White calls "scenic nationalism" oversaw the establishment of national parks and monuments. Resource and real estate development bolstered western economies, and invalids who went west for their health stayed on. In the years following World War II the Southwest exploded with often poorly managed growth. The westward movement of Americans continues today. For a variety of reasons, more and more people walk through the ruins of the Southwest. During the tourist season in Blanding or Cortez or Santa Fe, you are almost as likely to hear German or French as English.

Today more than ever, the Anasazi are "cool," as my nine-year-old son puts it. Rock art images are icons of pop culture appearing in advertising, on tee shirts, in rock videos, and as restaurant decor. The Anasazi have become an interior design concept. You can buy Anasazi beans in the grocery store. You can use a line of Anasazi hair-care products. With images from Anasazi rock art proliferating in the most unlikely places, the Kokopelli figure has become the smiley face of the 1990s. Satirizing and deploring all this, a recent *High Country News* editorial appeared under the title "Have a Kokopelli Day." Henry Miller, roll over.

Although many early explorers of the Southwest intuitively suspected the connection between the area's ancient ruins and the contemporary Native Americans of the region, and although science has increasingly acknowledged and documented it by tracing Puebloan tradition through fifteen hundred years, as far back as the Anasazi Basketmakers, the forces of public curiosity, market economics, government regulation, and scientific inquiry have seldom addressed the central religious concerns of the Puebloans. From the time the "locals" first started dynamiting the ruins in Arizona's Walnut Canyon looking for collectibles, vandalism and the wholesale looting of ancient sites have been for some a way of life in the Southwest. The pressure of development and the sheer volume of tourism also threaten the integrity of ancient sites. In Albuquerque, controversy continues to surround the proposed extention of a six-lane highway through Petroglyph National Monument. For members of the Five Sandoval Indian Pueblos, the threatened rock art sites are sacred, but Albuquerque Mayor Martin Chavez maintains that the sacredness of the land is compatible with development. "They say it's a seventeen-mile church," he observes. "Well, the Vatican has a road going through it." The dubious methods of early untrained excavators and the large-scale removal to museums and private collections of artifacts and burial remains ushered in the easy assumption that the ancient people of the region were up for grabs, that their material culture, even their bodies, were commodities, commercial or scientific resources to be mined from the desert like gold or coal. Puebloans today see this in the larger context of conquest, appropriation of Native American land, and denial of indigenous culture that has characterized the European occupation of the Americas. Today the vandalism and destructive looting continues and in fact has increased alarmingly since the 1970s. Shovels and even backhoes and bulldozers are often the tools of choice. Major auction houses continue to sell artifacts, always claimed by their sellers to have come legally from private land. Artifacts are even advertised on the Internet. "Treasure hunting" publications, imbued with the Indiana Jones mentality, implicitly encourage the displacement of ancient objects. In 1994, a housing development in Colorado advertised residential lots, each of which contained "numerous Anasazi sites."

This is only part of the story. Much of the impulse to protect ancient sites, as commendable as it is, is grounded in the premise that their primary value is archaeological or scientific. For the Native Americans of the Southwest, the meaning of these sites goes far deeper: They are sacred history. Priests make annual ritual pilgrimages to many ancient ruins to pray, to make offerings, to observe ceremonies of respect and continuity with the land and the past. Their actions are part of a vital and living religion that comes down from the lives of the ancients themselves and is so integral and persistent that it cannot be measured in years or otherwise scientifically quantified.

For non–Native Americans, the great and enduring question about the Anasazi has centered on their alleged disappearance. Why were the pueblos of Chaco Canyon or the cliff dwellings of Mesa Verde abandoned within a century of the apex of their construction? Before scientific answers were forthcoming, romantic clichés took over. John Bakeless, writing in his 1950 *America as Seen by its First Explorers,* suggests the sense of mystery that surrounded the once seemingly unaccountable disappearance of the ancient Anasazi. Bakeless describes Chaco Canyon as a place "where red men for centuries had built an isolated, peaceful civilization and then, sealing their houses, had vanished quietly, no man knows where or why."

Yet for many contemporary Pueblo people among the Zuni, the Hopi, the Acoma, and the pueblo communities of the Rio Grande Valley, these questions about disappearance are largely ridiculous, perhaps even dangerous. They know the ancient builders of today's ruins as their ancestors. They understand their own lives in part within an eight-hundred-year continuum represented by the ancient dwelling places. It is important to realize that popular notions about the "disappearance" of the Anasazi deny Native Americans connection to their own history. In a remote way, my own Native American heritage, although from the eastern forests and not the arid West, allows me to hear and understand this. It is likely that some of my ancestors built effigy mounds, if not alcove pueblos. Traditional Puebloans live within a complex and deeply meaningful network of honored relationships that bind together human existence, the geographical world, and all forms of organic life. They are also linked to those who lived before. Tessie Naranjo of Santa Clara Pueblo writes:

Our sense of social relationships leads us to respect all who have gone before us, our elders as well as our youth and those who will follow us. We also honor those people who have gone on and those objects that they created and with which they established an intimate relationship. This perpetual honoring of our ancestors allows us to remember our past and the natural process of transformation—breathing, living, dying, and becoming one with the natural world. We are never unrelated—not even in death.

The popular enthusiasm for everything Indian that began in the 1960s has been mainstreamed into a sometimes superficial and romantic enchantment with indigenous cultures. In particular it grew during the 1970s with the development of the so-called New Age movement. For many Native Americans, the specter of countless spiritual tourists chanting and drumming in their campsites, flocking to the "power spots" and "vortices" of Sedona, and congregating in Chaco Canyon like so many Daisy Millers come to view the Colosseum, is nothing short of a disturbing and arbitrary appropriation of their own revered traditions. Elizabeth Cook-Lynn characterizes the "absurd psychic/cultural discoveries of the 'New Age'" as based on the assumption that non–Native Americans "have no history, no past, no race, no religion, no ideals, no tribal responsibility." Equally sad is the irony that the Native American cultures American society so eagerly sought to destroy as recently as the 1950s seem to be enthusiastically coveted by it today.

Beyond this trendy appropriation of ancient and contemporary Native American lifeways lies more concrete danger. The treatment given Native American burial remains has been a particular source of sorrow and resentment among Native Americans. The Antiquities Act of 1906 was designed to protect ancient sites from vandalism, yet it authorized scientists to remove artifacts from public lands on the assumption that even Native American human remains were federal property. "It is most unpleasant work to steal bones from a grave," said anthropologist Franz Boas, "but someone has to do it." Increasingly, Native American leaders, lawyers, and writers have begun to call for the return of Native American remains from museums to the tribes. Negotiations have begun, and the Native American Graves Protection and Repatriation Act offers some hope that Indian religious freedom might someday actually be protected. Still, what non–Native Americans should find disturbing is the possibility that the large-scale abuse of sacred sites and human remains suggests not only an unconscious racism but also a profound estrangement among many Euro-Americans from any sense of their own religious connection to place and the past.

Even the term *Anasazi* is emblematic of the ongoing challenge. It has a nice ring to it. Furthermore, it has a respectable archaeological history. When in the 1930s archaeologists translated the term from Navajo as "the old people," few realized that a more accurate translation is "enemy ancestors." After its acceptance by scientists, *Anasazi* inevitably entered the vocabulary of popular culture, particularly during the last ten years as interest in ancient sites has grown dramatically. Indeed, in order to make the subject matter of this collection recognizable to readers, I had to use the word in the title.

For many Native Americans of the Southwest, however, "Anasazi" carries with it the legacy of cultural commodification and appropriation they continually battle. First of all, for many Puebloans, in part given the historical friction between the Navajo and the Puebloan Hopi, it is profoundly disrespectful that a Navajo word should be used to designate their ancestors. Furthermore, it is simply not an accurate reflection of how Puebloans think of their ancestors, who are regarded with a deep sense of kinship and certainly not as "enemy" ancestors.

Many Hopi resist reducing an explanation of their ancestors to one simple term but still prefer the name *Hisatsinom*, "the ancient people." The *Tewa*-speaking peoples of the Rio Grande Valley call them *Se'da*, "the ancient ones." Opinions vary among Puebloans concerning the use of the term *Anasazi*. In general, feelings run most strongly against its use at Zuni, Acoma, and particularly on the Hopi Mesas. The Hopi Cultural Preservation Office refers to the term as "inappropriate," and Tessie Naranjo of Santa Clara, although acknowledging the inappropriateness of the name, allows that "there are more important things to worry about" in Indian and non-Indian relations. The danger in the use of the term *Anasazi* for most of us, perhaps, is suggested in how the Hopi understand the people to whom the term is applied. Naming them as "ancient enemies" records and perhaps in a fundamental way sustains our modern inability to develop our own proper relationship and kinship to the land and the people who once inhabited it. There is a growing movement among the Pueblo people, and now among archaeologists as well, to substitute for *Anasazi* the more appropriate terms "Ancestral Puebloan" or "Ancient Puebloan." This is far more than shallow political correctness. It is accuracy and respect. Throughout the rest of this book I will make the switch, and I encourage you to do the same.

By observing ancient Puebloan sites, we all can learn something of what Native Americans already know about the true, surprisingly long timeline of human culture in North America. Even Henry Miller could not have overlooked it. The fact that Native American antiquity is still sometimes marginalized as primitive and immaterial to modern life suggests how we all have trouble stepping outside our own familiar sense of culture based on our own standards of value, achievement, and authenticity. For many people, antiquity continues to register as the marble of Rome and the statuary of Greece. There are real risks in that. Southwestern novelist Frank Waters writes:

> America is a peculiarly modern country. Without roots in its own ancient past, all its cultural traditions spring from Europe. But its umbilical cord with it has been cut. We are wholly the product of our own machine-made culture.

To say the least, the sense of isolation and dehumanization in Waters's characterization of contemporary American life sounds something short of nurturing and rich. Must this really be the price we pay for our modern ways? Maybe. But part of coming to terms with who we are as Americans, or perhaps more accurately as inhabitants of North America, regardless of race or ethnic origin, is coming to understand the real natural and human history of this place we claim as our home. What are the sustainable possibilities of where we live? The limitations? Who are our neighbors? Who has been here before us? What did they do? What did they think? If you're in Cincinnati, ask these questions about the Adena and the Hopewell. If you're in Charlotte, North Carolina, or Tahlequah, Oklahoma, ask it about the *Ani-yunwiya*, the Cherokee. If you're driving around Cortez, Colorado, ask it about the ancient Puebloans. The questions are as expansive as the territory of the original cultures.

When we read this language of long inhabitation left behind by the ancient Puebloans, we have to acknowledge on one hand that our "reading" is a subjective, individual experience. We must depart a personal distance from the objectivity of science, feel the sand in our shoes and the second degree sunburn on our necks as we stand among the ruined walls and try to think back into a world that was never ours. What would it have been like to live here eight hundred years ago? What would we have seen when we awoke in the morning? How can just being here influence our lives in a rapidly accelerating, technological, and sometimes baffling contemporary world? For over four hundred years people have wondered things like this. It's a very human thing to do in ancient places—merge them with our own lives, blend and confuse the horizon of our world with the horizon of another's and see if any of the territory is shared.

But on the other hand we must enter into this process with caution and respect. If we project too much of our world on another culture we are just looking in a mirror. If we try to borrow too freely from what is not ours, we are acting in the worst tradition of western history. We must respect the difference—acknowledge the distance.

When we accept Native American cultures on their own terms, we see the ancient ancestors as authentic precursors to our contemporary age, as men and women who found a way to live on this continent we now occupy with their descendents. This is the reality that the writers in this volume struggle with. Yes, they have limited perspectives defined by their own times and interests. Sometimes, it might seem to us, they get it all very wrong, other times wonderfully right. Like them, we too are bound by the horizon of our own lives. Still, the ruins, the rock art, the abandoned cornfields tell us fundamental stories of community, adaptation, and survival, especially if we develop our inclination to listen carefully.

By some estimates, the population of North America at the time of European contact was as high as 9,800,000. That's a lot of human lives—a lot of emotions, values, and goals. In varying ways, the writers assembled here take that habitation seriously, reflecting on the meaning and experience of these people who came before. As it was and is for them, so do the questions remain for us: How do we listen to the stories written in the stone as well as those written later on paper? How do we imagine them, fit them into our own lives, and learn from them without appropriating them from those lives in which they have their source?

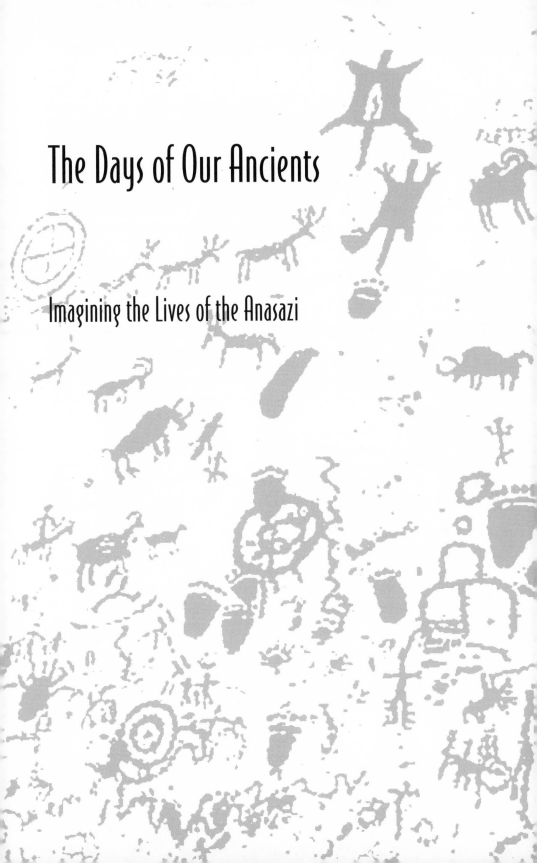

The Days of Our Ancients

Imagining the Lives of the Anasazi

✦

While attending graduate school at Stanford University in the early 1960s, N. Scott Momaday was encouraged by his mentor Yvor Winters to explore his Native American heritage in his writing. Momaday followed *House Made of Dawn,* which won the Pulitzer Prize for fiction in 1968, with *The Way to Rainy Mountain* (1969) and *Ancient Child* (1989). *House Made of Dawn* initiated a renaissance in Native American writing that continues to this day. Much of Momaday's work focuses on the discovery of the past through oral tradition and community and on the efforts of Native Americans to maintain the continuity of tradition in contemporary life. In this excerpt from "The Native Voice," the first chapter in the *Columbia Literary History of the United States* (1987), Momaday celebrates the persistence of narrative and how it resonates in the pictographs of Utah's Barrier Canyon.

f r o m

"The Native Voice"

N . SCOTT MOMADAY

Write vt I a (1): to draw or form by or as by scoring or incising a surface

—Webster's Seventh New Collegiate Dictionary

Imagine: somewhere in the prehistoric distance a man holds up in his hand a crude instrument—a brand, perhaps, or something like a daub or a broom bearing pigment—and fixes the wonderful image in his mind's eye to a wall or rock. In that instant is accomplished really and symbolically the advent of art. That man, apart from his remarkable creation, is all but impossible to recall, and yet he is there in our human parentage, deep in our racial memory. In our modern, sophisticated terms, he is primitive and preliterate, and in the long reach of time he is utterly without distinction, except: he draws. And his contribution to posterity is inestimable; he makes a profound difference in our lives who succeed him by millennia. For all the stories of all the world proceed from the moment in which he makes his mark. All literatures issue from his hand.

Language and literature involve sacred matter. Among sacred places in America, places of deepest mystery and ancient origin, there is one that comes to my mind again and again. At Barrier Canyon, Utah, there are some twenty sites upon which are preserved prehistoric rock art. One of these, known as the Great Gallery, is particularly arresting. Among arched alcoves and long ledges of rock is a wide sandstone wall on which are drawn large, tapering anthropomorphic forms, colored in dark red pigment. There on the geologic picture plane is a procession of gods approaching inexorably from the earth. They are informed with irresistible power; they are beyond our understanding, masks of infinite possibility. We do not know what they mean, but we know that we are involved in their meaning. They persist through time in the imagination, and we cannot doubt that they are invested with the very essence of language, the language of story and myth and primal song. They are two thousand years old, more or less, and they remark as closely as anything can the origin of American literature.

The native voice in American literature is indispensable. There is no true literary history of the United States without it, and yet it has not been clearly delineated in our scholarship. The reasons for this neglect are perhaps not far to find. The subject is formidable; the body of songs, prayers, spells, charms, omens, riddles, and stories in Native American oral tradition, though constantly and considerably diminished from the time of European contact, is large, so large as to discourage investigation. The tradition has evolved over a very long and unrecorded period of time in numerous remote and complex languages, and it reflects a social and cultural diversity that is redoubtable. Research facilities are inadequate, by and large, and experts in the field are few. Notwithstanding, the need is real and apparent.

Ancestors of modern American Indians were at the top of North America as early as 25,000 years ago. They were hunters whose survival was predicated upon the principle of mobility. Their dispersal upon the continent was rapid. In the hard environment of the far north there remains little evidence of their occupation, but they knew how to make fire and tools, and they lived as we do in the element of language.

American literature begins with the first human perception of the American landscape expressed and preserved in language. "Literature" we take commonly to comprehend more than writing. Writing, if we understand that word to mean visible constructions within a framework of alphabets, is not more than six or seven thousand years old, we are told. Language, and in it the formulation of that cultural record that is literature, is immeasurably older. Oral tradition is the foundation of literature. ▪

❁

According to his friend Charles F. Lummis, Adolf Bandelier not only was one of the pioneer archaeologists of the Southwest but was also perhaps the John Muir of scientific exploration in the region. Just as Muir ventured into California's Sierra Nevada with little more than the shirt on his back, during the 1880s Bandelier traversed the high desert on foot, slept in the open, and survived on the meager contents of a knapsack. Following his intellectual mentor, Henry Lewis Morgan, Bandelier used the evidence from his excavations at Pecos, New Mexico, to suggest relationships between the great cultures of Mexico and those to the north. Despite his distaste for romantic representations of Native Americans, Bandelier published *The Delight Makers* in 1890, a historical novel set in prehistoric times among the inhabitants of Frijoles Canyon, in what is now Bandelier National Monument in New Mexico. Hoping to persuade readers that Native Americans had developed complex and independent cultures before the arrival of Europeans, Bandelier explains that his goal in writing the novel was "to make the 'Truth about the Pueblo Indians' more accessible and perhaps more acceptable to the public in general." In the conclusion to *The Delight Makers,* reprinted here, Bandelier, perhaps more the imaginative novelist than the empirical archaeologist, takes the reader through vertiginous contrasts, describing Frijoles Canyon one minute as it appeared in 1890—uninhabited, its pueblos in ruins—yet in the next minute imagining it as it appeared seven hundred years earlier, alive with human activity.

f r o m

The Delight Makers

ADOLF BANDELIER

For a number of hours we have to follow the base of the huge potreros, crossing narrow ravines, ascending steep but not long slopes, until at about noon we stand on the brink of a gorge so deep that it may be termed a chasm. We look down to a narrow bottom and groves of cottonwood trees. To the north, the chasm is walled in by towering rocks; the Rio Grande flows through one corner; and on its opposite bank arise cliffs of trap lava and basalt, black and threatening, while the rocks on the west side are bright red, yellow, and white. The trail to the Rito goes down into this abyss and climbs up on the other side through clefts and along steep slopes. But we are not going to follow this trail. We turn to the left, and with the dizzy chasm of Cañon del Alamo to our right, proceed westward on one of the narrow tongues which, as the reader may remember, descend toward the Rio Grande from the high western mountains, and which are called in New Mexico *potreros*. The one on which we are travelling, or rather the plateau, or mesa, that constitutes its surface, is called Potrero de las Vacas.

For about two hours we wander through a thin forest. From time to time the trail approaches the brink of the rocky chasm of the Cañon del Alamo, near enough to have its echo return to us every word we may shout down into its depths. Suddenly the timber grows sparse and we behold an open space on a gentle rise before us. It is a bare, bleak spot, perhaps a quarter of a mile long, and occupying the entire width of the mesa, which here is not much broader. Beyond, the timber begins again, and in the centre of the opening we see the fairly preserved ruins of an abandoned Indian pueblo.

There are still in places three stories visible. The walls are of evenly broken parallelopipeds of very friable pumicestone, and the village forms the usual quadrangles. In the center is a large square; and no fewer than six, depressions indicate that the Pueblos had at one time as many as six circular subterranean estufas. In the ruins of the dwellings over four hundred cells are still well defined, so that the population of this communal village must formerly have reached as high as one thousand souls. Over and through the ruins are scattered the usual vestiges of primitive arts and industry—pottery fragments and arrowheads. Seldom do we meet with a stone hammer, whereas grinding slabs and grinders are frequent, though for the most part scattered and broken.

The spot is well selected for an abode of sedentary Indians. An extensive view opens toward the east, north, and south. We see in the east the mountains above Santa Fé, in the south the ranges at whose foot lie the ruins of Hishi. In the north the high plateaus above the Rito shut out a glimpse of the Puye, but a whitish streak in that direction indicates the top line of the northern cliffs that overhang the Rito de los Frijoles. Right and left of the village, not more than a hundred yards from each side, begin the rugged declivities of the sides of the potrero. If we want to go farther we can proceed to the west only, and there we soon get into timber again.

A few steps within that timber, and we have before us a strange sight. A wall of rudely piled stone slabs planted upright, flags laid upon them crosswise, and smaller fragments piled against and between them, form a pentagonal enclosure which at first sight reminds us of a diminutive Stonehenge. There is an entrance to it from the southeast—an open corridor flanked by similar parapets. The enclosing wall is not more than three feet high, and we easily peep into the interior.

Inside there are two statues carved out of the living rock. Although much disfigured today they still show a plain resemblance to the figures of two crouching panthers or pumas. They are life size; and the animals seem to lie there with their heads to the east, their tails extended along the ground. As we stand and gaze, our Indian goes up to the statues and furtively anoints their heads with red ochre, muttering a prayer between his teeth.

What may be the signification of this statuary? Do you remember the great dance at the Rito, and the painting on the wall of the estufa where the Koshare Naua sat and held communication with Those Above? Do you recollect that among these paintings there was one of a panther and another of a bear? The relation of the bear and panther of the estufa to the picture of the sun-father is here that of the two stone panthers to the sun himself. Their faces are turned to the east, whence rises the sun, in which dwells the father of all mankind, and the moon, which their mother inhabits. As in the estufa on the Rito, so in the outside world, the pictures of stone express a prayer to the higher powers, and here daily the people of the village were wont to make offerings and say their prayers.

We are therefore on sacred ground in this crumbling enclosure. But who knows that we are not on magic ground also? We might make an experiment; and though our Indian guide is not one of the great shamans, he might help us in an attempt at innocent jugglery.

Let us suffer ourselves to be blindfolded, and then turn around three times from left to right while our friend recites some cabalistic formula, incomprehensible of course to us.

One, two, three! The bandage is removed. What can we see?

Nothing strange at first. Surrounding nature is the same as before. The same extensive view, the same snow-clad ranges in the far east, the same silent, frowning rocks, the same dark pines around us. But in the north, over the yellowish band that denotes the cliffs of the Rito we notice a slight bluish haze.

A change has taken place in our immediate vicinity. The stone panthers and the stone enclosure have vanished, and the ground is bare, like all the ground in the neighborhood. Looking beyond we see that a transformation has also taken place on the spot where stood the ruin. The crumbling walls and heaps of rubbish are gone, and in their place newly built foundations are emerging from the ground; heaps of stone, partly broken, are scattered about; and where a moment ago we were the only living souls, now Indians—village Indians like our guide, only somewhat more primitive—move to and fro, busily engaged.

Some of them are breaking the stones into convenient sizes, for the friable pumice breaks in parallelopipeds without effort. The women are laying these in mortar made of the soil from the mesa, common adobe. We are witnessing the beginning of the construction of a small village. Farther down, on the edge of the timber, smoke arises; there the builders of this new pueblo dwell in huts while their house of stone is growing to completion. It is the month of May, and only the nights are cool.

These builders we easily recognize. They are the fugitives from the Rito, the little band whom the Tanos of Hishi have kindly received and charitably supported until a few months since, when they allowed them to go and build a new home. They came hither led on by Hayoue who is now their maseua; for each tribe, however small, must have one. Okoya is with him, and Mitsha, now Okoya's wife, comes up from the bottom with the waterurn on her head, as on the day when we first saw her on the Rito de los Frijoles.

And now we have, though in a trance, seen the further fate of those whose sad career has filled the pages of this story. We may be blindfolded again, turned about right to left; and when the bandage is taken from our eyes the landscape is as before, silent and grand. The ruins are in position again; the panthers of stone with their mutilated heads lie within the enclosure; an eagle soars on high; and our Indian points to it, smiles, and whispers—

"Look! see! the Shiuana are good!" ▪

Charles Fletcher Lummis is perhaps best known for his southern California magazine *Out West,* which first appeared in the early years of the twentieth century. Successful in enlisting the help of Theodore Roosevelt in order to preserve California's indigenous and colonial antiquities, Lummis was responsible for saving at least two then-crumbling Spanish missions. Lummis's interest in the Southwest also went much further afield, to New Mexico and the life and history of its original inhabitants. Lummis traveled widely with archaeologist Adolf Bandelier and after Bandelier's death in 1914 wrote a beautiful memorial preface to a reissue of *The Delight Makers.*

Lummis's *The Land of Poco Tiempo* (1893) is today his most widely read book. In the chapter "The Wanderings of Cochiti," Lummis recalls his impressions of the ancient sites of Frijoles Canyon, today part of Bandelier National Monument, where, it is reported, he had a penchant for entertaining School of American Research anthropologists around the campfire with a guitar that was, if nothing else, loud. In the passage from "The Wanderings of Cochiti" included here, Lummis integrates the ancient and contemporary life of New Mexico in an account of the ancient inhabitants of Frijoles Canyon, or *Rito de los Frijoles,* where centuries before the arrival of the Spaniards an ancient people had carved caves from the soft tufa rock and built multistoried pueblos on the canyon floor. Drawing upon the theories of Bandelier, Lummis describes the dwelling places of the ancient people he calls the *Cochiti,* suggesting that they were the probable ancestors of the modern *Queres-* (or *Keresan-*) speaking people of the nearby Cochiti Pueblo. *Tyu-on-yi,* the *Queres* word for the canyon, had by Lummis's time come more specifically to refer to the most prominent ruin within the canyon. The stone pumas Lummis describes remain today, still a site of worship for Puebloans.

---

f r o m

The Land of Poco Tiempo

C H A R L E S   F.   L U M M I S

The fable of the so-called cliff builders and cave dwellers, as a distinct race or races, has been absolutely exploded in science. The fact is, that the cliff dwellers and the cave dwellers of the Southwest were Pueblo Indians, pure and simple. Even a careless eye can find the proof in every corner of the Southwest. It was a question not of race, but of physical geography. The Pueblo cut his garment according to his cloth, and whether he burrowed his house, or built it of mud bricks or stone bricks or cleft stone, atop a cliff or in caves or shelves of its face, depended simply upon his townsite. The one inflexible rule was security, and to gain that he took the "shortest cut" offered by his surroundings. When he found himself—as he sometimes did in his volcanic range—in a region of tufa cliffs, he simply whittled out his residence. In the commoner hard rock canyons, he built stone houses in whatever safest place. In the valleys, he made and laid adobes. He sometimes even dovetailed all these varieties of architecture in one and the same settlement.

The Tyú-on-yi, the first known home of Cochití, is one of the unique beauties of the Southwest. As a canyon, it is but five or six miles long, and at the widest a quarter of a mile across. Its extreme depth does not exceed two thousand feet. There are scores of greater canyons in this neglected land; but there is only one Tyú-on-yi. At the *Bocas,* where it enters the gorge of the Rio Grande, it is deepest, narrowest, grimmest. A few hundred yards above these savage jaws was the townsite. A ribbon of irrigably level land a few rods wide, threaded by a sparkling rivulet, hemmed with glistening cliffs of white pumice stone fifteen hundred feet tall, murmurous with stately pines and shivering aspens, shut on the west by the long slope of the Jara, on the east by the pinching of its own giant walls—that is the Tyú-on-yi. That, but more. For along the sheer and noble northern cliff crumble the bones of a human past—a past of heroism and suffering and romance. In the foot of that stone snowbank new shadows play hide-and-seek in strange old hollows, that were not gnawed by wind and rain, but by as patient man. It is an enchanted valley. The spell of the Southwest is upon it. The sun's white benediction, the hush of Nature's heart, the invisible haunting of a *Once*—that utmost of all solitudes, the silence that *was* life—they wrap it in an atmosphere almost unique. It is an impression of a lifetime. The great cave villages of the Pu-yé and the Shú-fin-né, in their white castle buttes thirty miles up the river, are not to be compared with it, though they are its nearest parallel in the world. It is not only a much larger village than either of them, but with a beauty and charm altogether peerless.

Tyú-on-yi was a large town for the prehistoric United States—a town of fifteen hundred to two thousand souls. The latter figure was never exceeded by *any* aboriginal "city" of the Southwest. The line of artificial cave rooms is a couple of miles long, and in tiers of one, two, and three stories. With their "knives" of chipped volcanic glass for sole tools, the Cochiteños built their matchless village. First, they hewed in the face of the cliff their inner rooms. These were generally rectangular, about six by eight, with arched roofs; but sometimes large, and sometimes circular. Some were sole houses and had tiny outer doorways in the rock and as tiny ones from room to room within—a plan which has given rise, in ruins oftener seen by the theorizer, to the fable of cliff-dwelling pigmies. The builders, in fact, were of present Pueblo stature, and made these wee doorways simply for security. The man of the house could afford time to enter edgewise on hands and knees; an enemy could not. Some rooms combine cave and masonry, having an artificial outer wall. And some, again, were merely cave storehouses and retreats back of a stone brick house. Outside, against the foot of the cliffs, is the chaos of fallen masonry. The builders adopted a plan peculiar to this plateau. With their same flakes of obsidian they sawed the tufa into large and rather regular bricks, and of these exclusively laid their masonry in an excellent mortar of adobe. A restoration of the Tyú-on-yi would show a long line of three-story terraced houses of these tufa blocks against the foot of that weird cliff; the rafters inserted into still visible mortises in its face; without doors or windows in the ground floor, and abristle with the spar-like ladders by which the upper stories were reached, and, back through their rooms, the caves. None of the outer houses are now standing—the best of their walls are but four or five feet high—but the dim procession of centuries that has toppled them to ruin has dealt kindlier with the caves. The caked smoke of the hearth still clings—half fossil—on the low-arched roofs and around the tiny window smokeholes. The very plastering of the walls—for the home had already reached such painstaking that even the smooth rock must be hidden by a film of cement—is generally intact. The little niches, where trinkets were laid, are there; and in one house is even the stone frame of the prehistoric handmill. In several places are cave rooms with their fronts and partitions of tufa masonry still entire; and one lovely little nook, well up the canyon, has still a perfect house unlike any other prehistoric building in America— walled cave, wood-framed door and windows, and all. In this climate wood is almost eternal. Timbers that have been fully exposed since 1670 in the Gran Quivíra have not even lost their ornamental carvings, and beams of vastly greater age are still sound. Here and there down the slope, toward the brook, are the remains of the circular subterranean estufas wherein the male village dwelt; and in a strangely scalloped swell of the cliff is still the house of the Cacique—a very fair hemisphere of a room, cut from the rock, with a floor diameter of some fifteen feet. Not far away, beside the rivulet, are the ruins of a huge communal house—one of the so-called "round" ruins. Exploration always shows that these alleged circles are merely irregular polygons. There never was a round pueblo, though the estufas were very generally round and there were other small single buildings of the same shape. The usual stone artifacts are rarely to be found here, for roving Navajos have assiduously stripped the place of everything of aboriginal use. Only now and then a rude obsidian knife, an arrow point, or a battered stone axe rewards the relic seeker—beyond the innumerable fragments of ancient pottery.

So exceptionally complete are the links in a story which may very well go far back of William the Conqueror, that we even have legendary hints of the subdivisions of this immemorial village; and in a cave room of the cluster which has suffered most from the erosion of the cliff, I once stumbled upon gentle José Hilario Montoya, the now Governor of the new Cochití, wrapped in his blanket and in reverie. He had stolen away from us, to dream an hour in the specific house that was of his own first grandfathers.

We have no means of knowing just how long the strange white town of the Rito has been deserted, but it has been many, many centuries; for its hunted people built successive towns, and farmed and fought and had a history in each of six later homes before the written history of America began. Though eternally harassed by the Navajos, the Tyú-on-yi held its own, we are told, until destroyed by its own brethren. The conditions of life there (and in all prehistoric pueblos) and the interwarring of the various tribes are drawn with photographic accuracy of detail in that little read but archaeologically precious novel, *The Delight Makers.*

The survivors of the final catastrophe abandoned their ruined town in the Rito, and moving a day's march to the south, established themselves upon the tabletop of the great Potrero de las Vacas. They were now seven or eight miles west of the chasm of the Rio Grande, and on the summit of the tongue plateau between two of its principal side canyons. They were a mile from water—the sparkling brooklet which flows past the Cueva Pintada—and therefore from their farms. But feeling this inconvenience little so long as it gave safety, they reared among the contorted junipers a new town—essentially unlike the quaint combination-pueblo of the Rito, but like to a more common pattern. It was the typical rectangular stone box of continuous houses, all facing in. Here on the grim mesa, amid a wilderness of appalling solitude, they worried out the tufa blocks, and builded their fortress city, and fended off the prowling Navajo, and fought to water and home again, and slept with an arrow on the string. How many generations of bronze babies frolicked in this lap of danger; and rose to arrowy youth that loved between sieges; and to gray heads that watched and counselled; and to still clay that cuddled to the long sleep in rooms thenceforth sealed forever, there is no reckoning—nor when was the red foray, whereof their legends tell, of an unknown tribe which finished the town of the Mesa of the Cows. But when the decimated Quéres left that noble site, they left, beside their fallen home, a monument of surpassing interest. The Nahuatl culture, which filled Mexico with huge and hideous statues chiselled from the hardest rock, was never paralleled within the United States; for our aborigines had no metal tools whatever until after the Conquest. New Mexican work in stone (aside from the making of implements and beads) was confined to tiny fetiches which were rather *worn* than carved to shape, and to a few larger but very crude fetiches of softer rock. The only examples of life-size carvings, or of any *alto relievo,* ever found in the enormous range of the Pueblos, are the four astonishing figures which were, and are, the homotypes of the chase-gods of wandering Cochití.

A few hundred yards up the dim trail which leads from the ruined town of the Potrero de las Vacas toward the near peaks, one comes suddenly upon a strange aboriginal Stonehenge. Among the tattered piñons and sprawling cedars is a lonely enclosure fenced with great slabs of tufa set up edgewise. This enclosure, which is about thirty feet in diameter, has somewhat of the shape of a tadpole; for at the southeast end its oval tapers into an alley five feet wide and twenty long, similarly walled. In the midst of this unique roofless temple of the southwestern druids are the weathered images of two cougars, carved in high relief from the bedrock of the mesa. The figures are life-size; and even the erosion of so many centuries has not gnawed them out of recognition. The heads are nearly indistinguishable, and the fore-shoulders have suffered; but the rest of the sculpture, to the very tips of the outstretched tails, is perfectly clear. The very attitude of the American lion is preserved—the flat, stealthy, compact crouch that precedes the mortal leap. Artistically, of course, the statues are crude; but zoologically, they bear the usual Indian truthfulness. As to their transcendent archaeologic value and great antiquity, there can be no question. The circumstantial evidence is conclusive that they were carved by the Cochiteños during the life of the town of the Potrero de las Vacas.

The cougar, puma, or mountain lion—mo-keit-cha, in the Quéres tongue—is to the Pueblo the head of animate creation. In this curious mythology, each of the six like groups of divinities, "the Trues," which dwell respectively at the six cardinal points, includes a group of deified dumb animals. They are Trues also, and are as carefully ranked as the higher spirits, or even more definitely. The beasts of prey, of course, stand highest; and of them, and of all animals, the puma is Ka-béy-de, commander-in-chief. Under him there are minor officials; the buffalo is captain of the ruminants; the eagle, of birds; the crotalus, of reptiles. There are even several other animal gods of the hunt—the bear, the wolf, the coyote—but he is easily supreme. The hunter carries a tiny stone image of this most potent patron, and invokes it with strange incantations at every turn of the chase. But it was reserved for the Cochiteños to invent and realize a life-size fetich—therefore, one nearer the actual divinity symbolized, and more powerful. And from that far, forgotten day to this incongruous one, the stone lions of Cochití have never lost their potency. Worshipped continually for longer ages than Saxon history can call its own, they are worshipped still. No important hunt would even now be undertaken by the trustful folk of Cochití without first repairing to the stone pumas, to anoint their stolid heads with facepaint and the sacred meal, and to breathe their breath of power. ▪

⟨❂⟩

Born in Illinois, Mary Hunter Austin discovered the West on a barren and unsuccessful San Joaquin Valley, California, homestead in the 1880s. From this experience, however, Austin developed a deep passion for the desert and its Native American inhabitants. Encouraged and challenged by Charles F. Lummis, one of her first publishers, Austin became a prolific writer of essays and short stories and the author of many novels and nonfiction books. *The Land of Little Rain* (1903) established her as a significant voice in the tradition of American nature writing. She was an imposing and controversial figure in her day, acquainted with literary luminaries on both sides of the Atlantic, including Henry James, H. G. Wells, John Muir, Jack London, John Reed, and Mabel Dodge Luhan. Her lifelong interest in Native Americans arose from her interest in the regional identity of the American West and her sense of the need for human adaptation to the environment.

In this excerpt from her essay "The Days of Our Ancients," originally published in 1924 in the magazine *Survey* and included the same year as a chapter in her book *The Land of Journeys' Ending,* the modern experience of ancient ruins gives way to her desire to recapture the life of their former inhabitants and finally to Austin's sense of "Our Ancients" within the continuum of American cultural development. For Austin, it is the collective, communal life of the ancient Puebloans that brought them most meaningfully into history.

f r o m

"The Days of Our Ancients"

MARY AUSTIN

It was the nature of the country to which Our Ancients had come, in migrations not far separated in point of time, speaking at least four languages, but having a common origin legend and a common recognition of this Southwest as their Middle Place, that there was no easy way out of it.

Within their natural boundaries the Pueblo tribes settled or shifted, following their food, and from successive tarryings they swarmed. But by the end of the Small House period the trails of the various linguistic groups had become inextricably confused, issuing at intervals clear and well defined, and lost again like the track of desert creatures in the sand.

Where it issues at its most engaging is in the cliffs and caves of the San Juan drainage, and the Little Colorado. Not, however, as a phase of cultural evolution, but as a mere matter of convenience. There was no Cliff Dwelling age, but an easy adaptation to local advantages. Why dig a hole when there is a hole in a wall already dug for you? But because there is no important cliff dwelling without traces of corn culture, I am disposed to think it was the superiority of the inaccessible, solid-smooth rooms as storage vaults that led to their long continued use as homes. Every now and then the archeologist uncovers a wall cache of shelled corn, forgotten as long ago as the time an English king tended cakes in a cowherd's hut.

In the north there seems to have been a Small House period of cave dwelling, and a Tower House period after an interval in which cotton was added to the squash and beans and corn. Out of a cliff house in Utah, seed was taken of a distinct species, true Ancient of our tropical variety, and named *aborigeneum,* but how far it was from its native home there is no discovering.

Besides convenience there must have been an immense appeal of the cliff dwellings for their highness, the unstinted reach of vision, the sense of cuddling safety against the mother rock. How far from these aeyries, when the snow lay lightly as cloud on the junipers, they could trace the movement of the herds of elk and antelope. How comfortably they must have snuggled together around the three cornered fireplaces, when the torrent of the rain came falling like a silver curtain between them and the world, or the wolfish wind howled and scraped against the retaining wall!

It is more than likely that the same people moved in and out of their cave homes, as need or wishing drove them. At the *Rita de los Frijoles,* which is to say Bean Creek, the Keres who came into that shut valley with a well developed craft of stone working, preferred the cavate lodges, which at a later period they abandoned for the round, terraced pueblo, built up out of whole earth. And just as the Small House people clung to the sacred pits, so the town builders reverted to cave and crevice for their ceremonial chambers.

That was after the towns grew too large for the caves to hold, or after the enemy who might have driven them there had been vanquished or absorbed. Squeezed into the great cave of the Mesa Verde country there are towns that were able to afford streets, little plazas set about with public ovens, space between the cave and the house walls for the turkeys, rooms for milling and for meditation.

But it is difficult to write this period into any scheme of tribal evolution, there is such magic thrown over it by the wild splendor of the many colored cliffs from which the squared tops and ruined towers of the cliff villages peer down—eagles mewing about the perilous footholds, great trees rooting where once the slender ladders clung. You walk in one of the winding canyons of Southern Utah or Colorado, threaded by a bright stream, half smothered in chokecherry and cottonwood, where suddenly high and inaccessible, the sun picks out the little windows in the canyon walls, amid the smoke blue shadows, and you brush your eyes once or twice to make sure you do not see half naked men, deer and antelope laden, climbing up the banded cliffs, and sleek haired women, bright with such colors as they knew how to wring out of herbs and berries, popping in and out of the T-shaped openings like parakeets.

Clear October afternoons when the fleets of aspen gold at the bottoms of the canyons set sail for the ruined balconies and the gobble of the wild turkey sounds between the driving gusts, how can you be sure it does not come from the penned space behind the broken walls, how distinguish between the beat of your horse's hooves and the *plump, plump* of the mealing stones, or the roll of the medicine drums from the kivas?

Even more charged with the enchantment of mystery seem the cliff dwellings when you come upon them from above. Walking the level mesas between scant pines and silver dusted sage, you observe scarcely any human trace recognizable to the unpracticed eye. Here a low, squarish mound of surface stones shows where the Watchers of the Corn set up their towers, there a painted potshard kicked up from some stone rimmed area of wind sifted ash, mute evidence of a tender concern, marks for the knowing the place of incineration. Insensibly your feet stumble into the shallows of some ancient trail, and then suddenly the ground opens before you into a deep, many colored rift, murmurous with the ripple of a sunken stream, and the wind ruffled aspens. Midway of the cliff, or bent about the blind, rain blackened head of the canyon, the ruined towers beckon out of cavernous blueness. There must have been always this quality of enticement about these nested villages, even for the builders of them, so that you can well understand how, long after they were pulled by tribal necessities up over the clifftop to the building of walled towns, they returned to their sacred ceremonial cave as obstinately as the English return to Gothic for their religious architecture.

But for all their color of romance they remained simple and not over populous agricultural villages, so that if I wanted a marker for the age that built them I would not take it from the caves, but from a feature of their architecture that arose toward the end of the Small House period, out of the inner necessity of a tribal mind that was, at its profoundest, Oriental. All over the well timbered mesas of the McElmo, Pagose-Piedra and the upper Chama there arose a series of singular structures whose architectural evolution can still be traced, defining the period that produced them as the time of Towered Towns. They began before Our Ancients were fairly out of the cobblestone pits, and they do not disappear until the towns themselves have absorbed them, stretching up into seven-storied heights from whose tops the voice of the Cacique could be heard waking the village to its morning life.

From Hovenweep and Surouaro and Holly Canyon they spring. Round towers and square towers, towers squared on the sides and rounded on the corners, towers like Stronghold House thrust up on pinnacles of native rock, round towers at the outer corners of Great Houses as at Hovenweep, twin towers, set up over a cliff house, towers on the Mancos above cavate lodges, towers in the cliff villages at Far View and Spruce Tree Houses. The towers, I insist, grew out of an inner necessity of the tribes, that strange necessity of man to be responsible for his fellow man, of which the dawn impulse lies in the mind of the herd and the flock. Still in that region the leader of the browsing goats climbs up the boulder, on which the cacique of the Small House peoples sheltered his outlook with a round of heaped stone. But it was not for the enemy that he watched oftenest, if at all. He watched the game, antelope flashing their white rumps or scudding in great bands like cloud shadows across the grass mesas, blacktail trooping through shallow draws; but chiefly he watched the corn. He watched the crows settling over the young shoots, and between the glint of their wings he sent the glint of arrows and the twang of the bowstring, deeper than their quarreling caws. Many a mid-morning from his tower the voice of the watcher scattered the young men for turning aside the hooves of the mule deer, moving stealthily between the unfenced rows, ruining with selective bites the finest milky ears. No doubt he watched the sun and the stars, with whose orientation the times of his feasts were determined, and the lines of his ceremonial chambers set. But of all the necessities served by the Tower Houses, the keenest was the need of communication. From the tops of the towers went up smoke signals to the farthest confederated villages, but chiefly morning and evening Cacique or Pregonero cried prayers and the day's directions for a community that was always more communistic than anything of which we moderns have experienced.

The line at which our ancients crossed over from snuggling themselves into the environment as the wild hive into a hollow tree, and began to control it, is the line of the *acequia madre*. When a crop can flourish handsomely on the runoff of natural watersheds, a family may subsist satisfactorily by itself. But when a river is to be diverted in its course to irrigate the fields, then by the same tie that they bind the river to the service of the corn, men bind themselves to the indivisible utility. Rain falls on radical and conservative alike, but the mother ditch makes communists of them all.

That is, it makes for cooperative effort with psychological implications to which the term communism is a clumsy, crablike approach.

At the end of the Towered Town period, the homes of our Ancients in the land of their journey's ending, were mere clusters of more or less related, farmer groups, as slightly coordinated in respect to their civic functions as any pioneer crossroads, a state of things that we do as much as possible to disguise by calling their remains cliff cities, cliff palaces, Montezuma's castle and the like meaningless, falsely romantic terms. ■

D'Arcy McNickle was a member of the Confederated Salish and Kootenai Tribes of Montana, a trained anthropologist, founder of the National Congress of American Indians, and the first director of the Newberry Library Center for History of the American Indian. Although he wrote a number of historical and anthropological works as well as a biography of Oliver La Farge, McNickle is best known for his germinal novel *The Surrounded* (1936), a work in which the struggle between acculturation and traditional values anticipate the "Native American Renaissance" that would follow thirty years later. His posthumously published novel *Wind from an Enemy Sky* (1978) explores these issues further.

In 1954, McNickle wrote the historical novel *Runner in the Sun: A Story of Indian Maize,* a book for younger readers. Set in pre-Columbian times among the Puebloans of what is now the Southwest's Four Corners region, *Runner in the Sun* tells the story of a community imperiled by climatic change and internal division. The teenage boy Salt is sent by village elders to the Valley of Mexico to bring back a drought-resistant strain of corn. More than simply a rite-of-passage story for young people, McNickle's novel follows in the tradition of Bandelier's *The Delight Makers* as an important statement about the complexity of indigenous cultures. Furthermore, written during the Termination era of the 1950s, when the U.S. government sought to uproot Native Americans from their reservations, *Runner in the Sun* has been praised as an affirmation of the integrity and continuity of Native American communities. In the chapter reprinted here, as clan rivalries and internal power struggles begin to disrupt village life, the people discover that the spring on which they depend for survival is drying up. Although traditional Puebloan belief would suggest that this calamity arises from spiritual disharmony within the community, the boy Salt later finds that the water has been secretly diverted by the Spider Clan. McNickle shows traditional belief being made concrete in the actions of people.

---

f r o m

Runner in the Sun

D ' A R C Y   M c N I C K L E

That was the day of the summer solstice—the day on which the sun reached its farthest advance into the northern sky. On that day, and at the winter solstice as well, the village people felt uneasy. Partly, this uneasiness resulted from what they could see with their own eyes: each day in summer the sun rose and set at a place farther to the north. The Sun Watcher, whose task it was to observe this movement, peered through a slit in the Sun Tower at each rising and setting of the sun. On the wall opposite the slit, he made a check against markings which had been scratched into the stone by Sun Watchers long before his time. So the people knew of this movement of the sun northward in the summer, and they feared that if it did not check itself, it might desert the earth entirely. In the winter, it moved in the contrary direction and threatened to leave the world buried in snow and ice.

The principal cause of uneasiness, however, was the stories that were told of occasions when the sun disappeared out of the sky entirely. As the people watched in terror it seemed to die by degrees. True, it had always reappeared again, according to these stories, but such occurrences left men's minds with the unhappy feeling that the sun was a living substance, and like all living substances was mortal and was subject to whimsical behavior. Since their own lives, they knew, depended on the sun to warm their bodies and bring growth to their crops, they felt somewhat as children feel toward an elderly parent—they must be respectful and considerate.

Before dawn, runners had gone forth from each of the Seven Clan houses, or kivas. They would visit all the outlying shrines, some of which were at great distances, to place prayer feathers and offerings of sacred meal. They started early, because it was necessary to be back in the village before the sun reached its highest midday point.

Meantime, while the runners were out, officers of each of the Seven Clans took turns marching into the largest plaza, where they danced in two rows. They dressed bravely in many-colored knee-length aprons and sashes, and on their breasts and arms were ornaments of turquoise, shell, feathers, and animal teeth. The costumes were intended to be gay and bright, to persuade the sun that his earth children loved him and desired his presence. The songs they sang were quick and sparkling:

> Behold us here,
> Behold us here,
> Brothers all, ai-ay-ai.
>
> Here we sing,
> Here we sing,
> Brothers all, ai-ay-ai.
>
> Here is food,
> Here is food,
> Brothers all, ai-ay-ai.
> Ai-ay-ai-ai-ai-ai.
>
> Behold us here,
> Behold us here,
> Brothers all, ai-ay-ai.
>
> Here is rest,
> Here is rest,
> Brothers all, ai-ay-ai.
>
> Comes the sun,
> Sparkling sun,
> Brothers all, ai-ay-ai.
> Ai-ay-ai-ai-ai-ai.

The song would go on like that, without stopping, for several hours, as first one set of singers, then another, chanted the words. Even the smallest children were encouraged to join in these dances and songs, since the sun was fond of children.

As midday approached, the dancers began to leave the central plaza to return to their kivas. People who had been watching, retreated toward their houses. All who could, tried to be out of the direct glare of the midday sun. If a man found himself in the field, he sought a spreading tree or an overhanging rock, there to sit out the sun's climb to its zenith. On this day of the solstice, people waited through the high-noon period for word that the sun had arrived in his northern house and was content not to travel beyond.

The noise of the singing had died away, people everywhere in the village were moving out of sight—then it happened!

First one voice, then several voices, carried the news. The voices came from the far end of the village, toward the south, where the trail came up from the bottom of the canyon. People who had been on the point of entering their houses stopped in their tracks and looked down that way. Others, who were already inside, came out again. No one moved at first, but all stood watching. On a day when people were naturally uneasy, any unexpected happening filled the air with excitement.

Three women had reached the top of the trail and were running toward the village. Their hands were empty of water jars. They were screaming.

"Our spring! Oh, fathers! Our spring!"

As the three women reached the first house, wide-eyed and panting, other women moved forward in a group and swallowed them.

"What of the spring? What are you saying?" the women were asked.

A babble of sound followed. Meantime, other women were running forward. Men could now be seen standing in doorways or in the shadow of a building. They watched, but did not advance.

"What of the spring, Crane Woman?"

The woman thus called by name, eldest of the three, caught her breath and looked around.

"The spring, my people, is dead," she announced flatly.

The statement shocked everyone into silence. Minds groped with the words, turned them over and over. How could a spring die? What kind of nonsense was the woman talking?

After a moment, everyone talked at once, showering questions upon the three women. What had they seen? What happened?

Crane Woman was the first to collect her senses. She listened for a moment, started to answer a question, then threw up her hands and demanded silence.

"Peace! Peace! We have no time to stand babbling. The clan fathers must be told of this at once. Someone go to each kiva. Tell whomever you find that our spring has stopped flowing. It exists no more."

"At first, when we arrived to fill our jars, muddy water was flowing," the second woman explained. She too had sobered after the battering of questions. "We waited for it to clear. Then it stopped altogether."

The third woman of the group, hardly more than a girl but already a mother, was the last to speak out. Her voice was still strained. "We waited, and it seemed just to sink into the sand. We were frightened."

By that time, the first men had joined the group, and when they heard these reports they refused to believe them.

"Just wait, now," an old man said. He had a withered right leg and walked with the aid of a thick crutch which his bad leg wrapped itself around. He went by the name of Mountain Walker.

"Our clan fathers should not be disturbed here in the middle of the day. You women should take yourselves inside, away from the sun, instead of spreading this fantastic story about our spring drying up. What would we do without our spring?"

Crane Woman threw back her head. "Father, this is no time to worry about the sun, and if we don't tell this to the kiva leaders at once, we will all be sorry. I tell you, our spring is no more; it is dead, it runs no water. I saw it with my own eyes. These women, too. Ask them? Don't tell us we are spreading a fantasy! Just trot down there yourself, if you like."

"Peace, peace, woman!" the old man pleaded. "Obviously, I cannot trot anywhere. You say it ran dirty water first, then stopped. Perhaps a boulder fell from the cliff and blocked it for a while. It will flow again, just you see. In all our lifetimes, and the lifetimes of our fathers, our spring has never failed us. It cannot fail us now. Here, you young fellows, run down and look. Just see if the water hasn't worked its way around the boulder and started to flow again."

"There was no boulder—" Crane Woman started to protest, then stopped, as if she could not be sure. She looked at her two companions, but they only returned her stare. They could not remember whether they had seen a boulder lying in the stream or not.

"Maybe Mountain Walker is right. Maybe it will flow again," a voice came from the group of women.

"We are wasting time, and the kiva leaders will be angry," Crane Woman insisted, but she did not move away.

Two young men had already detached themselves from the group and were disappearing over the edge of the cliff. They would scramble down the log ladder and race for the bottom of the canyon.

The waiting group did not stand in its uncertainty for long, before men began to emerge from the seven kivas. The men of the Turquoise Clan came first. Some even had parts of their ceremonial dress still attached—anklets of eagle feathers, a kilt of black and red design. One man was absent-mindedly carrying an eagle-wing fan. The startling news had caught them as they were undressing.

Following close upon them, came men from the Water-Reed Clan, the Hawk Clan, the Stone Flute Clan, the Gray Badger Clan, the Yellow Rod Clan, and lastly the Spider Clan. Many of these had been taken by surprise too, since they came daubed with the white clay markings and bits of the ceremonial dress in which they had been performing. They streamed up the kiva ladders and out into the street.

The men of the Spider Clan were slower than the others in reaching the street, and only three came forth. Dark Dealer was not among these, though as War Chief and protector of the clan, he should have been among the first. People of the village did not recall this until later.

Now the houses too were emptying. On every terrace and rooftop, women and children and old people gathered in silent clusters. "What is it?" was asked everywhere. No one yet knew, or they would not talk about it. "Something. Just wait," mothers told their young ones.

Star Climber had been in his own Turquoise kiva when the Sun Crier, the man who kept vigilance for the clan and made public announcements, scrambled down the ladder and held a whispered conversation. Whatever he said reached only to the ears of the leaders in the center of the room, but from their startled expressions and sharp exclamations, Star Climber knew that a terrible thing had happened. He had come to the kiva, as a dutiful young man should, to help the elders remove their cumbersome dance costumes and do whatever else was required. It filled him with dismay, therefore, when these sober, meticulous men cast aside costumes without regard and sprang for the kiva ladder. All without saying a word to him.

He climbed to the plaza, not sure in his mind whether to leave the kiva unprotected, but pulled strongly by the desire to know what was happening. He could see men hurrying toward the place where the trail came up from the canyon. . . .

At last he reached the fringe of the crowd. The women had made way for the men pouring up from the kivas, and all waited at the corner of the last building of the village. The runners who had been sent into the canyon to verify the stories told by the three women were just then coming into view.

The head of the trail was above the village and anyone coming up from the canyon was immediately visible in the village. The young men waved their arms and shouted something which Star Climber at least could not hear clearly. Then they ran forward and were encompassed by the crowd.

"It is true, O fathers," one gasped. "Our spring has stopped flowing."

His breath gave out, and the second runner continued: "We looked for a boulder or rock slide, but there was nothing. The water—just stopped."

"A few pools still hold water," the first speaker resumed. "I think the women should go with their jars. Before it disappears into the ground."

A profound silence fell upon the crowd. If the sun had fallen out of the clear sky on that equinoctial day, the people could not have been more deeply shocked. The spring was life, as was the sun. To be deprived of either, they knew in their hearts at once, meant the end of life. Without water, where would they go? What would they do? Each man and woman pondered these questions as if they had been passed from mouth to mouth, though no word was uttered.

It was Trailing Cloud, the Sun Watcher of the Turquoise Clan, who broke into the shocked silence. His eyesight was dim and his legs unsteady, but his voice was a firm check on their mounting fear. He spoke as if the future were already clear and he knew what each must do.

"Let a woman from each of the clans go with storage jars and collect the water in the pools. Then see that each family gets a fair share. When the pools have been drained, let men from the clans dig pits in the sand. These may fill by morning. But someone will need to watch, to see that the water does not seep away and that no one takes more than his share."

The elder paused for thought, then resumed. "We must get word at once to the man up there." All looked toward the rock shelter in the cliff, knowing that he meant the Holy One. "Shield will go to him. We will ask his help."

He squinted at the crowd that pressed around him. "I cannot tell who is here. I do not see Eldest Woman. Is she here?"

The men looked over the crowd, then at each other. No one had seen her.

"Then send for her," the old man ordered. A younger woman hurried from the crowd. Eldest Woman had been known to refuse to come at the bidding of a man.

Trailing Cloud's mouth quivered, but he held firm. "Tell the Rain Makers to prepare their prayer sticks and their holy meal. We will go down to the spring and speak for the lives of our people."

All at once his strength failed. "I want to sit down," he rasped irritably. His assistants led him to some stone steps where the street climbed up between houses.

The crowd fell apart then. The Rain Makers of each clan went to their kivas to prepare for the ceremony at the spring. Others could not decide whether to go below and see with their own eyes, or whether to wait. Most of the crowd simply stayed together, saying little, scarcely moving. They stood in the full glare of the midday sun and thought nothing of it.

Women, meanwhile, were arriving with jars of all sizes, including some very large storage jars which when filled would be too heavy for a single person to carry up the trail. These would be left below and water would be dipped from them into smaller vessels. Men with digging tools of sharp sticks and stone hand shovels came out of the houses and started down the trail.

"This may be the end of our ancient village," Trailing Cloud spoke as though from a dream. His kiva leaders, the Fire Chief, Tobacco Chief, and Sand Chief stayed with him. At a little distance, the boy, Star Climber, squatted on his heels. He was fearful of approaching too close to the leaders, because of the dread things he might hear, and equally fearful of not being on hand if they should ask for him.

"The people will survive," the old man went on, held in the grip of his dreaming vision. "But they will have to scatter. Who knows what will become of us? By tonight we will start runners out. They will have to range far and wide, to places we have never been, in search of living water. We know all the waters nearby; they are small streams, not enough for all our people, or they flow for only a short time each year."

Then he shook his head and came back to one thought, from which he never strayed far. Many that day kept returning to the same thought.

"This is strange, indeed. Our spring has never failed us before. In my lifetime, and in my father's lifetime, and I do not know for how long before that, the spring never failed. It almost seems as if someone among us has offended the Cloud People and our Guardian Spirits in some grievous way. But who among us will want to say who is responsible for such a thing! Who among us understands such things!"

The Rain Makers were now returning, but they were troubled. For each clan there was a Rain Maker Chief and two assistants. Now they came with their cedar branches, their prayer sticks topped with kingfisher feathers, their pouches filled with water-washed stones, and their reed flutes. All were together and ready, except for the men from the Spider Clan. They had waited at the Spider Clan kiva and finally sent someone to ask for the Rain Chief. No one could say where he was. The sun was now halfway across the afternoon sky. What were they to do?

Trailing Cloud rose shakily to his feet. In his heart he knew that something was very wrong; a chill crept through his body. But a decision had to be made, and he would make it. He reached out to find a shoulder for support.

"We will go below," he said in a voice turned weak. "We will go without Spider Clan, though never before have we acted without all the clans together. Send word throughout the village that all are to come below, to pray for our spring and for our people."

Then he asked again for Eldest Woman, and when it was reported that she had been sent for and could not be found, a tremor went through his body. Clearly, it was an evil day.

Criers called through the village and their voices echoed back as they spread the word.

The clan leaders went first, and as they filed out of the village, they began to chant of the Far Reaching One and the Dawn Sky Woman, for these were the first Beings and all things came from them. First the clan leaders took up the chant and were heard until, group by group, they started down the log ladder and their voices were lost in the chasm. Then, as people of the village followed after the leaders, they continued the chant, until their voices were also lost. It took some time for the village to empty itself. No one hurried. The people walked in what seemed a reluctant procession, as if their minds already assured them that they would fail in this attempt. Finally, all had departed and their singing came more faintly, echoed back from the far side of the canyon.

The people of the Spider Clan had not joined in the procession, but at the time no one seemed to notice that.

Since the early 1960s, Pulitzer Prize–winning poet Gary Snyder has crafted his experiences with the natural world, Beat subculture, and Asian philosophy into carefully detailed and evocative work. With *The Practice of the Wild* (1990), he established himself as one of our foremost living essayists in the tradition of American nature writing that includes Henry David Thoreau, John Muir, Aldo Leopold, and more recently Edward Abbey and Ann Zwinger. In "Anasazi," first published in 1972 and reprinted as part of his 1974 collection *Turtle Island*, Snyder repopulates the landscape in the tradition of Bandelier and McNickle. Using a mosaic of precisely wrought images, he imagines an ancient Puebloan cliff dwelling as it might have been, alive again in the experiences of the people.

"Anasazi"

GARY SNYDER

Anasazi,
Anasazi,

tucked up in clefts in the cliffs
growing strict fields of corn and beans
sinking deeper and deeper in earth
up to your hips in Gods
            your head all turned to eagle-down
            & lightning for knees and elbows
your eyes full of pollen

            the smell of bats.
            the flavor of sandstone
            grit on the tongue.

            women
            birthing
at the foot of ladders in the dark.

trickling streams in hidden canyons
under the cold rolling desert

corn-basket   wide-eyed
            red baby
            rock lip home,

Anasazi

※

Although his training was in civil engineering and technical writing, not archaeology, Franklin Barnett in the years following World War II developed a deep commitment to understanding the prehistory of the American West. His work has been published by the Albuquerque Archaeological Society and the Museum of Northern Arizona, and in 1973 Barnett completed his *Dictionary of Prehistoric Indian Artifacts of the American Southwest.* He wrote reports of the excavations of Matli Ranch Ruins and the Fitzmaurice Pueblo ruin in Yavapai County, Arizona. Like Adolf Bandelier and D'Arcy McNickle, Barnett attempts to recover through the medium of fiction what life might have been like among the ancient Puebloans in his historical novel *Crooked Arrow: A Novel of Southwestern Prehistoric Indians of the 13th Century* (1977). In Chapter Thirteen of *Crooked Arrow,* reprinted here, Barnett's central character, the young man Ah-ee, attempts to provide for his community in the midst of a changing climate.

f r o m

Crooked Arrow

FRANKLIN BARNETT

Ah-ee and his brothers spent most of the remainder of the day discussing ways to help the people who remained at the pueblo. The only practical help would be furnishing meat, where there had been none for so long. There must be one more extensive hunt which would cover all of the game country they had ever known or heard of.

Most of the big hunters were gone, and many of those who remained were quite young. But the brothers all agreed that the young hunters could be taught the tricks of the trail, even as older hunters had taught them such tricks many summers before.

Ah-ee was made the leader of this hunt, which they all felt would probably be their last in this area. Their hope was to provide some meat for those who had practically none for several moons.

In three days' time, all was in readiness. There were seven hunters and five warriors in the main body of the hunting party. Six boys were to be taken along to carry extra arrows, what little food there was, and to help bring back the carcasses of animals as they were killed. They would then return to the hunting party. One of the young boys was Quaant's older son, Di-qu. The boy was large for his age, and while Memah was not too sure she wanted Di-qu to go on such a trip, she realized this was his first step to manhood.

Ah-ee's plan for the hunt was based upon what he and his brothers knew of as the best areas to hunt, as well as those areas they had heard of.

The hunting party left the pueblo during the middle of the third day. They started through the country of the huge jumble of granite boulders, and on to the north. One of the warriors was out in front of the group as a lookout. From time to time, he glanced back at Ah-ee, who would signal the direction to take. The party moved at a fast pace through this area where there was nothing to be hunted.

The next day, the three brothers moved abreast, but several paces apart. All unnecessary noise and talking was held to a minimum. The hunters hoped to find animals of some sort at any time. Except for two rabbits and five prairie dogs, game was nowhere to be seen.

That night, all of the hunters agreed that the real hunting areas were still to the north and west, toward the foothills of the mountains at the north end of the big valley.

Early morning of the following day was a more successful time. Without knowing it, they had camped only a short distance from a small stream. Quaant and his son, Di-qu, and one of the other boys had wandered off to the north before the party was grouped for the day's hunt. Di-qu, who had been in the lead, held up his hand, halting the other two. Quaant quietly moved forward.

Straight in front of them stood two deer, drinking from a small spring near the edge of a narrow meandering stream of water. Quaant fitted an arrow into his bow, carefully aimed, and drew back his bow. At this instant, both deer raised their heads, and alert to the slight sound and movement. Now he released his arrow. The deer nearest Quaant and the boys jumped high into the air, then fell heavily to the ground, there to thrash his legs helplessly. In a moment, he lay still. The second deer bounded off into the underbrush in long, graceful leaps. The hunter fitted a second arrow into his bow, but did not get a chance to shoot.

Quaant quickly removed the entrails and the head from the deer he had killed. His son and his friend had already cut a pole on which to carry the trussed deer. The three moved back to camp, carrying the carcass.

"Now we know there is at least one more deer around here," said Ah-ee. Each of the men was sure he would be the one to kill the other one. Ah-ee picked two of the older boys to take the deer to the pueblo. The boys were cautioned not to loiter, but to hurry both going and returning. Ah-ee drew a map on the ground showing where the pueblo was, where they were now, and where the party would be by the time the boys returned.

No more game was sighted through the day. In the late afternoon, Ah-ee decided that since they were so close to the small pueblo, he and some others would go and see the place. He knew he probably would never come near here again. When they were asked, everyone in the party wanted to see the small pueblo where Ah-ee and Cu-mo were born. Cu-mo, Quaant, and Di-qu, had special reasons. Cu-mo, because of who he now was, and Quaant and his son, because Memah came from here.

During the trip to the small pueblo, they killed four rabbits and ten prairie dogs. The party prepared a camp in the old pueblo dance area. Tonight there would be a feast. On the next day, they would show the area to those who had not seen it before.

Ah-ee and Cu-mo were silent. They were near their home pueblo, and the place was full of memories. Everything had started from here.

The following morning, some of them went through many of the houses in the pueblo. Neither Ah-ee nor Cu-mo would go into any of them. As Chief Bacht said when he and the remainder of the people from here came through the big pueblo to the south, many of the houses had been burned out, and the roofs had fallen in. In the short time since the departure of those people, debris and sand had blown in and filled the houses half way up the walls.

After the rest at the small pueblo, the hunting party moved to the hills and juniper forest to the northwest. This was country with which Ah-ee was familiar. But now times had changed. Even in this previously lush area, the drouth had affected the vegetation, which affected every animal.

Ah-ee changed directions of the hunting party to the south. They began to follow the foothills, and to search each draw where in previous summers there had been springs and small streams.

With the change of direction, there was also a change of fortunes. Now some small game was occasionally seen, and some were shot for the meal at the end of the day. But a large rocky draw provided the excitement of the day.

One of the young hunters had been scouting in the area of the draw, located between two rocky, almost vertical cliffs on either side. The upper end of the draw contained large boulders, which were piled one upon another, and formed the area into a small boxed canyon.

As the young man progressed beyond the entrance of the area, he saw four deer grazing at the far end. Carefully withdrawing, he got behind the cover of a large boulder and called Ah-ee with the hoot of a night owl. Ah-ee, in turn, signaled Cu-mo and a young hunter who was near him, and those two converged on Ah-ee. The three moved stealthily toward the young hunter who had signaled. After a hasty consultation, the four spread out in a line to cover the width of the draw, and crept forward in slow deliberate motions.

Quaant signaled to two of the young hunters and two warriors near him to form a support line, and follow Ah-ee, Cu-mo and the others. Everyone advanced as carefully as possible. Bows were fitted with arrows.

The first line of hunters came within bow range of the deer, when the large buck, the leader of the small herd, raised his head. As the buck gazed around him, the hunters froze in position. Soon the buck lowered his head and continued to graze. As he did so, the first line of hunters moved closer to their prey.

At an almost imperceptible signal from Ah-ee, each bowman in the first line raised and aimed his arrow at the deer directly in front of him. They released their arrows simultaneously. Two of the deer dropped immediately, while a third staggered, then ran crazily in a zig-zag line down the draw. The fourth deer was only slightly wounded, and dashed down the draw in a series of gigantic leaps. Both deer ran between the hunters in the first line.

Here Quaant's strategy became apparent. As the two deer moved down the draw, the second line of hunters rose and completed the kill of the four deer.

When the deer were headed for the pueblo on the shoulders of excited boys, Ah-ee turned to Cu-mo and said, "This is why it is good we teach our brother Quaant how to hunt, so we kill all four deer we see."

Now everyone relaxed. It had been many months since Ah-ee had expressed even the slightest sign of levity.

Quaant, not to be outdone, answered, "I follow both of my brothers, so there will be enough meat for pueblo. If I do not, then there is only half as much." In an assumed haughty manner, he continued, "Now we leave so I can get the rest of the animals in hills near here." Grinning, he waved the others to move out ahead.

The change of fortune was short-lived. As the hunting party went farther south, they killed only two more deer and one antelope. There just were not any more animals.

Except for several small mammals which were shot the last two days of the hunt, there was nothing else. The hunters brought the small animals to the pueblo with them.

Head Priest Ba-te-wa called a meeting of leaders to get a final report of conditions from Ah-ee. When the number of hunters and the country covered were taken into account, the few animals they killed were only those that for some reason could not leave this parched country. The priest also noted that even with so many families gone, the amount of meat brought in looked like more than it really was. There were fewer people to feed. ■

Although Robert Frost was born in San Francisco, his name is virtually synonymous with New England. Frost's poetry evokes the beauty and peace of the rural landscapes of Massachusetts and New Hampshire and also the complexity of human emotional engagement with them. His reputation as the quintessential American poet of the twentieth century began with *A Boy's Will* (1913) and *North of Boston* (1914). Following his reading at the inauguration of John F. Kennedy in 1961, Frost's *In the Clearing* (1962) demonstrated the poet's creative vigor even when he was well into his eighties.

Frost's son-in-law, Willard Fraser, took many excursions with friends Earl and Ann Axtell Morris on archaeological digs along the La Plata River and on the Navajo Indian Reservation in Arizona. When Morris presented Frost with an ancient Puebloan arrowhead from near the La Plata, Frost repaid the gift with this poem.

"A Missive Missile"

ROBERT FROST

Someone in ancient Mas d'azil
Once took a little pebble wheel
And dotted it with red for me,
And sent it to me years and years—
A million years to be precise—
Across the barrier of ice.
Two round dots and a ripple streak,
So vivid as to seem to speak.
But what imperfectly appears
Is whether the two dots were tears,
Two tear drops, one for either eye,

And the wave line a shaken sigh.
But no, the color used is red.
Not tears but drops of blood instead.
The line must be a jagged blade.
The sender must have had to die,
And wanted some one now to know
His death was sacrificial-votive.
So almost clear and yet obscure.
If only anyone were sure
A motive then was still a motive.
O you who bring this to my hand,
You are no common messenger
(Your badge of office is a spade).
It grieves me to have had you stand
So long for nothing. No reply—
There is no answer, I'm afraid,
Across the icy barrier
For my obscure petitioner.
Suppose his ghost is standing by
Importunate to give the hint
And be successfully conveyed.
How anyone can fail to see
Where perfectly in form and tint
The metaphor, the symbol lies!
Why will I not analogize?
(I do too much in some men's eyes.)
Oh slow uncomprehending me,
Enough to make a spirit moan
Or rustle in a bush or tree.
I have the ochre-written flint,
The two dots and the ripple line.
The meaning of it is unknown,
Or else I fear entirely mine,
All modern, nothing ancient in't,
Unsatisfying to us each.
Far as we aim our signs to reach,

Far as we often make them reach,
Across the soul-from-soul abyss,
There is an aeon-limit set
Beyond which we are doomed to miss.
Two souls may be too widely met.
That sad-with-distance river beach
With mortal longing may beseech;
It cannot speak as far as this.

Poem composed on receipt of an Anasazi arrowhead from the La Plata district, southern Colorado, a gift from Earl H. Morris █

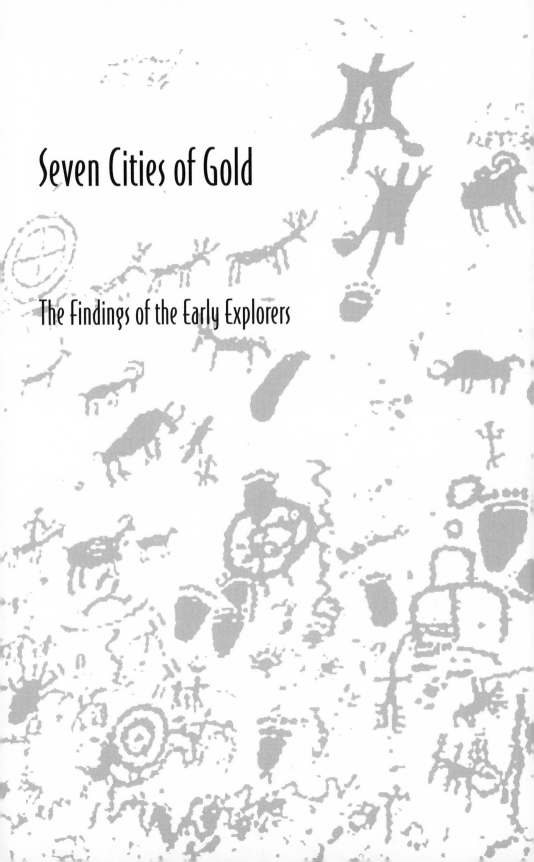

Seven Cities of Gold

The Findings of the Early Explorers

✺

One of the first Europeans to write about the American Southwest, Pedro de Castaneda chronicled the 1540 expedition of Francisco Vásquez de Coronado in search of the legendary Seven Cities of Cibola, a journey that took him north from Mexico City to the pueblos of New Mexico and as far as north-central Kansas in search of another mythic land, Quivira. Setting out to confirm missionary priest Fray Marcos de Niza's dubious account of treasure-laden golden cities far to the north, Coronado led three hundred soldiers and priests, hundreds of American Indians and slaves, and great herds of livestock into country then almost wholly unknown to Europeans. Accompanying the expedition was the Moor Estevanico, who had made a remarkable journey across the continent with Cabeza de Vaca in the 1530s and who claimed special knowledge about the location of Cibola. Although the expedition brought back a wealth of information about the geography of the Southwest, it failed to find any gold. Cibola turned out to be the pueblos of Zuni. Quivira turned out to be, well, Kansas.

If the inhabited sixteenth-century pueblos were a disappointment to the Spaniards' dreams of plunder, the ruins of the abandoned pueblos they encountered along the way seemed nearly irrelevant. They were looking, after all, for cities of gold, not of red earth, as is made evident in this account by Casteneda of Coronado's visit to Casas Grandes, in present-day Chihuahua, Mexico.

f r o m

The Coronado Expedition, 1540-1542

PEDRO DE CASTANEDA

The general, as has been said, started to continue his journey from the Valley of Culiacan somewhat lightly equipped, taking with him the friars, since none of them wished to stay behind with the army. After they had gone three days, a regular friar who could say mass, named Friar Antonio Victoria, broke his leg, and they brought him back from the camp to have it doctored. He stayed with the army after this, which was no slight consolation for all. The general and his force crossed the country without trouble, as they found everything peaceful, because the Indians knew Friar Farcos and some of the others who had been with Melchior Diaz when he went with Juan de Saldibar to investigate. After the general had crossed the inhabited region and came to Chichilticalli, where the wilderness begins, and saw nothing favorable, he could not help feeling somewhat downhearted, for although the reports were very fine about what was ahead, there was nobody who had seen it except the Indians who went with the negro, and these had already been caught in some lies. Besides all this, he was much affected by seeing that the fame of Chichilticalli was summed up in one tumbledown house without any roof, although it appeared to have been a strong place at some former time when it was inhabited, and it was very plain that it had been built by a civilized and warlike race of strangers who had come from a distance. This building was made of red earth. From here they went on through the wilderness. . . . ▨

After attacking the Zuni Pueblo of Hawi-kuh in 1540, Coronado sent one of his lieutenants, Hernando de Alvarado, to investigate the country to the east. On his way to Acoma along the rugged lava flows of the Ojo Caliente valley, Alvarado came across indications of an ancient civilization, the ruins of whose cities he compared to Spain. Contemporary Zunis do not claim to know the precise sites to which Alvarado refers in his official report of his mission, but there is a chance that he may have stumbled upon what is today known as the Village of the Great Kivas, located on Zuni land south of Gallup, New Mexico.

f r o m

The Report of Hernando de Alvarado

HERNANDO DE ALVARADO

We set out from Granada on Sunday, the day of the beheading of Saint John the Baptist, the 29th of August, in the year 1540, on the way to Coco. After we had gone two leagues, we came to an ancient building like a fortress, and a league beyond this we found another, and yet another a little farther on, and beyond these we found an ancient city, very large, entirely destroyed, although a large part of the wall was standing, which was six times as tall as a man, the wall well made of good worked stone, with gates and gutters like a city in Castile. Half a league or more beyond this, we found another ruined city, the walls of which must have been very fine, built of very large granite blocks, as high as a man and from there up of very good quarried stone. Here two roads separate, one to Chia and the other to Coco; we took this latter, and reached that place, which is one of the strongest places that we have seen, because the city is on a very high rock, with such a rough ascent that we repented having gone up to the place.

Born in 1645 in what is today northern Italy, Eusebio Francisco Kino entered the Society of Jesus in 1665. When he was thirty-six years old he was sent as a missionary to Mexico City and on to the northern Spanish frontier. After establishing a mission to the American Indians at Nuestra Señora de los Dolores in Sonora, Mexico, Kino went on to conduct some forty expeditions into the wilderness of Pimeria Alta, a Spanish administrative region made up of what is today northern Sonora and southern Arizona. Following in the footsteps of the famous Fray Marcos, Kino was a true explorer-priest and is often credited as the discoverer of the sources of the Rio Grande, Colorado, and Gila Rivers. Although he worked to convert the Pima people to Christianity, he also is said to have actively opposed the brutal enslavement of American Indians in Spain's colonial silver mines. In this excerpt from *Kino's Historical Memoir of Pimeria Alta,* Kino relates his 1694 visit to the ruins at Casa Grande on the Gila River, today in central Arizona. He also alludes to the similarly named Casas Grandes ruins described by Castaneda.

It is clear that, for Kino, the ancient ruins on the Gila at least at one time must certainly have been the legendary Seven Cities of Cibola, even if the Native people who may first have described them to Fray Marcos had neglected to mention that they were already abandoned by the time the Spaniards arrived.

f r o m

Kino's Historical Memoir of Pimeria Alta

EUSEBIO FRANCISCO KINO

In November, 1694, I went inland with my servants and some justices of this Pimeria, as far as the *casa grande,* as these Pimas call it, which is on the large River of Hila that flows out of Nuevo Mexico and has its source near Acoma. This river and this large house and the neighboring houses are forty-three leagues beyond and to the north-west of the Sobaipuris of San Francisco Xavier del Bac. The first rancheria, that of El Tusonimo, we named *La Encarnacion,* as we arrived there to say mass on the first Sunday in Advent; and because many other Indians came to see us from the rancheria of El Coatoydag, which was four leagues further on, we named the latter *San Andres,* as the following day was the feast of that holy apostle. All were affable and docile people. They told us of two friendly nations living farther on, all down the river to the west, and to the northwest on the Rio Azul, and still farther, on the Rio Colorado. These nations are the Opas and Cocomaricopas. They speak a language very different from that of the Pimas, though it is very clear, and as there were some who knew both languages very well, I at once and with ease made a vocabulary of the said tongues, and also a map of those lands, measuring the sun with the astrolabe.

The *casa grande* is a four-story building, as large as a castle and equal to the largest church in these lands of Sonora. It is said that the ancestors of Montezuma deserted and depopulated it, and, beset by the neighboring Apaches, left for the east or Casas Grandes, and that from there they turned towards the south, and southwest, finally founding the great city and court of Mexico. Close to this *casa grande* there are thirteen smaller houses, somewhat more dilapi-dated, and the ruins of many others, which make it evident that in ancient times there had been a city here. On this oc-casion and on later ones I have learned and heard, and at times have even seen, that further to the east, north, and west there are seven or eight more of these large old houses and the ruins of whole cities, with many broken metates and jars, charcoal, etc.

These certainly must be the Seven Cities mentioned by the holy man, Fray Marcos de Niza, who in his long pilgrimage came clear to the Bacapa rancheria of these coasts, which is about sixty leagues southwest from this *casa grande,* and about twenty leagues from the Sea of California. The guides or interpreters must have given his Reverence the information which he has in his book concerning these Seven Cities, although certainly at that time, and for a long while before, they must have been deserted. ▪

Advised to take a trip west for his failing health in 1831, Josiah Gregg not only recovered but stayed. Turning his back on his medical training, he went on to become a merchant in Santa Fe and a correspondent during the war with Mexico (1846–47). He died in 1849 on his way to the goldfields in California, probably of exposure or starvation. Gregg's *The Commerce of the Prairies* (1844) draws upon his travels on the Santa Fe Trail, which was at the time the main trade route between the United States and the Mexican province of Nuevo Mexico.

A mix of objective treatise and remarkable anecdotes compiled from his extensive notebooks, *Commerce* is an engaging portrait of the mid–nineteenth century frontier and its people. Gregg praises the freedom and personal responsibility that the wilderness engenders, but he deplores romanticized depictions of the West that imply the "unvarnished facts" are somehow not enough. That the ancient pueblos were built by a mysterious "vanished people" would be consistent with Gregg's suspicions about the romantic; his suggestion that there is a historical connection between the abandoned pueblos of Pueblo Bonito and Casas Grandes and the existing pueblos of the Hopi (Moqui) and the Rio Grande Valley might be read as an early rejection of this popular myth. More likely, however, Gregg is merely subscribing to the once-popular theory that the indigenous peoples who built the pueblos in the north were the descendants of the Aztec ruler Montezuma.

f r o m

The Commerce of the Prairies

JOSIAH GREGG

All the Indians of New Mexico not denominated Pueblos—not professing the Christian religion—are ranked as *wild tribes,* although these include some who have made great advances in arts, manufactures and agriculture. Those who are at all acquainted with the ancient history of Mexico will recollect that, according to the traditions of the aborigines, all the principal tribes of Anahuac descended from the North: and that those of Mexico, especially the Azteques, emigrated from the north of California, or northwest of New Mexico. Clavigero, the famous historian heretofore alluded to, speaking of this emigration, observes that the *Azteques,* or Mexican Indians, who were the last settlers in the country of Anahuac, lived until about the year 1160 of the Christian era in Aztlan, a country situated to the north of the Gulf of California; as is inferred from the route of their peregrinations, and from the information afterwards acquired by the Spaniards in their expeditions through those countries. He then proceeds to show by what incentives they were probably induced to abandon their native land, adding that whatever may have been the motive, no doubt can possibly exist as to the journey's having actually been performed. He says that they travelled in a southeastwardly direction towards the Rio Gila, where they remained for some time—the ruins of their edifices being still to be seen, upon its banks. They then struck out for a point over two hundred and fifty miles to the northwest of Chihuahua in about 29° of N. latitude, where they made another halt. This place is known by the name of Casas Grandes (big houses), on account of a large edifice which still stands on the spot, and which, according to the general tradition of those regions, was erected by the Mexican Indians, during their wanderings. The building is constructed after the plan of those in New Mexico, with three stories, covered with an *azotea,* or terrace, and without door or entrance into the lower story. A hand ladder is also used as a means of communication with the second story.

Even allowing that the traditions upon which Clavigero founded his theoretical deductions are vague and uncertain, there is sufficient evidence in the ruins that still exist to show that those regions were once inhabited by a far more enlightened people than are now to be found among the aborigines. Of such character are the ruins of Pueblo Bonito, in the direction of Navajo, on the borders of the Cordilleras; the houses being generally built of slabs of fine grit sandstone, a material utterly unknown in the present architecture of the North. Although some of these structures are very massive and spacious, they are generally cut up into small, irregular rooms, many of which yet remain entire, being still covered, with the *vigas,* or joists, remaining nearly sound under the *azoteas* of earth; and yet their age is such that there is no tradition which gives any account of their origin. But there have been no images or sculptured work of any kind found around them. Besides these, many other ruins (though none so perfect) are scattered over the plains and among the mountains. What is very remarkable is that a portion of them are situated at a great distance from any water, so that the inhabitants must have depended entirely upon rain, as is the case with the Pueblo of Acoma at the present day.

The general appearance of Pueblo Bonito, as well as that of the existing buildings of Moqui in the same mountainous regions, and other Pueblos of New Mexico, resembles so closely the ruins of Casas Grandes that we naturally come to the conclusion that the founders of each must have descended from the same common stock. The present difference between their language and that of the Indians of Mexico, when we take into consideration the ages that have passed away since their separation, hardly presents any reasonable objection to this hypothesis. ■

After *The Journals of Lewis and Clark,* John Wesley Powell's 1875 *The Exploration of the Colorado River and Its Tributaries* is certainly the most remarkable adventure narrative in the literature of the American West. Setting off in 1869 from what is today Green River, Wyoming, with a small company of explorers, the one-armed Civil War veteran navigated the unknown canyons of the Colorado River from a captain's chair bolted to the deck of his small boat, the *Emma Dean.* Anyone who has floated the Colorado rapids can appreciate Powell's descent, which was without benefit of maps or guidebooks. To this day, river runners read from Powell's journal in their camps.

Originally composed on brown paper and bound along the way in shoe leather, the journals formed the basis for a series of articles in *Scribner's* magazine in 1874, and the complete account was published in the next year. Powell's knowledge of the Colorado Plateau was unsurpassed in his day, and as a founder of the U.S. Geological Survey and director of the Bureau of Ethnology, he worked tirelessly to promote an accurate picture of the arid West. A careful interpreter of what he saw, Powell records his impressions of the ancient building sites within the Grand Canyon in this passage.

f r o m

The Exploration of the Colorado River and Its Tributaries

JOHN WESLEY POWELL

August 16—We must dry our rations again today and make oars.

The Colorado is never a clear stream, but for the past three or four days it has been raining much of the time, and the floods poured over the walls have brought down great quantities of mud, making it exceedingly turbid now. The little affluent which we have discovered here is a clear, beautiful creek, or river, as it would be termed in this western country, where streams are not abundant. We have named one stream, away above, in honor of the great chief of the Bad Angels, and as this is in beautiful contrast to that, we conclude to name it Bright Angel.

Early in the morning the whole party starts up to explore the Bright Angel River, with the special purpose of seeking timber from which to make oars. A couple of miles above we find a large pine log, which has been floated down from the plateau, probably from an altitude of more than 6,000 feet, but not many miles back. On its way it must have passed over many cataracts and falls, for it bears scars in evidence of the rough usage which it has received. The men roll it on skids, and the work of sawing oars is commenced.

This stream heads away back under a line of abrupt cliffs that terminates the plateau, and tumbles down more than 4,000 feet in the first mile or two of its course; then runs through a deep, narrow canyon until it reaches the river.

Late in the afternoon I return and go up a little gulch just above this creek, about 200 yards from camp, and discover the ruins of two or three old houses, which were originally of stone laid in mortar. Only the foundations are left, but irregular blocks, of which the houses were constructed, lie scattered about. In one room I find an old mealing stone, deeply worn, as if it had been much used. A great deal of pottery is strewn around, and old trails, which in some places are deeply worn into the rocks, are seen.

It is ever a source of wonder to us why these ancient people sought such inaccessible places for their homes. They were, doubtless, an agricultural race, but there are no lands here of any considerable extent that they could have cultivated. To the west of Oraibi, one of the towns in the Province of Tusayan, in northern Arizona, the inhabitants have actually built little terraces along the face of the cliff where a spring gushes out, and thus made their sites for gardens. It is possible that the ancient inhabitants of this place made their agricultural lands in the same way. But why should they seek such spots? Surely the country was not so crowded with people as to demand the utilization of so barren a region. The only solution suggested of the problem is this: We know that for a century or two after the settlement of Mexico many expeditions were sent into the country now comprising Arizona and New Mexico, for the purpose of bringing the town-building people under the dominion of the Spanish government. Many of their villages were destroyed, and the inhabitants fled to regions at that time unknown; and there are traditions among the people who inhabit the pueblos that still remain that the canyons were these unknown lands. It may be these buildings were erected at that time; sure it is that they have a much more modern appearance than the ruins scattered over Nevada, Utah, Colorado, Arizona, and New Mexico. Those old Spanish conquerors had a monstrous greed for gold and a wonderful lust for saving souls. Treasures they must have, if not on earth, why, then, in heaven; and when they failed to find heathen temples bedecked with silver, they propitiated Heaven by seizing the heathen themselves. There is yet extant a copy of a record made by a heathen artist to express his conception of the demands of the conquerors. In one part of the picture we have a lake, and nearby stands a priest pouring water on the head of a native. On the other side, a poor Indian has a cord about his throat. Lines run from these two groups to a central figure, a man with beard and full Spanish panoply. The interpretation of the picture writing is this: Be baptized as this saved heathen, or be hanged as that damned heathen. Doubtless, some of these people preferred another alternative, and rather than be baptized or hanged they chose to imprison themselves within these canyon walls. ■

✸

The post–Civil War years saw an acceler-
ated interest in scientific exploration of the American West. Earlier surveys undertaken by Josiah Whitney and Clarence King in California served as models for the
great postwar surveys directed from Washington, D.C. *New York Tribune* reporter
Ernest Ingersoll was traveling with Ferdinand Hayden's U.S. Geological Survey
party in Colorado in 1874 when he heard rumors from local miners about the ruins
of an ancient civilization in Mancos Canyon, in the state's southwest corner. Accompanied by the survey's photographer, William H. Jackson, Ingersoll visited the
ruins and electrified an East Coast reading public with accounts of what he had
seen. Ingersoll's *Tribune* article brought the ancient Pueblos to America's con-
sciousness for the first time, unleashed a flood of interest from archaeologists, and
anticipated the discoveries by the Wetherill brothers on Mesa Verde. This excerpt is
reprinted from Ingersoll's 1885 *The Crest of the Continent: A Summer's Ramble in
the Rocky Mountains and Beyond.*

f r o m

The Crest of
the Continent

ERNEST INGERSOLL

Photographs and sketches completed, we pushed on, rode
twenty miles or more, and camped two miles beyond Un-
agua springs. There were about these springs, which are at
the base of the Ute mountain, the tallest summit of the
Sierra ù Late, formerly many large buildings, the relics of
which are very impressive. One of them is two hundred feet
square, with a wall twenty feet thick, and enclosed in the
center a circular building one hundred feet in circumfer-
ence. Another, nearby, was one hundred
feet square, with equally thick walls, and
was divided north and south by a very heavy partition. This
building communicated with the great stone reservoir
about the springs. These heavy walls were constructed of
outer strong walls of cut sandstone, regularly laid in mortar,
filled in with firmly packed fragments of stone. Some por-
tions of the wall still stand twenty or thirty feet in height,
but, judging from the amount of material thrown down, the
building must originally have been a very lofty one. About

these large edifices were traces of smaller ones, covering half a square mile, and out in the plain another small village indicated by a collection of knolls. Scarcely anything now but white sage grows thereabouts, but there is reason to believe that in those old times it was under careful cultivation. Evidently these thick walls were the foundations of old terraced pueblos, an unusually large community having grown up about these plentiful springs, just as at Taos, San Juan, Zuñi, and the present Moqui villages in Arizona.

Our next day's march was westerly, leaving the mesa bluffs on our right and gradually behind. The road was an interesting one, intellectually, but not at all so physically—dry, hot, dusty, long and wearisome. We passed a number of quite perfect houses, perched high up on rocky bluffs, and many other remains. One occupied the whole apex of a great conical boulder that ages ago had become detached from its mother mountain and rolled out into the valley. Another, worth mention, was a round tower, beautifully laid up, which surmounted an immense boulder that had somehow rolled to the very verge of a lofty cliff overlooking the whole valley. This was a watchtower, and we learned afterward that almost all the high points were occupied by such sentinel boxes. From it a deeply worn, devious trail led up over the edge of the mesa, by following which we should, no doubt, have found a whole town. But this was only a reconnaissance, and we could not now stop to follow out all indications.

Not far away the odd appearance of a cliff attracted my attention, and leaving the party I rode over the bare, white, rocky floors which capped all the low, broad ridges, to find a long series of shallow grottos in the escarpment filled with houses, some of which were roofed over, but most consisting simply of walls carried to the ceiling of the light, dry cavern in the sandstone, often only one or two houses occupying each of the small caves, whose openings were in the same water worn stratum, and only a few feet or yards apart. Still more curious examples of these cave dwellings have been seen since in the same neighborhood, and lower down. For example, on the San Juan, in 1875, Holmes and Jackson discovered, halfway between top and bottom of a bluff where a stratum of shaly sandstone had been weathered and dug out to a depth of six feet, leaving a floor and a projecting ledge overhead, a continuous row of buildings, though none have their front walls now remaining. Doorways through each of the dividing walls afforded access along the whole line. A few rods upstream a little niched cave house, 14 x 5 x 6, divided into two equal compartments; a small, square window, just large enough for one to crawl through, was placed midway in the wall of each half. "We well might ask whether these little 'cubbyholes' had ever been used as residences" [the report notes] "or, whether, as seems at first most likely, they might not have been caches, or merely temporary places of refuge. While, no doubt, many of them were such, yet in the majority the evidences of use and the presence of long continued fires, indicated by their smoke-blackened interiors, prove them to have been quite constantly occupied. Among all dwellers in mud-plastered houses, it is the practice to freshen up their habitations by repeated applications of clay, moistened to the proper consistency, and spread with the hands, the thickness of the coating depending upon its consistency. Every such application makes a building perfectly new, and many of the best sheltered cave houses have just this appearance, as though they were but just vacated."

The grandest of all these cave shelters, perhaps, was that in the Montezuma canyon, the main building of which was forty-eight feet long, and built of well smoothed stones. "In the rubbish of the large house," says the report, "some small stone implements, rough, indented pottery in fragments, and a few arrowpoints were found. . . . The whole appearance of the place and its surroundings indicates that the family or the little community who inhabited it were in good circumstances and the lords of the surrounding country. Looking out from one of their houses, with a great dome of solid rock overhead, that echoed and re-echoed every word uttered with marvelous distinctness, and below them a steep descent of one hundred feet, to the broad, fertile valley of the Rio San Juan, covered with waving fields of maize and scattered groves of majestic cottonwoods, these old people, whom even the imagination can hardly clothe with reality, must have felt a sense of security that even the incursions of their barbarous foes could hardly have disturbed."

But I cannot linger over these extremely interesting and instructive ruins, nor stop to tell of the variety and skill shown in their architecture, in their storage of water and food, in their means of defense, in their manufacture of utensils, and the art with which their life was adorned. Out of the hundreds of leveled pueblos, cave houses, towers, water reservoirs and wasted fields which once bore bountiful harvests, I have only culled one here and there. I may say that not only every canyon which cuts down through the mesa to the Rio San Juan and into all of its lower tributary valleys, but many of the plateaus between, are occupied by the ruins which show an Indian occupation previous to the present savages, and of a different rank, if not of another race.

Particularly accessible to the ordinary tourist are the ruins to be seen in the Animas valley, about twenty-five miles south of Durango. These are said to consist of a pueblo three hundred and sixteen feet long by nearly one hundred wide, which evidently rose to the height of many stories. Some of the lower rooms in this great house are still standing, and skeletons and relics of great interest have been taken from them. In the center of the ruins is a subterranean, cistern-like chamber, described as about sixty feet in diameter, and plastered everywhere within with hard cement. This, probably, was the main estufa of the village. Other lesser ruins and remains of farming operations are scattered about the vicinity, and are well worthy of exploration.

Just who and what were these aborigines (if so they were, which is very doubtful), opinions differ; but that in the Village Indians of New Mexico and Arizona we see today their lineal descendants, seems indisputable.

Traditions are few, that have any value, but the partial and imperfect researches which have already been made in the Southwest enable us to make out dimly some strangely tragical scheme of history for this race of men whose sun set so long ago. ■

No one knows exactly why Frederick Chapin visited Colorado's Mesa Verde area during the summers of 1889 and 1890, exploring the rugged mesas and canyons and the cliff dwellings that had recently been discovered and "pot hunted" by local residents. Perhaps it was an interest in antiquities, perhaps the love of mountains and climbing that had already surfaced in his 1889 book *Mountaineering in Colorado: The Peaks about Estes Park.* In any case, Chapin recorded his observations of Mesa Verde in 1892 in *The Land of the Cliff Dwellers,* and Gustaf Nordenskiöld, usually credited with undertaking the first systematic excavations in the area, named the mesa between Soda Canyon and Navajo Canyon "Chapin's Mesa" in his honor. Here Chapin gives us a look at early travel on the mesas, presenting a sharp contrast to the experience that today's tourists have on steep, winding but paved Park Service roads.

f r o m

The Land of the Cliff Dwellers

FREDERICK H. CHAPIN

The Mesa Verde* is the name given to the high plateau which rises above the Mancos and Montezuma valleys to a height of from fifteen hundred to two thousand feet. Roughly speaking, it is about twenty by thirty miles in extent, and thus contains over six hundred square miles.

The surrounding country to the north and west has been eroded, leaving this plateau standing alone. It would seem, when observed from below, as if the top were nearly level; but this is far from the fact: the surface is undulating. Moreover, Mancos Canyon cuts through the entire length of the plateau, and as the side canyons head near the outer rims, the seeming solid mass is but a shell. The work of erosion is still going on, at least in winter, when volumes of water from the melting snows flow down the canyons and over the cliffs. The capping is of sandstone, and the greater part of the plateau is built up of layers of this same material, though this geological formation is interlaid with strata of friable nature which are more easily eroded, leaving the firmer rock standing as sheer precipitous walls. The top of the Mesa, except on the highest points, is covered with a scrubby forest of juniper and piñon trees. Indian and game trails lead through this open forest in every direction.

There are several ways of ascending or descending with pack-mules and horses—an important consideration, as a journey without pack animals is out of the question; for blankets and provisions should be taken for a stay of several days. One route is to descend the main canyon of the Mancos to a point between Cliff and Navajo canyons, where a good Indian trail leads to the plateau. It is not so steep nor so difficult as that leading to the opposite mesa.

---

*This plateau was named the "Mesa Verde" by Dr. J. S. Newberry when he, as geologist, accompanied the exploring expedition of Capt. J. N. Macomb. At that time its sides were covered with grass.

Another trail leads from Mancos Valley to Point Lookout. This is much traveled by cattle, and the paths are well worn. A third leads from the Montezuma Valley and was never used except by Indians until we passed over it in September 1890. It is not easy to find, especially in making the descent. Our party tried to get down the cliffs in many places before we discovered the true route. We wasted several hours, and descended in vain to considerable distances at different points of the Mesa's edge, and were as often obliged to climb up again. At last we found an encampment of Indians, of a party which had come from Ute Mountain, and descended by their trail.

The summit of the plateau is very dry, water being found in but few places. Occasionally it remains in "tanks" some time after a rainfall. These tanks are of special interest, from the fact that they were used by the cliff dwellers. In some cases they were walled up to increase their capacity, and, where the sides were steep and slippery, steps were cut in the rock to enable the carriers to descend and bail out the water. Similar natural cisterns are also found in dry streams in the bed of the canyons. Once we searched long for such a place, riding till late in the night over an almost impassable trail; and we should have been obliged to camp without water if we had not discovered some cattle belonging to the Utes, which gave us the clew, following which we came to a tank.

On the Mesa, near the brink of Cliff Canyon, not far from the great ruin, is such a tank; but while camping there we gave it up to our animals, as there is a good spring in a short box canyon near at hand, from which we could conveniently draw up the water over the cliff with lassos.

On another occasion we suffered from extreme thirst. Our canteens were empty, and we searched in vain for tanks on the Mesa. We separated, and followed the brink of canyons, looking below for pools. Search for ruins was given up; we were engrossed with our search for water. Finally one sighted it in a pool below, and answering his call, we gathered on the edge of the canyon. There, down in the depths, was a little round, yellow, dirty-looking puddle. It did not look inviting, but we knew it was good, for it was rainwater, and there were no signs of alkaline incrustations near it. We descended at breakneck speed, and spent an hour by its side.

It is difficult to find places of descent for horses and mules into the tributary canyons. The walls, except near the western rim of the plateau, are very abrupt, and when one rides along the Mesa, he frequently finds that he has arrived at a jumping-off place, for he is between two of the branches. The easiest places of descent are by the main canyons.

The Navajos have kept sheep and horses on the Mesa, using for a corral the area between two box canyons, which is cut off from the main plateau by a fence of juniper trees.

There are many ruins on the Mesa, but they are so dilapidated that it is impossible to form an idea of their construction. A tower is yet standing between the forks of Navajo Canyon and another on the brink of one of the tributaries. This latter is a very picturesque sight when observed from the ravine below; it commands a good view, and may have been used as a place of lookout. The places of burial were near the houses, and here it is that we find such an abundance of broken pottery, while a most fascinating variation is the search for arrowheads. I found a number of very pretty specimens in an hour's time spent among some of these mounds. Similar ruins are found at the base of the Mesa, among the sandhills of the northern side.

Let me finally describe one of our journeys across the Mesa. Our camp was on the brink of Cliff Canyon. We reached it long after dark; and after the usual hard riding after stray horses, we got everything to rights, and whiled away the evening hours by a huge fire. Such a blaze as juniper and piñon pines make!—a fire easy to build, and of lasting brilliancy.

The next morning dawned warm and bright, with a pleasant light breeze. We were up at sunrise, and off at eight o'clock, delaying only to photograph the camp and pack animals. Our route lay to the north, along the mesa summit, and between Cliff and Navajo Canyons, which here run nearly parallel with the main one. We passed near the ends of many tributaries of these gorges, which showed that while it was a comparatively easy matter to get out of this country to the north, to come back to any given point from that direction would be impossible to any one not familiar with all the arms of the different canyons. Reversing the case of a mouse and a wire trap, it is easy enough to get out, but difficult to get in.

We observed no traces of ancient roads on the Mesa, nor of irrigating ditches; but we passed the ruins of what appears to have been a large reservoir.

At about ten o'clock we were at the heads of Navajo and Cliff Canyons; and soon we were so near the west end of the Mesa that we caught a glimpse of the broad Montezuma Valley. All the morning we followed trails leading through the extensive chaparral of juniper and piñon trees. The piñons were loaded with nuts, which are good eating. The Indians make flour from them, and subsist on it in certain seasons. Flying about were many piñon birds. The trails were made by Indians, deer, or cattle. We caught sight of three deer in the morning, and our dog brought a wild steer to bay, which threatened at one time to run us down.

About noon we reached the summit of the Mesa, at a point about an hour south of the promontory which marks the entrance to Mancos Canyon. A most remarkable view was unfolded. Over the pastoral scenes of the valley of Mancos, beyond the deep canyons of the Dolores River, far away in the north, loomed the snowy crests of the San Juan Mountains: Lone Cone, and the San Miguel on the left, then the Ouray group, with the grand peaks which we had climbed, flanked on the south by the mountains of Silverton and the Needles of the Rio de las Animas. Far away in the east rose range upon range which we could not identify with certainty. In the west were the Blue Mountains of Utah, Sierra Abajo, and Sierra la Sal. To the south and southwest stretched the great system of labyrinthine canyons, and far beyond were the Carisso Mountains of New Mexico. Here, within sight of our valley, and within a few hours' ride of it, we were able to while away the midday hours, and—as perhaps the former inhabitants of this strange land may have done at this same outlook—watch the panorama. . . .

Looking over the wide stretch of country, we recalled the fact that to the early explorers this land seemed a desert. And well indeed it might. Over the wide arid plains stretch miles of waste acres covered with sagebrush and greasewood. Yet all along the tops of the great Mesa over which we had been riding, pottery is strewn and signs of a primitive race are found. Its numbers must have been large, or the period of their stay prolonged.

It has been inferred by some writers that there must formerly have been a greater annual rainfall, in order that such a population could have been supported by agricultural employment; but judging from so much evidence that we found in the way of tanks and fragments of large water jars, it would appear that the country was lacking in water even when occupied by the cliff dwellers. And the hypothesis of a change of climate therefore becomes unnecessary. That the vanished race could have gained subsistence by tillage of the soil, seems evidenced by what the farmers of Mancos and Montezuma Valleys are doing. This success shows what the lowlands at least, are capable of producing, with irrigation. We find, however, no vestiges of ditches on the Mesa, and there is not much water to turn into such channels, if they did exist. Yet, on the tableland on which thrive such forests of juniper and piñon, enough grass grows to support much game and many cattle; and the time may come when the land, grasped by the oncoming mightier race, will be overturned and tilled, and all along the broad tablelands and in many of the fertile canyon beds we shall see the tasselled maize bend, and fields of wheat wave to the breeze. Then it will no longer seem incredible when we read that the country once supported a great population, a people well advanced in many arts, and who conceived of certain forms of beauty, even though they lacked the ability to reproduce them in artistic shapes. And may we not imagine them a race who loved peace rather than war, but who, hard-pressed by a savage foe, fought stubbornly and long, and died rather than desert their romantic fortresses among the canyon cliffs? ▪

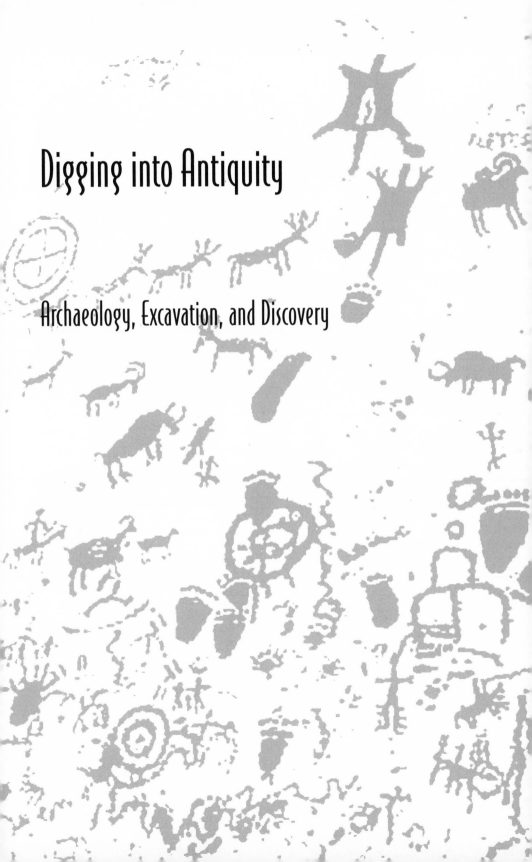

Digging into Antiquity

Archaeology, Excavation, and Discovery

✸

Richard Wetherill was a Quaker rancher and farmer in southwestern Colorado's Mancos Valley before he turned amateur archaeologist. From 1888, when he stumbled upon Cliff Palace on Mesa Verde while looking for lost cattle, to the moment of his murder in 1910 in Chaco Canyon, Wetherill was at the archaeological forefront of this rugged era. He found the ruins of Kiet Siel in today's Navajo National Monument and excavated Basketmaker sites in Grand Gulch. He undertook the investigation of Pueblo Bonito in Chaco Canyon and, along with his wife, Marietta, worked for its preservation by claiming the area as a homestead.

In his 1957 biography *Richard Wetherill—Anasazi: Pioneer Explorer of Southwestern Ruins*, Frank McNitt provides valuable insight into the early days of western archaeology. McNitt's biography of Wetherill also includes important primary documents, including early newspaper and journal articles and even a collection of Wetherill's love letters. Wetherill's younger brother Al, often quoted by McNitt, told his own story in an 1948 article published in the *Durango Herald-News,* and his account of the famous early days of exploration on Mesa Verde now appears in his autobiography, *The Wetherills of the Mesa Verde* (1977).

This passage from McNitt's *Richard Wetherill—Anasazi* describes Richard Wetherill's entry into the history of archaeology.

f r o m

Richard Wetherill— Anasazi

FRANK McNITT

With every changing season the ranchers of Mancos Valley moved their cattle to get the best grass and water. The Dolores River and Dove Creek country was favored for some of the larger herds during most of the year, but a number of cattle owners wintered their stock as far south as the San Juan. The hard winters always presented a problem. Snow drifted deep in the Mancos and Montezuma valleys, making grazing there impossible; the sheltered slopes and small canyons of the mountains to the east offered a refuge for a few of the ranchers. The Wetherills wintered their cattle in Mancos Canyon and the side canyons of Mesa Verde. Although the Utes regarded this region as their own, they assured the Wetherills that Alamo stock could graze unmolested.

Mancos Canyon was a winding gorge, half a mile wide and fifteen hundred feet deep. The shallow, narrow river twisted through it between deep banks, with towering cliffs of sandstone rising sheer on either side and talus of huge, fallen boulders and sand mounds at their base.

A leaden sky, heavy with snow, could add to or just emphasize the lonely, utter silence. Crows flapped about the cliffs and a hawk circling high, slowly gliding on the air currents, was an occasional hunter. Long-eared rabbits were alert to sudden death from above. A change in the wind's direction caused a sighing among the fir and piñon on the mesa's summit, and from far below brought a faint murmuring of water as the river slipped between ice-frosted banks. At intervals the stillness would be ravelled by the screech of an unseen jaybird.

Time had no beginning and no end. Day turned to night to be succeeded by day again in endless cycle, but time itself was meaningless. Yesterday was the same as tomorrow. Five hundred years ago could have been a moment of yesterday. Only the seasons changed; the cliffs and the canyons were changeless.

A small thing occurred to mar this atmosphere of timelessness. In the river gorge, close to the mouth of Johnson Canyon, Richard in 1884 or 1885 built a cabin, a winter camp, where he and one of his brothers stayed while watching the cattle. They took turns but most often it was a job for Richard and Al. Sometimes John or Clate Wetherill, or Charlie Mason or Jim Ethridge would appear, leading a packhorse with provisions to keep the cabin hands supplied for another month. Whoever came usually stayed for a day or two. Often at such times Richard or Al would ride off into the canyons for hours, searching for mounds and cliff dwellings. They found many, Al making the first discovery of importance—the ruin they called Sandal House.

Charlie Mason, the husband of his sister Anna, was company for Al on a number of these excursions. Once, after finding a cliff house rich with relics, they brought a small collection of pottery and stone implements back to Alamo Ranch. Benjamin Wetherill either sold or gave this collection, the first of which there is any mention, to the wife of a Denver stationer and bookseller named Chain. Years afterward, Al Wetherill wrote of these first discoveries:

"There were six of us [the five brothers and Charlie Mason] actually involved off and on in the explorations of the region. My father never was well enough to give more than moral support and deep interest in the proceedings. Richard, the oldest, was always spokesman for the group, acting in the capacity of head of the household when my father was not able to do so himself. Because we were reared in strict Quaker style, we never questioned Richard's authority."

Standing in the cabin door watching the cattle graze, Richard could look out across the river, and see the mouth of Cliff Canyon nearly opposite. It was one of the deepest and most impenetrable of all in Mesa Verde. Thus he was standing one day when approached by his friend Acowitz. For years the Ute had lived in a hut close by.

The old man's eyes followed the direction of Richard's gaze. Then he spoke. He would tell his friend a secret, he said, a thing unknown to white men. Deep in that canyon and near its head were many houses of "the old people—the ancient ones."

"One of those houses," said Acowitz, "high, high in the rocks, is bigger than all the others. Utes never go there. It is a sacred place."

Richard was intrigued. How would he find it? he demanded. But the Ute shook his head as though he had already said too much.

"I could tell you, but I warn you not to go there. When you disturb the spirits of the dead, then you die too." That is all Acowitz would say.

During the winter of 1887 Richard and Al entertained a visitor at the winter cabin, a Dr. Comfort. The doctor had come from Fort Lewis on the promise he would be shown some of the cliff dwellings. Early one morning Dr. Comfort and Richard rode into Johnson Canyon while Al, alone and on foot, forded the river and started in the opposite direction, into the Mesa Verde. Sixty-one years later, Al described his adventure:

"On this particular day we weren't hunting stray cattle but were on the lookout for ruins. I went up and around and across canyons and mesa tops until nearly dusk. I was about all in, but I thought I'd make just one more climb and across the top to see what there might be in a branch canyon which I passed earlier in the day. By the time I had reached the other canyon, I was through! I was too tired to be interested in new canyons or what they might have in them and besides it was getting dark and I had a long way to go back to join the others. I decided to follow the bed of the branch canyon as being the most direct route to the meeting place."

Al had walked half a mile when, looking up through an opening in the heavy brush and the treetops, he said he was startled to catch a partial glimpse of a cliff dwelling that filled the recesses of an immense cave.

"I stood looking at the ruins in surprised awe. I had hoped to find some unexplored dwellings—but this discovery surpassed my wildest dreams. I gauged the steep walls of the canyon against my tired legs and the ebbing daylight and turned slowly away. They would wait—they had waited for hundreds of years for the moment of discovery.

"I met Dr. Comfort and Richard near the mouth of the fork. They had become anxious and started out to look for me. I told them about the ruins and we intended to return promptly to see how extensive they were. But the pressure of ranch duties once more had the priority rating and we were unable to do anything about the new find at that time."

Al Wetherill was a truthful man, untroubled by hallucinations. Nevertheless his "discovery" when alone and stumbling with fatigue, would be enough to stir up an unending controversy years later.

A year went by. It was winter again and a day of lowering sky. Richard and Charlie Mason were on the top of Mesa Verde tracking strays that had wandered off with a bunch of wild cattle. The men had reached the summit after driving their horses across the icy river and then up a precipitous switchback climb between Navajo and Soda canyons. Now, following the tracks, they found themselves in a place where neither had been before. It was snowing, large, drifting flakes that blurred their vision. Making progress more difficult, a barrier of underbrush scratched and snared the legs of their panting horses. The cattle tracks fanned out or narrowed according to the terrain, sometimes taking the riders closer than they liked to the edge of an abyss. It was December 18, 1888.

Richard and Mason dismounted to rest the horses at a place overlooking a small branch canyon, and then walked out on a windswept point of bare rock. The gulf yawning below them was so deep that a dislodged stone would have plummeted down and struck at last without audible echo. A snow-powdered dark green carpet of tree-tops ascended the bottom of this gorge into a wider, distant canyon. Suddenly, with an exclamation of astonishment, Richard grasped Mason's arm.

Nearly opposite them, half a mile away and just below the far mesa's brown caprock, was a long, deep opening in the cliff face. Mirage-like in the falling snow and outlined against the cave's darkest shadows, were ghostly traceries of the largest cliff dwelling either had ever seen. The walls rose and fell in broken terraces, pierced here and there by the black, sightless eyes of doorways. Near the center, rising austerely in the afternoon's pale light, a tapering tower of three stories, beautifully round, dominated the entire ruin. It was all as compact, as complete and unreal as a crenelated castle.

The strays were forgotten. Richard and Charlie Mason turned away and started back around the edge of the smaller canyon, keeping the horses as close to the rim as they dared. They broke a fresh trail through the underbrush until they reached a clearing directly opposite the great cave. Here the cliff dropped away abruptly for thirty feet or more, but the problem of descent was quickly solved. Finding several dead trees, they lopped off the limbs to within a foot or so of the trunks, joined the sections together with their lariats and then lowered the whole improvised ladder over the cliff. By this means they reached the bottom.

Now, standing in the silence of the ruin, they could begin to gauge its size. The walls rose in tumbled splendor above them for several levels and to the height of a tall pine—reached into the shadows beyond the round tower for two or three hundred yards. The cabin they had left that morning could be tucked away in a corner of this crowded cave. They moved, scarcely speaking, but their voices magnified in hollow echoes across piles of rubble. Behind them, from one room to the next, they left footprints in dust for centuries undisturbed by any human.

Then, or soon afterward, Richard thought of the name. Cliff Palace. Nothing else would quite do. For several hours he and Charlie Mason explored the ruins with mounting excitement, with the realization they had discovered a prehistoric wonder of architecture undreamed of by their world.

Four hundred people or more once lived here and when they left they took only light possessions that could be carried easily. In the feathery dust of one room the explorers found a stone ax, the heavy blade still lashed securely to the wooden handle. In other rooms were pottery bowls, mugs and large jars for cooking or carrying water, left as though the owners had just set them down and might return at any moment.

The thought occurred: whoever they were, these people had fled after a siege—and there was some evidence to support the idea. Roof beams had been pulled out of almost all of the rooms and not a trace of the timbers remained. That could mean, they reasoned, that attackers had attempted to destroy the village after overcoming its defenders. On the other hand there was little else to suggest there had been siege and violence. They did discover three skeletons in the rubble. After a battle, was that enough?

They left the skeletons as they had found them but took a few pieces of the pottery, eager now to discover if other large ruins were close by. Snow still fell over the mesa and with not too many hours of daylight left, they separated, after agreeing to meet and camp near the place where they had first seen Cliff Palace.

Dusk closed in and they met, first gathering and piling piñon branches for a fire against the oncoming cold. Then, stamping in the snow and flailing his arms over the ruddy glow, Charlie Mason could report nothing more than his nearly frozen hands and feet. Richard had been luckier.

He told of another ruin he had found in the late afternoon, not as large as Cliff Palace but in better condition. After they parted, Richard said, he rode north and then west across the mesa, emerging finally on the rim of a deep canyon. Following its curve he sighted a second large cave and within it a cliff dwelling rising in places to three stories. The light was darkening. Across the front of the cave was a fringe of spruce trees, clinging to a steep slope. One of these, a tree of great height, had sprouted up through an outer retaining wall and for this reason Richard named the ruin Spruce Tree House.

When morning came and they started back for Spruce Tree House they lost their way and presently came to the edge of Navajo Canyon. There, almost at their feet, was a third large cliff dwelling; Richard named it Square Tower House. Built in a curving recess at the base of the cliff, it was smaller than Spruce Tree House but remarkable for a square tower thrusting four stories high among a cluster of rooms and circular chambers. They inspected it hurriedly and then went on, finding several small ruins in the same vicinity before deciding, after measuring a dwindling supply of food, to turn back toward winter camp in Johnson Canyon.

On their return they encountered the camp of three acquaintances—Charles McLoyd, Howard Graham and Levi Patrick. Richard and Mason stopped long enough for some warming coffee while Richard drew a rough map in the snow showing where they had found Cliff Palace. When he finished, the listening men were determined to see it for themselves; they waited only long enough to be joined by John Wetherill. The four of them packed in on foot with enough food to last several days, while Richard and Charlie Mason continued toward the cabin.

A short time after the McLoyd party returned, the men combined forces for a systematic search, not only of Cliff Palace but of any other ruins they could find in Mesa Verde. For Richard, it was the turning point of his life. Before this, exploring had been a pastime. Now it was to become a passion that consumed his time, his energy and all of his resources. He had discovered a lost civilization. ▪

During the era of Richard Wetherill's work excavating ancient Puebloan sites, the line was fine indeed between science and pot hunting, and the excitement of frontier discovery mingled freely with an early impulse toward preservation. Today Wetherill remains a particularly controversial figure—by some accounts a cattle rustler, a desecrater of sacred sites, and sometimes

an all too vigorous entrepreneur who was willing to capitalize on early archaeological expeditions and the wholesale removal of ancient artifacts. Still, Wetherill died with only $73.23 in his bank account.

Included here is an 1890 letter from Wetherill to Frederic Ward Putnam, director of the Peabody Museum at Harvard University, in which Wetherill promotes his discoveries—and gets his East Coast geography a little mixed up.

A letter to
F. W. Putnam

RICHARD WETHERILL

Mancos, Montezuma Co. Col.
April 7th 1890

Prof. F. W. Putnam
Cambridge Conn

Dear Sir—

Through the kindness of Frederick W. Chapin, of the Hartford Archaeological Society, I received your address, and the request that I send you a short description of one of the Cliff houses, and a list of the relics found there. I also received a number of pamphlets from you, which I have not yet had time to study.

We recognize the fact, the principal scientific value of collections existed in the circumstances of their original position, or reference to the implements or objects with which they are associated, and we worked accordingly, with a view to throw as much light upon this subject as possible, we explored a great number of cliff houses in the Mancos and its tributaries.

We found in the first cliff house explored by us in the Mancos Canyon, where visitors and tourists have been going for the past fifteen years, that nearly everything of value had been overlooked, and during all this time a great amount of dirt and rock had been handled, back and forth.

This house is situated upon the west side of the Mancos River on the side of the mountain 150 feet above the river bottom. It has twelve rooms on the ground floor, was originally three stories high, a portion of the walls still standing above the first story, the walls of which are in a good state of preservation.

The rooms range in size from 3 x 6 to 10 x 12 feet. There is a circular room 21 feet in diameter, at the n.e. corner of the house which is plastered on the inside with mud mixed with cedar bark, and corn husks.

We found in this house a great number of sandals, bone implements, skeletons, feather cloth, matting, pottery, baskets, bands &c.

I think a visit to the Mancos Canyon would amply repay any one interested in prehistoric man.

In a single letter it is impossible to give even a faint outline of the extent of the ruins. We explored 182 houses and 250 miles of cliffs, and have secured the largest and most interesting collection of cliff dweller relics in the world.

Hoping to see you in our beautiful valley during the present season I am

Very truly yours
Richard Wetherill

Before his untimely and less-than-romantic death in 1900, when he choked on a fish bone at the age of forty-three, Frank Hamilton Cushing had established himself as certainly the most colorful anthropologist of his day. Sent by the Smithsonian Institution in 1879 to study the Zuni in New Mexico Territory, Cushing abandoned the objectivity of the pure scientist to live as the Zuni themselves did. He was eventually accepted as a member of the community and the Bow Priesthood. Cushing's method of "participant observation" offered unique insights into the Zuni worldview and way of life, and his presence at the pueblo provided the Zuni, then struggling with government officials and mercenary traders, with a valuable mediator. He stayed until 1884.

In this excerpt from his 1890 lecture "Life at Zuni," delivered to an appreciative and curious audience in Buffalo, New York, Cushing describes the origins of his interest in the Zuni and suggests that living Pueblo people are descended from the ancient builders of the cliff dwellings then being discovered in the Southwest.

f r o m

"Life at Zuni"

FRANK HAMILTON CUSHING

Fifteen years ago, one winter night, I fell asleep before my desk in the old tower of the Smithsonian Institution. I dreamed that I was far away in a country I had never seen or heard of. There the sun was brighter, the air clearer; the valleys, vast and twilit, were like cracks down to the foundation rocks of the world. The mountains rising from these ruptured plains were as flat as the plains they rose from, and rising from the level tops of these were others whence towered here and there, smaller mountains hundreds of feet high, rock-bound yet at first sight as round and pointed as the tent of a titan. But when one climbed to their tops, the points were broken off, revealing great craters yawning wider and wider downward into darkness, whence the voice of man or the cry of beast rolled back like the sonorous tones of far-off Buddhist bells.

On the edge of the smallest of these hollow mountains I was contending with two strangers, a rope around my body; they were holding me back and I straining forward. All at once I was spinning and dangling at the end of the rope, my hands burning, my heart beating, my eyes staring down into the twilight. Then I stood on a solid rock-strewn bottom, at my feet a strange, time-eaten idol, while, my vision slowly clearing, farther down in a smoky nook I saw a pagan altar surrounded by hundreds of painted wands, some with half-decayed plumes fastened to them, still faintly fluttering in the chill, chill eddies of the subterranean air which seemed the echo wind of another age. All was so wonderful, so strange and silent and ancient down there, the whole land was so solemn and weird and desolate and still that I was awed beyond measure, yet happy to the verge of ecstasy, as I stooped to pick up the great-headed, greenish, flat-faced, square-eyed, crooked little idol at my feet—so happy that I awoke, dazed to find myself empty-handed, my head pillowed among the papers on my writing table in the tower of the old Smithsonian! Again and again thereafter I dreamed this dream, and others like it, until weary of its weird fascination.

One day, six months later, as I was passing a great screen of photographs displayed in the government exhibit of the geological surveys at the Centennial Exhibition [Philadelphia, 1876] next to the one that I had charge of, my eye chanced to fall on a little watercolor sketch of a dancing Indian. As I looked, I became fascinated, for in the mask this figure wore—flat-faced, green paint, and all—I descried a face like that of the idol I had dreamed of. Beneath the figure was written "Katchina Dancer of Zuñi, New Mexico."

It may be that the chill of a windy winter night caused me to dream of wild and desolate lands, the height of my tower home, of mountains, the clang of an iron door left unlatched six flights below, of hollow, reverberating mountains, and my studies among the relics and idols of primitive man gathered the world over, of an idol stranger than any I have studied—while my joy was only that of every born collector and student of olden things. Again it may be that these things only aided me to see the things that resembled them far away in time and station; who knows? Be all this as it may, my eyes were first turned towards Zuñi by a vision of the night, else it is more than likely the exploration which I was bent year in and year out on accomplishing would have led me almost anywhere else than Zuñi; for at that time I longed to study the old dead cultures and monuments of Mexico, Central America, and Peru, told of by Stephen Prescott and others. I had conceived the idea of seeking among still existing tribes of those southern lands the descendants of the ancient builders and of living their lives, if need be, to overcome their secrecy in regard to the lore of their land. Now my fancy took another turn. I began to hear of the cliff and mesa ruins of our great Southwest. I heard also that the race who reared them were supposed to be related to the peoples I had wished so much to study. When I learned the little then known of the Zuñi and other pueblo Indians of New Mexico and Arizona, I believed some of them would turn out to be themselves the children of the cliff dwellers. Never after that did I abandon the idea of someday visiting them to acquire knowledge which would guide me farther on in my quest of the golden sun worship. ▪

Gustaf Nordenskiöld was twenty-two years old in 1891 when he arrived in the United States from Sweden. Son of Arctic explorer A. E. Nordenskiöld, Gustaf had been trained in chemistry and mineralogy at the University of Uppsala. Like his father, he had been drawn to the north and was a member of a geological expedition to Spitsbergen in 1890. Diagnosed with tuberculosis after his stay in the Arctic, Nordenskiöld embarked on a grand tour of Europe to regain his health and soon continued on to the United States. While there, he visited important museum collections and met with leading scientists, planning a cross-country trip to San Francisco and eventually to Japan.

In Denver, however, Nordenskiöld's plans changed when he learned about the cliff dwellings of Mancos Valley discovered in 1888 by Richard Wetherill and Charlie Mason. Bankrolled by his father, the young man drew upon his background in geology to undertake the first scientific excavations of the Mesa Verde area. The results were a book, *The Cliff Dwellers of Mesa Verde* (1893), and the assembly of an extensive collection of Puebloan artifacts and materials. Nordenskiöld's letters from his stay in Colorado were compiled in 1991 by Irv Diamond. As this letter to his father suggests, Nordenskiöld's excavations were early on the source of controversy. Vilified by local residents as a foreign looter, Nordenskiöld was forced into extensive legal and even diplomatic efforts to clear his name. All charges were finally dropped, and today Nordenskiöld is remembered for his contributions to the early archaeology of Mesa Verde. Most of the artifact collection he assembled is housed in the National Museum in Helsinki, Finland.

---

f r o m　　　　　*At the campsite in Navajo Canyon, 23 August 1891*

Letters of Gustaf Nordenskiöld

GUSTAF NORDENSKIÖLD

Thank you for your letter, Father, which I finally received yesterday. I have recently fallen into some difficulties with the authorities, but everything has been cleared up now. One of the area's two largest merchants became dissatisfied with me, since I bought all of my supplies from the other. He sent some sort of report to interested authorities, stating that a foreigner was busy destroying some of the most beautiful ruins. The result of this was a public notice in the Mancos post office, to approximately the following effect:

> Nobody is allowed in this reservation for the purpose of procuring Indian (!) relics from Aztec (?) ruins . . . No foreigner is allowed on the Indian land without permission . . . fine 1000 dollars.

"1000 dollars" had a negative effect upon me. I rode in haste to the nearest military station, where I obtained without difficulty a pass which allowed me to be on the reservation, but which also had the inconvenient addendum that "this pass do not [sic] include any right of making excavations in the ruins."

Through an influential acquaintance in Durango who is a good friend of the Indian agent, I received the message that no one would hinder me in my excavations as long as no ruins were destroyed. In the meantime, I have sent home the items I have already obtained, just to be sure. My plans now are as follows: until the end of September, I shall stay here in the Mancos area, occupied mainly with studying the cliff ruins. By that time, I should have a rather beautiful collection from there. After that I will go directly to the Grand Cañon in Colorado [sic] and from there by horseback through Arizona, New Mexico, Texas, and possibly a bit of old Mexico, to the East Coast, and from there take the shortest route home, whence I ought to arrive at around Christmastime. I may need some more money, but will be arriving home with a profit of 3000 or 4000 crowns, perhaps more, if I can get my collections out of here. A good camera will probably cost me about 100 dollars. My camera there at home, with all its equipment, has cost over 500 crowns. My collections here are increasing all the time. Beautiful stone tools, more crania, woven items, etc. I am presently employing 4 men for a total of 7 dollars per day in wages. To feed them and myself costs about $1.50 a day. I own 5 horses, representing a total value of 150 dollars. One has run away, and another is poorly saddle trained. The climate and the lifestyle here has the most healthful effect upon me.

If I tell people that I am traveling for the sake of my health, they laugh at me. I am beginning to get fat (I have had to let out my underwear by 4 inches). How much did you get for my newspaper articles? I'll send more of them in the form of letters to Mamma. If any of my collections are unpacked, please see to it that bones from the different skeletons are not mixed up; they have been packed each in a separate sack. Has the phosphate report been printed anywhere? I am impatient to get more letters from home. My address is still the same, at least until the middle of September.

Many greetings. Pappa's devoted Gustaf. ■

Ann Axtell Morris accompanied her husband, archaeologist Earl Morris, on many of his excavations, most notably in Canyon de Chelly, Canyon del Muerto, and during his restoration of the great kiva at Aztec in 1933. Ann Axtell Morris balanced the dry commentary of scientists with her own engaging, richly human account of life in the field. *Digging in the Southwest* (1940) is her chatty, witty, intelligent, sometimes glib, but often genuinely humorous book. In it, Morris satirizes archaeologists as she praises their accomplishments. In the following excerpt, she recounts meeting Charles and Anne Morrow Lindbergh during their 1929 airplane excursion of the Southwest and relates the famous couple's contributions to the archaeology of Puebloan sites.

f r o m

Digging in the Southwest

ANN   AXTELL   MORRIS

All the world knows about the great service Colonel Lindbergh did archaeology in his discoveries of ancient Yucatan cities, jungle-buried these many hundred years. But not many people are aware of the reaction of this initial archaeological venture on the Colonel himself. One taste of the age-old fascination was enough to make an addict of him. So we were not surprised to read a much belated newspaper notice in August, 1929, that the Lindberghs were taking a southwestern air cruise with headquarters at Dr. Kidder's camp near Pecos, New Mexico.

A few days later the echoing cliffs around Antelope Cave picked up a distant buzz as of myriad bees. Most of the men were out at work somewhere, but the two of us left in camp kept our eyes peeled toward the canyon bend anticipating an automobile full of visitors—an event rare enough to be very exciting. The buzz became louder, receded, came again, and finally swelled to a gigantic roar. No auto ever sounded like that, and when finally our searching eyes came to rest it was upon the first airplane ever to swoop over Canyon del Muerto.

"The Lindberghs!" Bud Weyer and I shouted together and wildly flapped our arms, forgetting how pebble-small we would appear from such a height. Sick with disappointment, we watched the plane disappear up canyon. But a few minutes later back it came, and from the circling tactics we knew that they were searching for some specific thing, which was in all probability ourselves. This time Bud and I flapped dishtowels, which were the largest, whitest things at hand, but still without any more success than if they had been pocket handkerchiefs. Back and forth went the seeking plane, and we were frantic at our helplessness. Then I had an inspiration and dashed out to a white Indian horse hobbled before the cave. Using his large white expanse of back to supplement my towel, I wigwagged with the latter. The horse plunged and I flapped; then finally the combination caught a Lindbergh eye. It was almost as if the very beat of the motor changed—at any rate they saw us and we knew they saw us. A few more circles and they flew away, and we were left regretting the narrow tortuous canyon bottom which made such an impossible landing field.

A couple of days later Earl and I had to leave for the railroad in order to collect some official visitors. A terrible storm broke in the meantime, and our way back to Chinlee was made with the greatest difficulty. Once at Chinlee, the difficulty magnified to impossibility, for the canyon was running high. For two days we champed at the bit on the foaming banks while all the rain that had fallen on a near range of mountains poured off into the De Chelley–Del Muerto channel.

The morning of the third day the torrent had somewhat abated, but it was clear that autos would not be able to negotiate passage for at least two days more. So, bowing to the inevitable, we hired a wagon and four large mules. By supper time this speedy vehicle finally dragged its weary length to the end of the ninth mile and we were home again at Antelope Cave.

The men who had been left at the digs had a tale to unfold! It seems that, just after we had left, the plane, which we had chosen to think of as belonging to the Lindberghs because it made it more interesting, came back again. They heard it roaring up and down the country in the late afternoon. It circled again over camp, still high in the air to be well clear of tricky canyon air currents, and when the plane's occupants were sure that they had been noticed, down from the lofty heights came tumbling a small heavy white sack. Inside was a cocoa tin full of letters addressed to Earl and me.

In the meantime the plane had disappeared from sight and, most curiously, had as suddenly passed out of hearing. Dusk was falling, and supper was in progress. It was nearly dark when two people were spotted wading toward camp. Oscar said that the only thing in his mind was that if two people were so plucky and so poverty-stricken as to *walk* up Del Muerto they at least deserved a good meal. He went out to meet them in the deepening dusk. There was a tall young chap and a girl. The tall young chap most politely inquired if this was the Morris camp, whereupon he mentioned rather diffidently that Dr. Kidder had sent him, ending, even more diffidently, with, "My name is Lindbergh."

To us southwesterners so far from the paths of planes and airfields the Lindbergh name was almost a hallowed myth. Such an encounter in such a place was breathtaking to say the least. I asked Oscar what he said then. "Well," he answered, "I was pretty surprised, so I just said, 'My name is Tatman. Won't you stay for supper?' " Which was doing very well indeed under the circumstances.

They did stay for supper and all night and all the next day, reveling both in archaeology and isolation. It seems that when they came back to bring us our Pecos mail, they had spotted a flat area of ground reasonably clear of trees and brush, directly above and opposite our camp. And, what amazed us tremendously after all our residence and explorations in the district, they had sighted from the air a little trail zigzagging straight up the canyon wall just around the corner.

They put the plane down on their informal field, only paying one small rip in one wing where a cedar had snagged it. A more hopeless country for landing a plane could hardly be thought of—canyon cut and timbered over every yard. It was extraordinary good fortune that the only clear spot for scores of miles in every direction should have been so close and so conveniently served by a goat trail.

On the original flight the Lindberghs had located a cave in the neighboring Canyon de Chelly, high in the rim, containing cliff houses, which they photographed. As far as Dr. Kidder knew, it had never been explored before, and he told the Lindberghs so. This naturally excited them, so the next morning with Omer and Bud they started out. They reclimbed the trail, walked over to De Chelly, and began following the rim of that canyon in an endeavor to find the cave. It proved to be very difficult, for the spot they wanted to find was beneath them and of course out of sight. The photographs were the only guide, but even with their help the problem was obscure. The terrain from the air looked far different from its aspect close at hand. The party had to follow each bend and promontory in order to check their position, which meant miles and miles of additional walking.

The sun became blisteringly hot and the ground rougher as the hours passed. Mrs. Lindbergh wore loose riding boots, which, although satisfactory enough as the crow flies, proved a distinct liability for ground work. More than all this, the pace was set by a leader who was eager and further blessed by a famous pair of extremely long legs. That day our camp was completely and absolutely "sold" on the subject of Anne Lindbergh. They still tell with enthusiasm of her pluck and determination. She kept up the pace, laughed as she was doing it, and never once mentioned a blister as big as a silver dollar on each heel till she returned to the Kidder camp and borrowed their medicine kit. The next week I walked to the same cave over a much more direct route and properly shod. But by the time I had covered the eleven miles to the place and the eleven miles in return, with a couple of goat climbs thrown in, I had to close my teeth hard in order to approach the Spartan standard set by the other Anne.

When the cave was finally found it turned out to be a little beauty. The original trail led down from the top, for by now it is and perhaps always was impossible of access from below. The cave itself consists of triple ledges of rock, perpendicularly below one another, with three separate cliff dwellings upon them. Each is made up of houses of several rooms, and the upper two are in perfect condition. Behind one of them was a dead Navajo, but he was very dead—quite mummified—and as he was armed with a rawhide shield painted blue, it was apparent that he was practically archaeological in age. This took the curse off, so it was possible for the four hungry explorers to enjoy their lunch in his vicinity.

Digging was very poor, however. Very little débris was left in the caves; the trash pile which undoubtedly had cascaded from the front in olden times had completely weathered away. Such earth as remained yielded the usual bits of string, corncobs, and broken pottery, but nothing spectacular. The view was of a quality that compensated, though. The little houses were delightful, and there was that indescribable feeling of satisfaction to be derived from setting foot "where white man had never trod before."

Late in the afternoon they all returned to where the plane was parked—probably the first time in its history that protection from souvenir hunters had not been necessary. The two boys watched it sail away into the east and returned to camp.

When we arrived some days later, everybody was still bubbling from their delightful surprise. The cocoa tin was pried open and the letters from Pecos read which established, as one of them said, "the first air mail service between Pecos and Del Muerto." Among the lot were some corking air pictures of the canyon signed by Colonel Lindbergh.

The boys retailed one most amusing occurrence. It is our habit to carry along great quantities of newspapers on our expeditions to use to pack specimens in. There is a certain particularly flamboyant Western sheet which is printed on such poor stock that it crumples very satisfactorily. In the present instance we had bought many pounds of old numbers, the major portion of which were all of one date. And when the Lindberghs arrived, the camp was plastered from end to end with infinitely repeated headlines, "Anne and Lindy Married." The boys furtively turned them over as fast as they could, and I suspect they were much more embarrassed about it than the principals themselves. ▪

Neil M. Judd was a Smithsonian Institution archaeologist who conducted major excavations in Chaco Canyon and Navajo National Monument, working with some of the greatest names in archaeology. Author of a history of the Bureau of American Ethnology, Judd also wrote *Men Met Along the Trail: Adventures in Archaeology* (1968), the highly readable and vivid memoir of a life lived on the cutting edge of the scientific study of the Southwest's ancient sites. The "men met along the trail" are a virtual Who's Who of American archaeology. Here Judd describes the 1917 restoration of Betatakin ruin in Tsegi Canyon of the Navajo National Monument. As part of his account he relates his version of an often repeated and variable anecdote, the Native American response to World War I. While you're in the ruins, you are also in the political world beyond.

f r o m

Men Met Along the Trail

NEIL M. JUDD

In 1916, Congress authorized an Interior Department appropriation of $3,000 to cover the preservation and repair, under supervision of the Smithsonian Institution, of prehistoric ruins in Navajo National Monument, Arizona. Early in March, 1917, I was unexpectedly named to represent the Institution on this joint undertaking, and, because Interior Department funds were involved, I was sworn in as a disbursing agent of the Bureau of Indian Affairs, a prominent unit of Interior.

While receiving instructions and advice from a Bureau representative who had never been west of the Alleghenies, I was also informed of the diversity of reports which I was expected to submit during field work. There were daily reports, weekly reports, monthly reports, and bimonthly reports. Each had its own designated color, with a specified number of carbon copies; each was to be neatly typed, double space. Midway of these instructions I interrupted to say that a single report upon conclusion of my assignment would have to suffice. And it did.

I boarded a train at Washington, D.C., on March 16, 1917 (unexpended funds had to be returned to the Treasury by June 30, the end of the fiscal year). I reached Flagstaff, Arizona, three days later, hired five chance laborers from a street corner, and left with them on the twentieth by automobile for Tuba City, seventy-five miles distant, western agency for the Bureau of Indian Affairs. Sheltered from wintry winds by the old octagonal trading post at Tuba, we transferred to John Wetherill's four-horse freight wagon, driven by his faithful Navajo teamster, Chischili-begay. From Tuba it was seventy-five or eighty miles to the Wetherill trading post at Kayenta with two nights in the open on snow-covered ground, and from Kayenta by saddle horse and pack mule another fifteen or twenty miles to Betatakin, our first objective. Thus, within a week, I utilized four means of transportation—the best the country offered—to reach my destination.

Chischili-begay was a long-haired Navajo who spoke no English. If he understood what was wanted, he never asked questions. He did what had to be done. About 1907, when a Ute raiding party attacked the Wetherill-Colville trading post at Oljeto, Chischili-begay was sent for help, and, riding through Monument Valley at a gallop, he was shot at by one of the Utes. The ball missed its mark but broke the pommel of his saddle. As late as 1923, that broken saddle still hung in Wetherill's store.

Although the congressional appropriation clearly anticipated repair and preservation of all three major ruins on the Monument, I knew that such an undertaking was utterly impossible within our allotted time. Thus I resolved to restrict our efforts to Betatakin because it was most accessible to tourists and, for this very reason, perhaps in greatest need of early stabilization. All three ruins were responsibilities of the National Park Service, but there was no Service man present in 1917.

Betatakin (Hillside House in Navajo) had been discovered in early July, 1909, by Professor Byron Cummings, then of the University of Utah, and I was one of his student assistants. The date was July 5, as I recall, or a day or two either way. Professor Cummings and his party were returning from explorations in upper Segi Canyon when his chief guide and interpreter, John Wetherill, stopped to chat with a Navajo family beside the trail and, incidentally, to inquire about any nearby ruins. The Segi and its branches were all new to John Wetherill in 1909; it was his first trip through the canyon.

The woman of the household (Navajos are matrilineal) described a large cave dwelling in a gorge across the way, and one of the men agreed to lead us to it. Dean Cummings paid five dollars for this service, but the Navajo, typical of his kind, advanced only partway, then indicated direction by thrusting out his chin and sat down beside the trail to await return of the others. As a Navajo he would have nothing to do with the Anasazis, "the ancient ones," and dared not enter a ruin for fear of the *chindies,* ghosts of the ancient people.

Our examination at that time was very superficial, for Wetherill was in a hurry to return to his home at Oljeto whence he was to leave next day on a business trip to Gallup. Also, being on sabbatical leave from the university, Professor Cummings expected to return in the fall to examine the ruin more minutely. During our hurried tour we found a stone pipe on a bench in one of the ceremonial rooms, a couple of fragments of basketry, and numerous potsherds. Potsherds were everywhere, hundreds of them.

Betatakin occupies a high-vaulted cave at the end of a box canyon, an unnamed south branch of the main Segi. Cliffs of reddish-brown Navajo sandstone arch above the ruin and wall the canyon. "Navajo," a geological designation for a variety of sedimentary sandstone, was singularly appropriate in this instance since we were in Navajo country and all our neighbors were Navajos. On the occasion of that 1909 visit I naturally had no thought that eight years later I would be back again, to assist the Interior Department in preserving Betatakin for the future.

At an elevation of seven thousand feet the Betatakin area is no warm resort, especially in early spring. In March, 1917, we broke trail through two feet of snow to establish camp among scrub oaks below the ruin, the flattest bit of ground anywhere around. Since there was no forage for our saddle animals we sent them back to Kayenta, leaving ourselves isolated and afoot. Not anticipating so much winter, I had come unprepared and had to borrow tents from Wetherill and Colville. The tents were of lightweight canvas; the ground, wet and cold. A raised hearth lifted coffeepot and Dutch oven above the snow, but only the great ruin and its empty rooms provided shelter when the wind blew and ice formed on the canyon stream.

Initially, in 1917, we tested the talus slope for burials, then cleared away tons of blown sand that had settled below a mid-cave seepage zone. A band of columbine greened the upper part of this seepage; in the lower half, a thicket of scrub oaks had taken root, covering the wreckage of shattered walls. In its prime, Betatakin consisted of perhaps 150 rooms or more. From the number of families those rooms represented, there should have been several deaths each generation; but, as at other major Navajo

Monument ruins, we found no discoverable burial place either in the talus or about the dwellings.

During clearing operations we happened upon a former village spring and readied it for use again. Broken timbers and building stones suitable for repairs were piled to one side. When it was noticed that some of the ancient mortar had outlasted the sandstone blocks it bound together, we began experimenting with different proportions of sand, clay, and rock. Eventually we were able to duplicate that ancient mortar and thereafter employed it with great satisfaction in all our repair work and rebuilding of walls.

Betatakin fills a broad, southward-facing cave. Its Navajo name, Hillside House, was well chosen for, except at its two extremes, the cave floor has a slope of approximately forty-five degrees, thus requiring seatings to support house walls built upon it. To meet this requirement the ancient builders pecked with stone hammers a succession of shallow cups, lateral depressions the size and depth of an oyster shell. Half a dozen were needed for the average wall. These hand-pecked seatings are a distinct feature of every Navajo National Monument ruin with which I am acquainted, for every cave in that particular region has a downward- and forward-sloping floor. Only by providing basal supports could the builders erect a stone-and-mud wall on such a slope.

Stonework for front walls normally rose three to five feet above their seatings, to floor level of the room under construction. Very often the outer end of that room consisted of wickerwork—wattled willows plastered inside and out with mud. However inadequate wickerwork may seem to us, it obviously answered the purpose since it is to be found everywhere. Side walls, whether of wickerwork or masonry, invariably stood upon a series of notches rising with the slope. Thus, in all our repairs we were at pains to provide suitable seatings for walls, both at the end of a room and at its side. And all our seatings, cut with steel chisels, purposely exceeded in depth what would have satisfied the ancient masons.

In late April messengers brought news of United States entry into World War I, and a few days later an Indian policeman from the Bureau agency in Tuba City appeared with papers from a too-zealous local draft board informing the six of us—the only strangers in Navajo County—that we had all been selected for the armed services. A foot-loose Indian who had become a regular weekend visitor at our camp was curious to know what all this war talk was about. When he asked who the Germans were and why Washington was going to fight them, I did my best to oblige; with an inadequate knowledge of his language I managed to get the idea across. I told him that from Betatakin by saddle horse it was two days' ride to Shiprock, then three or four days to Santa Fe. From Santa Fe it would take a good rider twenty-five or thirty days to reach New York and, from there, a whole week in a big boat to get across the big water. After that, about three more days of riding to get to where the Americans and Germans were fighting.

After studying this prospect for a moment or two our guest replied: "You tell Washington the Germans never did anything to us Navajos and we are not mad at them, but if Washington wants to fight the Mexicans we will all go." ∎

A true adventurer of the early-twentieth-century American West, Marietta Wetherill is usually eclipsed by the reputation of her famous husband, Richard Wetherill, memorialized as the discoverer of the ruins on Mesa Verde and a central figure in early southwestern archaeology. In 1900, Richard filed a homestead claim in Chaco Canyon in New Mexico, by many accounts with the primary intention of protecting its ruins, and Marietta accompanied him there to operate a small trading post. They lived in a house built near the outer west wing of Pueblo Bonito. Marietta became very close to the Navajo of the area and was eventually adopted into the Chee Clan.

Marietta's account of her life was recorded in the 1950s by Lou Blachly, an interviewer for the Pioneers Foundation, a commercial organization that compiled testimonies of western old-timers. In 1992, Kathryn Gabriel transcribed and edited these tapes for *Marietta Wetherill: Reflections on Life with the Navajos in Chaco Canyon.*

Shortly after their marriage in late 1896, Richard interrupted the couple's honeymoon in Mexico to undertake excavations in Utah's Grand Gulch. With a developing interest in archaeology herself, Marietta went along. The 1897 expedition to Grand Gulch focused on excavating burial sites of the newly discovered preceramic Basketmaker Culture, named by Richard when he visited the area in 1893. Archaeologists of the 1890s thought the Basketmaker Culture might represent a culture earlier than and perhaps wholly distinct from the Puebloans. Funeral basketry, textiles, and the preserved bodies of the dead were unearthed by the expedition and shipped to museums Back East. Here, Marietta describes how the newlyweds shared their camp bed with several of these mummies.

"The Princess Mummy and Other Burials"

MARIETTA WETHERILL

Mr. Wetherill went to Grand Gulch [in 1893–94] and discovered the Basketmakers, another tribe of people who lived in the Mesa Verde country and also in New Mexico, Arizona, and Colorado. He named these early people for their great weaving. Scientists thought everyone they dug up belonged to one tribe. Mr. Wetherill readily found more than one tribe; their heads were a different shape and they made different kinds of material in their homes. They didn't make pottery and they lived together differently than the cliff dwellers.

When somebody tells me a tribe is pureblooded, I shake my head and say there ain't no such thing. Man is very promiscuous, you know. These Indians traded back and forth, and stole or sold slaves from the Horn up to the Bering Strait. You can't tell me there's such a thing as a thoroughbred Indian, whatever tribe he is. I look at those children that are brother and sister, and they don't look any more alike than my brother and I do. I've bred horses and I know how long it takes to get a thoroughbred.

When we got into Grand Gulch there our trouble began. The trail used by the Paiute was in no shape to bring in pack horses and we had to stop for several days while the men worked on it to make it passable. The pack horses wore panniers, or side boxes, that carried pans, coffee pots, canned goods, and a keg of sourdough.

We had four or six Harvard boys. One boy's parents decided the trip would give him something to do for the winter and he brought along a tutor to make sure he stayed out of trouble. They told us they would want crackers in their soup. Mr. Wetherill couldn't get oyster crackers but settled for soda crackers—about twenty-five pounds worth.

We had [forty] animals with us. We took along extra horses because Mr. Wetherill was such a horse lover and refused to push a horse further than it could go. We also brought horses for eating. We heard there would be no game down there and we couldn't drive cattle in, and they would be skin poor by the time we got down in there, anyway. I don't think those boys ever knew they were eating horse. . . .

After we got the trail into Grand Gulch fixed, we started down. One of the wranglers said, "It would break a snake's neck to crawl through that canyon." That's how crooked the trail was. Mr. Wetherill and the horsemen went first, followed by the pack animals. I should have been close to Mr. Wetherill, but I wanted to stay back to watch everyone as they went down the trail. Was I a coward?

Suddenly I heard a big racket up front and the horse that was packed with two boxes of soda crackers and a sack of grain across the top went over the side. The horse had gone around a narrow bend and his box touched the solid rock. It scared him and he tried to turn around but he slipped off. Crackers and grain and horse went clear to the bottom with a thump, killed him instantly, right now.

I was scared and so was my horse. Those trails were so narrow I was glad I parted my hair in the middle. There was no room to get off my horse because of the solid rock on one side and that drop on the other. "Billy," I said to the horse. "You be careful if you was ever careful in your life. I'll let you have the reins perfectly loose and I'll set square and steady on you and hang onto the horn of this saddle and I won't even breathe when we go around that place." We made it all right.

Mr. Wetherill didn't want that horse down there dying, so he sent Clate down to see if the horse was dead and to take the pack saddle off him. A two-year-old colt fell off the trail before Clate could get to the bottom. I never could see any sense in it. He ran into the horse in front of him and his hind feet lost footing and he went down. I couldn't eat any supper that night, I just crawled into my bedroll and stayed there.

We got to the bottom that day with everything else and made our camp. There was a group of us and we needed quite a bit of room. The next morning everybody got up early to see this great gulch and we were never disappointed. In every curve there was evidence of people having lived there.

We came to a cave that went way back, and right in front of it were the remnants of a small room. We measured every cave, every grave, and took photographs of everything we did. If I make mistakes it's because I don't remember and didn't pay attention but I should say it was six or eight feet across. I was the one measuring and taking notes. "This looks like a turkey pen," Mr. Wetherill said, and he decided to excavate it.

They dug a little ways down and found they were coming to a body. Usually after they dug the first shovelful, they saw a rim of pottery or maybe a knee, and they got the brushes out. They used whisk brooms and a finer brush and then all the digging was done with a small garden trowel in those days. Mr. Wetherill insisted on photographing and measuring before he ever started to dig. I measured from front to back then the height by holding up a stick and measuring the stick.

They found this marvelous mummy in there. They called the mummy Joe Buck after one of the fellows on the trip. I don't know who did it but the boys all blamed me when [Orion or Oscar] Buck got mad every time anybody would say that mummy looked like him. The mummy was covered first in a plain turkey feather blanket. The warp of those blankets was yucca string, and the feathers were taken off the quill and wound around the string. That was covered with another blanket with little bluebird feathers in it. The marvel of marvels was a blanket made of cotton, beautifully woven and intricate as a design in red, black, yellow and white.

The men lifted the blankets off the mummy and carefully laid them between the canvas. Carefully, they took him out of his grave. He'd been a large man and his knees were drawn up. Mr. Wetherill found that he had been cut from hip to hip and sewed up with string made from human hair. You could see where it had begun to knit together. Mr. Wetherill turned him over and found a stone atlatl point six inches long sticking out of his hip. They had cut into his hip to get that point out and couldn't find it. The scar had begun to heal before he died.

We moved camp further down the canyon and went to another burial cave, this one more wide-mouthed and five or six feet above a stream that ran when there was water. These burials had been dug straight down into the bottom of this cave. They were two-and-a-half feet across the top but round and lined with mud and baked. And then they put the bodies in those little pots. They broke all the tendons in the elbows and the shoulders and the knees, and the back was bent over and the neck was broken and pushed right over. They mashed them down into those little earthen pots that they'd made there and then put a flat stone on the top. Somebody had been there before us and taken the bodies out of most of them. We only found a very few with the bodies still inside them, but the skeletons were lying in the cave. You couldn't walk in that cave without stepping on human bones they were so thick in there.

I found one skull of a man who wasn't very old when he died. The teeth were still good and the skull was thick. It must have been shot right under the chin because the arrow point stuck out the top of the skull. Never knew what hit him.

We moved camp again and I'd been with Mr. Wetherill all day measuring some caves and we were just about ready to go home. It was getting warmer then and the sun shone in and it was full of soft clean sand. Mr. Wetherill looked around the cave and said, "It doesn't look like many people have lived in here, if any, but someone might have camped here occasionally." He walked behind a rock leaning up against the cliff wall, and thought it would make an awful good burial. "You're not in a hurry to go home, are you?" he said.

He dug a little and then carefully scooped away the windblown sand and finally brushed away the sand with a whisk broom. "Yes, here's a basket," he exclaimed. The basket was rather coarsely woven and at least as tall as I am, five-foot one-and-a-half. "I believe I'll dig a little bit around the edge here. Would you mind getting on your pony and telling Clate to bring the camera?" Everyone had already gone to camp and had taken everything with them.

I got down as fast as Billy would go and told Clate. By that time the sun was down and it was almost dark. I grabbed my flashlight while Clate saddled his horse. Clate tried to take pictures but it was too dark. They dug all around the basket and lifted it off. I was just in agony to see what was underneath it.

Under the basket was another basket and beneath that was a turkey feather blanket with bluebird feather spots. Under that was another feather blanket with yellow spots from wild canaries, perhaps. A smaller basket, which had a design similar to an Apache basket I have, laid at one end.

"Oh, she's alive!" I said when Mr. Wetherill lifted the basket from her face. I couldn't believe she was dead. You can't imagine how quickly these mummies begin to wither when the air gets to them.

"She sure does look asleep, doesn't she?" Mr. Wetherill said.

We called her "Princess." Her body was painted yellow, and her face was painted red and her hair was long. She had sandals [another time Marietta said she wore moccasins] on her feet and a necklace of shell beads. She lay in another basket a bit larger than the one covering her. Moisture never reached that little grave. She had just dried.

One night it commenced to snow. This was my first experience of sleeping with a mummy. If we didn't get them in out of the snow, the mummies would have been destroyed. Our tent [made of large canvas tarpaulin] didn't offer much room and Mr. Wetherill was worried. "What would you like to do?" he asked me. "Would you like to have them at your head, or at your feet?" I said I would have them at my feet. So that night we slept with four mummies at the foot of our beds.

We wrapped the mummies in muslin in those long tarpaulin bags and packed them with grass and snapped them all shut. It rained for several days and they sure did smell. Every time it was sunny I got our beds out and aired them. ■

❈

Although Clyde Edgerton's five previous novels are set in the rural South, in the darkly comic and extensively researched western novel *Redeye* (1995), he moves to the turn-of-the-century Southwest in a narrative based loosely on the early discoveries of the Wetherill brothers and Gustaf Nordenskiöld. In this passage, rancher Abel Merriwether has unearthed the mummified body of an ancient Pueblo child and brought it to the Copeland family's frontier funeral parlor. Desperate to comfort her aged mother, who is lost in a mournful second childhood, Mrs. Copeland gives the long-dead child into the care of the old woman. Marietta Wetherill's account in this volume of the actual discovery of a mummified body suggests the events that Edgerton might have drawn upon to fashion his macabre satire of the early entrepreneurial pot-hunting days of southwestern archaeology.

f r o m

Redeye

CLYDE EDGERTON

When I got back to the ranch, Star was out by the irrigation ditch with the girls.

"Mr. Merriwether's back," she said. "Wait till you see what he found up there. He brought it in a tow sack."

Three or four Mexicans and Juanita was on the porch circling around something. I got up there as fast as I could. It was a baby they'd set up in a chair, a almost perfect mummified baby tied and wrapped onto a big snowshoe-looking baby board that still had straps for the mama's back. Its head was sticking up out of all the wrappings, turned sideways, and its mouth was open more on one side than the other. It looked like a little girl. She looked almost alive, except she was staring out of little dark holes where here eyes had been—made her head look hollow. Ears and nose was still there. At some time, when she was buried I guess, her neck had been painted red and her face and bald head yellow. Between her eyes up on her forehead was a little red cross, almost disappeared. She was all wrapped in a feather cloth that still had color in it—from bluebirds and yellow birds it had to be, or maybe parrots, but at the same time, you could tell by the faded and rotten parts of the wrapping that she had to be real, real old.

While I was standing looking, Juanita came out and said Mr. Merriwether wanted to see me in his office.

"Sit down," he said when I got in there. He was on his settee with his feet up and some open letters on the couch beside him and some other things. "Did you see it?"

"Yessir."

"I can't imagine anything like that more perfect, but I need to talk to you." It was kind of like I was a grownup. "First look at this." He pulled a very large jar out of a towsack. "Look at that. Take it. Be careful."

I took it. It was lighter than it looked. White with black meanderings.

"The form is the best I've seen," he said. "Very admirable work."

It was big and almost perfectly round with a little hole on top that had a short neck and little loop handles on each side. "But it was never baked enough," he said. "Almost as if the baking were interrupted. Put your finger right there. See? It's soft. And the ornament is sloppy . . . and here, look at this." He pulled a basket out of the sack. "Look at the tightness of the weave of this. You don't see anything like that done today—anywhere in the Southwest. These things were in the trash pile down the cliff, *hidden* in there—not thrown away, but hidden. The next time we go in, I'm going to have somebody do nothing but the trash piles down below, because . . . but look at this." He pulled out a black, shiny bird, as big as my hand, a crow it looked like, with turquoise eyes and collar. He handed it to me. My frog was in my pocket. I started to show it to him, and then figured no, I'd better not. I'd been keeping it too long.

"It's made from jet," he said. "I've never seen another like it. It had to be brought in, traded in from somewhere. I've sent Andrew to the library in Denver to see if he can find out anything about where it might have come from. I think maybe Mexico. But I can't imagine *when*. Did you see the miniature bow and arrow on the porch?" he said.

"No."

"It was with the little princess."

"She was in the trash pile, too?"

"No, but I did find two skeletons there—packed into jars, children, with bones broken to get them in there. The little princess was in a very small room up high. One of those we talked about getting into—with the door mortared closed. It took me a day to get in there, and the room had been airtight I'm sure, because you saw what condition she's in. She had two bowls, a ladle, and a miniature bow and set of arrows in there with her. It was actually more of a hole than a room, but there she was, about perfect, which is why I need to talk to P.J. Because from the time I got her out until nightfall I'm afraid she withered, just the tiniest bit. What we've got to do is get her in an airtight coffin with a glass cover and that's what I want P.J. to do for me. I need you to go tell him, and take her with you. I can show you how to tote her."

He was kind of getting me in on helping him out and telling me all of these things, so I felt he liked me, and I decided maybe I ought to just say something about what all Mr. Blankenship was planning. "Do you know about Mr. Blankenship's plan?" I said.

"I'm not sure. Which plan?"

"He wants to bring in tourists. He's got some kind of setup with the railroads and he thinks people would come in and pay to be took up to see the cliff dwellings. That's what he's been talking about."

"I hope it doesn't come to that but, on the other hand . . ." He picked up an open letter on the couch beside him. "The Smithsonian refuses, flat refuses to help with the first nickel for any kind of exploring in the Southwest. But if we can get some photographs of the princess to them, and of this bowl and the bird, and some other relics, then I don't see how they can refuse. I need to hire some people to go back in there. We could use twice as many as we had, and dig in that one ruin for years."

I wondered again if I should show him my frog, but I decided not to. He showed me how to take Princess, in a canvas bag, on my back. It was a pretty day and I rode easy so as not to shake her apart or anything. It's not far to Mr. Copeland's, but I stopped where Bobcat Creek crosses the road and took a little rest and ate biscuits and venison that Mrs. Merriwether had give me in a paper sack. I laid back in the grass beside Princess and while Sandy grazed I drifted off to sleep and dreamed about the Mountain Meadows Massacre. There was skeletons all over the ground, painted yellow, and somebody was walking through a field, picking them up with one hand, and holding them up. They looked stiff and held together, the whole skeleton, not falling apart. I woke up and got to worrying a little bit about keeping that frog with me so I put it under this big rock at the base of a big cottonwood right where the creek and road intersected. I was thirsty and so I took a drink from the creek and then we headed on toward Mr. Copeland's.

I had to be careful about the dogs not getting at Princess, so I went ahead and put her down on the table in the corpse—tree—room. I had her propped up so everybody could see her when they come in the kitchen door. Sister was the first one, then Mrs.

Copeland came in just before Brother rolled Grandma Copeland up the ramp outside. Brother and Grandma had been playing dog.

After he backed her in there and turned her around, Grandma looked at the baby mummy—then let out this cry like some kind of high-pitched old war whoop, and held her arms out. I'd never heard her make any noise at all, except for this little grunt she did while she was eating. We didn't know what was wrong at first. Mrs. Copeland tried to talk to her, but all she would do is reach out toward the mummy. Then she let out one of those cries again with Mrs. Copeland down in her face trying to calm her down, and Sister, standing there, says, "Give her the baby doll. She wants the baby doll."

Grandma Copeland was crying, so Mrs. Copeland lifted the mummy and passed it down to her sitting there in her wheelchair and she took it in her lap facing her and slowly lowered her head until it was touching the mummy, and she started talking a kind of baby talk, but you couldn't understand it. Her voice was up real high and al-most like singing.

"She thinks it's hers," said Mrs. Copeland. "She lost four. She must think it's the one that lived a little while. One lived a little while, you know. Here, Grandma, let me put it back now. This is not your baby, Grandma. This here is a mummy."

Mrs. Copeland was bending down, but when she tried to take it away, Grandma Copeland held on tight and let out this high wailing sound.

I was thinking if they didn't watch out they was going to pull it apart, and I was thinking how Mr. Merriwether had said we had to get it in a airtight glass case right away. I figured we couldn't put Grandma in there with it. Or maybe we could if Mr. Blankenship got in on it.

Later, Mrs. Copeland sent me after Star at her cabin and they took turns sitting with Grandma Copeland in the tree room with her holding the mummy in her lap. She would turn it one way and then the other like she was trying to get it comfortable. She tried once to get it out of the wrappings, but it was wrapped tight and you couldn't get at it very good.

Mrs. Copeland said wait till Mr. Copeland got home and let him decide what to do since Grandma was *his* mama. I had Brother and Sister on the porch shelling peas when he come riding up in the buggy about sundown. He stopped by the saddle store for a few minutes and checked on things before he came on over to the house.

"We got another mummy out in the corpse room," I said. "Mr. Merriwether brought it back and wants you to make a coffin with a glass top. It's a baby, and in bet-ter shape than the other one."

"Grandma thinks it's alive," said Brother. "She thinks it's her baby."

"Pearl Jane," said Mr. Copeland.

We could see in from the kitchen—Grandma and Mrs. Copeland in Grandma's room. Mrs. Copeland put her finger up to her lips, so we tiptoed in there. Grandma was in her rocking chair by the window, asleep, and at first I couldn't figure it out, but then I saw: Grandma Copeland's dress was unbuttoned up top and she was . . . she was *nursing* the mummy—or had been trying to. We just all stood there staring. Her head was back and she was snoring.

"She just went to sleep," Mrs. Copeland whispered. "I'm afraid to take it or she might start hollering again."

"Her name was Pearl Jane," said Mr. Copeland. "Y'all stand back, let me do this." He went over and picked up the baby real easy and Grandma Copeland didn't budge. He put it on the bed. "Bumpy, help me move this bed over against the wall so she won't push it off." We pushed the bed against the wall. "Y'all move on in the kitchen," he said quietlike.

"Mr. Merriwether wanted you to put it in a glass case," I said.

"I can't do that right now. Can't you see that? Get in the kitchen."

We heard him wake her up. "Mama," he said. "Pearl Jane's in the bed now, and it's time for you to go to bed with her. She's sick. She ain't feeling good at all."

And we could hear him getting her in the bed. Then he come to the door. "Has she eat supper?"

"Lord no. I forgot," said Mrs. Copeland. "Here." She got a ham biscuit off the side table and handed it to him.

Mr. Copeland gave her the bread and chewed up the ham for her, then Grandma laid down in bed beside the mummy and we all went in and said good night and she seemed just as calm as she could be, blinking her eyes up at us and gumming her food.

"I think she'll be all right now," said Mr. Copeland. "Let's go eat."

"How you gone to get it away from her?" I asked him on the way over to the house.

"Well, tonight when I go out there to set her on the pot, first thing I'll do is get the mummy and hide it, and then when I wake her up, or in the morning, I'll just say, 'Pearl Jane has died, Mama,' and that I'm making a coffin for her. And if we have to, we'll have a little funeral service. Sing a song and so forth. I'll have to start on a baby coffin after supper. But I ain't got no glass top that will fit . . . well, yes, I've got those two big panes that didn't fit the hearse. What's for supper?"

"Sister," said Mrs. Copeland, "go back and get them ham biscuits from the kitchen. We got corn, tomatoes, squash, and onions." Then she stopped on the house steps. "P.J., I want you to add on a new kitchen. I ain't been able to use that kitchen but once this week. You ought to be able to do it if you're making so much money in Mortuary Science."

"I'll start soon, in the next week or so. But I got to get on that little display coffin tonight so the mummy don't wrinkle no more." ■

One of the great masters of the craft of nature writing, Barry Lopez has won the National Book Award for nonfiction and the John Burroughs Medal for the best book on natural history. His work includes *Winter Count* and *Arctic Dreams*. In his 1976 *Desert Notes: Reflections in the Eye of a Raven,* Lopez turns to the arid landscapes of the Southwest. One of his most remarkable and vexing pieces of writing, the short story "The Blue Mound People," has its roots in physical anthropology and natural history but finally suggests that the impulse to understand ancient cultures empirically can be profoundly difficult. The story relates an unidentified narrator's experience with the remains of a nearly indecipherable ancient culture. Clearly the invention of Lopez's imagination, the Blue Mound People nevertheless suggest the complexity we face when attempting, as outsiders, to understand the lives of the ancient Puebloans of the Southwest.

"The Blue Mound People"

BARRY HOLSTUN LOPEZ

Once there was a people here who numbered, at their greatest concentration, perhaps two hundred. It has been determined by a close examination of their bones and careful reconstruction of muscle tissues that although they looked as we do they lacked vocal cords. They lived in caves ranged in tiers in the bluffs of the east on the far edge of the desert and because of this some of their more fragile belongings, even clothing, can still be examined intact. The scraps of cloth that have been found are most frequently linen, some of them woven of over a thousand threads to the inch, cloth the thickness of human hair. As nearly as can be determined, there were no distinctions in clothing between the sexes;

everyone apparently wore similar linen robes of varying coarseness and sandals made of woven sage.

Also found in the caves were the usual implements: mortars and pestles, cooking knives, even some wooden bowls that, like the cloth, are oddly preserved. The knives are curious, made of silver and inlaid with black obsidian glass along the cutting edge. A number of glass and crystal shards have been found in the dirt on the floors of the caves, along with bits of bone china and porcelain. Some intact pieces have been uncovered and the workmanship is excellent. A pair of heavily worked pewter candlesticks together with scraps of beeswax were also located.

The caves, though with separate entrances, are linked by an odd and, it seems, needlessly complicated maze of interconnecting hallways. Nothing has been found in these hallways except where they juncture with caves; here a storage area seems to have existed, a sort of back porch. It has been theorized that the maze itself might have been a defensive network of some sort.

Other than the sharp implements apparently used in the preparation of food, there are no other weapons of any sort to be found. This at first puzzled archeologists, who had determined by an examination of shallow refuse pits that the cave people lived on a mixed and varied diet of meat and vegetables. Not only were no hunting implements found (not even ropes or materials for building snares), there were, it has been determined, too few animals nearby to account for the abundance revealed in an examination of the refuse pits and larder areas. Further complicating the issue of sustenance is the lack of evidence that soil suitable for farming was available to provide the many cultivated varieties of melon, tomato, cucumber, celery and other vegetables for which we have found fossilized seeds. Nor could there have been enough water without some form of irrigation (and there was no river at that time for that) to support such agriculture. In fact, a series of drillings has revealed that only enough water was available to support perhaps sixty to eighty people over the course of a year without exhausting the water table.

Radiocarbon dating has pinpointed the time of inhabitance at 22,000 ± 1430 years BP. Again, a projection of game populations and climatic conditions for this period indicates that the cave people were living a life of apparent plenty in an area that, clearly, could not support such an existence. It has been suggested that these people hunted and farmed abroad but preferred to live at the edge of the desert and traversed great distances in order to do so, but this suggestion has not been taken seriously. The nearest area with sufficient water and soil suitable for farming lies sixty miles to the northeast. Also there is this: the major source of meat, after rabbits and, strangely, geese, was a diminutive antelope, an extremely wary creature so widely scattered that it could not be effectively hunted by men on foot. Only very occasionally could such animals be tricked into running off a cliff or trapped in a piskun. It has been conjectured that they traded for their food but this is highly unlikely.

The question of how they provided for themselves remains unanswered.

Other questions also remain. For instance, no cause of death has been determined for the 173 sets of remains, but it is believed that they all died within the period of a year. All but one was arranged in a crypt in the walls of the caves. The one who was not was found sitting on the floor with his back against an intricately woven cedar bark backrest. This man was in his forties and was apparently working on a piece of beaded cloth when he died. It has never been suggested where his white alabaster beads came from.

What these people did is also a mystery; just as there are no hunting implements, so there are no agricultural tools. Nor is there evidence of elaborate religious ceremonies nor extensive artwork nor are there tools or ovens to work the glass and metal objects found in the caves (and it is extremely unlikely that these were obtained in trade as we know of no other cultural group with such skills in existence at this time).

Some believe that a key to understanding these people lies in determining the purpose of a series of blue earth mounds. These mounds of deep blue-grey dust are about a foot high and are perfectly conical in shape but for the rounded tops. One was found in each cave and the remains of four of them have been detected out on the desert, approximately a mile from the caves. At the heart of each one, toward the base, a hard white stone was found, perfectly round, smoother than dry marble, as if it had been washed for hundreds of years in a creek bed. These stones are gypsum-like but of a different crystalline structure and extremely light. There is some reason to believe that they are the fossilized remains of some sort of organism.

It is for this reason, of course, that these people are referred to as the People of the Blue Earth or the Blue Mound People. They cannot be associated, either geographically or by the level of certain of their crafts with any of their supposed contemporaries. And a number of questions continue to pose themselves. In spite of their anatomical inability to speak, we find no evidence of any other system of communication. No paintings, no writings, no systems of marking, no sequences of any sort. And there is, of course, no source for the linen cloth. There are no objects which might be called toys or evidence of any games, although several lute-like instruments have been found. Almost everything else is quite common in design but the materials from which some things have been made are unusual. There are, as I have indicated, pieces of china and glass, even sterling silver, but, as I have noted, no evidence of their fabrication. A careful sifting of cave soils has revealed fragments of oak and leather furniture but no evidence of fire pits, as, indeed there was at that time apparently no wood or other fuel close by. As nearly as can be determined, food was prepared on rock slabs outside the caves with perhaps some glass device to concentrate the rays of the sun. Inside the caves there was, it seems, no source of heat.

A single scrap of papyrus-like paper has been found and objects for which no explanation has been set forth (among them a smooth red sandstone disc and an enormous turtle shell) have also been appearing.

Further analysis of the cave soils and a closer examination of the surrounding area continues, but you can see the problem. We are dealing here with a people entirely out of the order of things and, for this reason, we should be forgiven any sort of speculation. An artist with an eastern museum, for example, has completed a series of drawings based on anatomical studies; he has given these people blue-grey skin and white hair with soft grey eyes. His pictures are very striking; the eyes have a kind, penetrating quality to them. He is perfectly free to do this.

But I have my own ideas.

The alkaline desert was here at the time these people were, this I have on the best scientific authority, even though the area surrounding the desert was swamp-like and no reasons can be given for the existence of a desert in this area at that time. It is obvious to me, then, that these people lived with some unusual arrangement in this desert; conditions were harsh in the extreme, and their food and water (not to mention linen, silver, and glass) had to come from somewhere else. I do not think it facetious at all to suggest, especially to anyone who has seen these caves, then, that in exchange for food, water, and other necessities these people were bound up in an unusual relationship with the desert. I have examined the caves closely enough myself to have determined that these were both a comfortable people, free from want, and a sedentary or perhaps even meditative people. This seems most reasonable.

I think it will be found too that the blue mounds with their white stone hearts have more to do with the desert than they have to do with the people alone. I think they might even be evidence of a bond between the people and the desert. I assume that the desert was the primary force in this relationship, but I could be wrong. It could have been the people who forged this relationship; we have no way of knowing exactly what they were capable of doing. Perhaps they were blue-skinned, and each had the thought of the desert at his heart, like the white stone in the blue earth, maybe this is the meaning. Perhaps this is what they are trying to say, that the desert is only a thought. I don't know.

There have been other suggestions, of course, mostly of a religious nature, but it is all conjecture. Many, of course, have avoided any mention of the blue mounds. In the years since I first discovered the caves I have noticed that they have been shifting a little to the north each year although the wall they are set in seems solid. I am apparently the only one to have noticed this. I have also been here recently when the caves were gone. ▪

Anthropologists and detectives? Yes, of course. Readers of contemporary detective fiction have found in Tony Hillerman a skillful and unique craftsman of the genre. In over a dozen novels, Hillerman places his Navajo Tribal Police detectives Joe Leaphorn and Jim Chee on the trail of mystery and murder. It is the character of the Navajo, the construct of the reservation, and the traditions and tribal experiences of the people, however, that give Hillerman's novels their real power. For his Navajo detectives, solving the crime inevitably involves complex intercultural events and is often as much a matter of restoring the Navajo sense of wholeness or beauty as it is bringing a criminal to justice. Hillerman has made the vandalism of ancient Pueblo sites a central issue throughout his fiction. In the opening chapter of A Thief of Time (1988), an unfortunate anthropologist encounters the legendary Kokopelli, whose image is so frequently represented in southwestern rock art. Or is it the Kokopelli?

f r o m

A Thief of Time

TONY HILLERMAN

The moon had risen just above the cliff behind her. Out on the packed sand of the wash bottom the shadow of the walker made a strange elongated shape. Sometimes it suggested a heron, sometimes one of those stick-figure forms of an Anasazi pictograph. An animated pictograph, its arms moving rhythmically as the moon shadow drifted across the sand. Sometimes, when the goat trail bent and put the walker's profile against the moon, the shadow became Kokopelli himself. The backpack formed the spirit's grotesque hump, the walking stick Kokopelli's crooked flute. Seen from above, the shadow would have made a Navajo believe that the great *yei* northern clans called Watersprinkler had taken visible form. If an Anasazi had risen from his thousand-year grave in the trash heap under the cliff ruins here, he would have seen the Humpbacked Flute Player, the rowdy god of fertility of his lost people. But the shadow was only the shape of Dr. Eleanor Friedman-Bernal blocking out the light of an October moon.

Dr. Friedman-Bernal rested now, sitting on a convenient rock, removing her backpack, rubbing her shoulders, letting the cold, high desert air evaporate the sweat that had soaked her shirt, reconsidering a long day.

No one could have seen her. Of course, they had seen her driving away from Chaco. The children were up in the gray dawn to catch their school bus. And the children would chat about it to their parents. In that tiny, isolated Park Service society of a dozen adults and two children, everyone knew everything about everybody. There was absolutely no possibility of privacy. But she had done everything right. She had made the rounds of the permanent housing and checked with everyone on the digging team. She was driving into Farmington, she'd said. She'd collected the outgoing mail to be dropped off at the Blanco Trading Post. She had jotted down the list of supplies people needed. She'd told Maxie she had the Chaco fever—needed to get away, see a movie, have a restaurant dinner, smell exhaust fumes, hear a different set of voices, make phone calls back to civilization on a telephone that would actually work. She would spend a night where she could hear the sounds of civilization, something besides the endless Chaco silence. Maxie was sympathetic. If Maxie suspected anything, she suspected Dr. Eleanor Friedman-Bernal was meeting Lehman. That would have been fine with Eleanor Friedman-Bernal.

The handle of the folding shovel she had strapped to her pack was pressing against her back. She stopped, shifted the weight, and adjusted the pack straps. Somewhere in the darkness up the canyon she could hear the odd screeching call of a saw-whet owl, hunting nocturnal rodents. She glanced at her watch: 10:11, changing to 10:12 as she watched. Time enough.

No one had seen her in Bluff. She was sure of that. She had called from Shiprock, just to make doubly sure that no one was using Bo Arnold's old house out on the highway. No one had answered. The house was dark when she'd arrived, and she'd left it that way, finding the key under the flower box where Bo always left it. She'd done her borrowing carefully, disturbing nothing. When she put it back, Bo would never guess it had been missing. Not that it would matter. Bo was a biologist, scraping out a living as a part-timer with the Bureau of Land Management while he finished his dissertation on desert lichens, or whatever it was he was studying. He hadn't given a damn about anything else when she'd known him at Madison, and he didn't now.

She yawned, stretched, reached for her backpack, decided to rest a moment longer. She'd been up about nineteen hours. She had maybe two more to go before she reached the site. Then she'd roll out the sleeping bag and not get out of it until she was rested. No hurry now. She thought about Lehman. Big. Ugly. Smart. Gray. Sexy. Lehman was coming. She'd wine him and dine him and show him what she had. And he would have to be impressed. He'd have to agree she'd proved her case. That wasn't necessary for publication—his approval. But for some reason, it was necessary to her. And that irrationality made her think of Maxie. Maxie and Elliot.

She smiled, and rubbed her face. It was quiet here, just a few insects making their nocturnal sounds. Windless. The cold air settling into the canyon. She shivered, picked up the backpack, and struggled into it. A coyote was barking somewhere over on Comb Wash far behind her. She could hear another across the wash, very distant, yipping in celebration of the moonlight. She walked rapidly up the packed sand, lifting her legs high to stretch them, not thinking of what she would do tonight. She had thought long enough of that. Perhaps too long. Instead she shought of Maxie and Eliot. Brains, both. But nuts. The Blueblood and the Poorjane. The Man Who Could Do Anything obsessed by the woman who said nothing he did counted. Poor Elliot! He could never win.

A flash of lightning on the eastern horizon—much too distant to hear the thunder and the wrong direction to threaten any rain. A last gasp of summer, she thought. The moon was higher now, its light muting the colors of the canyon into shades of gray. Her thermal underwear and the walking kept her body warm but her hands were like ice. She studied them. No hands for a lady. Nails blunt and broken. The skin tough, scarred, callused. Anthropology skin, they'd called it when she was an undergraduate. The skin of people who are always out under the sun, working in the dirt. It had always bothered her mother, as everything about her bothered her mother. Becoming an anthropologist instead of a doctor, and then not marrying a doctor. Marrying a Puerto Rican archaeologist who was not even Jewish. And then losing him to another woman. "Wear gloves," her mother had said. "For heaven's sake, Ellie, you have hands like a dirt farmer."

And a face like a dirt farmer too, she'd thought.

The canyon was just as she remembered from the summer she had helped map and catalog its sites. A great place for pictographs. Just ahead, just beyond the cottonwoods on the sheer sandstone wall where the canyon bottom bent, was a gallery of them. The baseball gallery, they called it, because of the great shaman figure that someone had thought resembled a cartoon version of an umpire.

The moon lit only part of the wall, and the slanting light made it difficult to see, but she stopped to inspect it. In this light, the tapered, huge-shouldered shape of the mystic Anasazi shaman lost its color and became merely a dark form. Above it a clutter of shapes danced, stick figures, abstractions: the inevitable Kokopelli, his humped shape bent, his flute pointed almost at the ground; a heron flying; a heron standing; the zigzag band of pigment representing a snake. Then she noticed the horse.

It stood well to the left of the great baseball shaman, mostly in moon shadow. A Navajo addition, obviously, since the Anasazi has vanished three hundred years before the Spanish came on their steeds. It was a stylized horse, with a barrel body and straight legs, but without the typical Navajo tendency to build beauty into everything they attempted. The rider seemed to be a Kokopelli—Watersprinkler, the Navajos called him. At least the rider seemed to be blowing a flute. Had this addition been there before? She couldn't remember. Such Navajo additions weren't uncommon. But this one puzzled her.

Then she noticed, at each of three feet of the animal, a tiny prone figure. Three. Each with the little circle representing the head separated from the body. Each with one leg cut away.

Sick. And they hadn't been here four years ago. These she would have remembered.

For the first time Eleanor Friedman-Bernal became aware of the darkness, the silence, her total isolation. She had dropped her backpack while she rested. Now she picked it up, put an arm through the carry strap, changed her mind. She unzipped a side pocket and extracted the pistol. It was a .25 caliber automatic. The salesman had shown her how to load it, how the safety worked, how to hold it. He had told her it was accurate, easy to use, and made in Belgium. He had not told her that it took an unusual ammunition that one always had to hunt for. She had never tried it out in Madison. There never seemed to be a place to shoot it safely. But when she came to New Mexico, the first day when there was enough wind to blow away the sound, she'd driven out into the emptiness on the road toward Crownpoint and practiced with it. She had fired it at rocks, and deadwood, and shadows on the sand, until it felt natural and comfortable and she was hitting things, or getting close enough. When she used up most of the box of cartridges, she found the sporting goods store in Farmington didn't have them. And neither did the big place in Albuquerque, and finally she had ordered them out of a catalog. Now she had seventeen bullets left in the new box. She had brought six of them with her. A full magazine. The pistol felt cold in her hand, cold and hard and reassuring.

She dropped it into the pocket of her jacket. As she regained the sandy bottom of the wash and walked up it, she was conscious of the heaviness against her hip. The coyotes were closer, two of them somewhere above her, on the mesa beyond the clifftops. Sometimes the night breeze gusted enough to make its sounds in the brush along the bottom, rattling the leaves on the Russian olives and whispering through the fronds of the tamarisks. Usually it was still. Runoff from the summer monsoons had filled pools along the rocky bottom. Most of these were nearly dry now, but she could hear frogs, and crickets, and insects she couldn't identify. Something made a clicking sound in the darkness where dead tumbleweed had collected against the cliff, and from somewhere ahead she heard what sounded like a whistle. A night bird?

The canyon wound under the cliff and out of the moonlight. She turned on her flash. No risk of anyone seeing it. And that turned her thoughts to how far the nearest human would be. Not far as the bird flies—perhaps fifteen or twenty miles as the crow flew. But no easy way in. No roads across the landscape of almost solid stone, and no reason to build roads. No reason for the Anasazi to come here, for that matter, except to escape something that was hunting them. None that the anthropologists could think of—not even the cultural anthropologists with their notorious talents for forming theories without evidence. But come they had. And with them came her artist. Leaving Chaco Canyon behind her. Coming here to create more of her pots and to die.

From where Dr. Friedman-Bernal was walking she could see one of their ruins low on the cliff wall to her right. Had it been daylight, she remembered, she could have seen two more in the huge amphitheater alcove on the cliff to her left. But now the alcove was black with shadow—looking a little like a great gaping mouth.

She heard squeaking. Bats. She'd noticed a few just after sundown. Here they swarmed, fluttering over places where runoff had filled potholes and potholes had bred insects. They flashed past her face, just over her hair. Watching them, Ellie Friedman-Bernal didn't watch where she was walking. A rock turned under her foot, and she lost her balance.

The backpack cost her enough of her usual grace to make the fall hard and clumsy. She broke it with her right hand, hip, and elbow and found herself sprawled on the stream bottom, hurt, shocked, and shaken.

The elbow was most painful. It had scraped over the sandstone, tearing her shirt and leaving an abrasion that, when she touched it, stained her finger with blood. Then her bruised hip got her attention, but it was numb now and would punish her later. It was only when she scrambled back to her feet that she noticed the cut across the palm of her hand. She examined it in the light of her flash, made a sympathetic clicking sound, and then sat down to deal with it.

She picked out a bit of the gravel imbedded in the heel of her hand, rinsed the cut from her canteen, and bandaged it with a handkerchief, using left hand and teeth to tighten the knot. And then she continued up the wash, more careful now, leaving the bats behind, following a turn back into the full moonlight and then another into the shadows. Here she climbed onto a low alluvial ledge beside the dry streambed and dumped her pack. It was a familiar place. She and Eduardo Bernal had pitched a tent here five summers ago when they were graduate students, lovers, and part of the site-mapping team. Eddie Bernal. Tough little Ed. Fun while it lasted. But not much fun for long. Soon, surely before Christmas, she would drop the hyphen. Ed would hardly notice. A sigh of relief, perhaps. End of that brief phase when he'd thought one woman would be enough.

She removed a rock, some sticks, smoothed the ground with the edge of her boot sole, dug out and softened an area where her hips would be, and then rolled out the sleeping bag. She chose the place where she had lain with Eddie. Why? Partly defiance, partly sentiment, partly because it was simply the most comfortable spot. Tomorrow would be hard work and the cuts on her palm would make digging difficult and probably painful. But she wasn't ready for sleep yet. Too much tension. Too much uneasiness.

Standing here beside the sleeping bag, out of the moonlight, more stars were visible. She checked the autumn constellations, found the polestar, got her directions exactly right. Then she stared across the wash into the darkness that hid what she and Eddie had called Chicken Condo. In the narrow stone alcove, Anasazi families had built a two-story dwelling probably big enough for thirty people. Above it, in another alcove so hidden that they wouldn't have noticed it had Eddie not wondered where an evening bat flight was coming from, the Anasazi had built a little stone fort reachable only by a precarious set of hand- and footholds. It was around the lower dwelling that Eleanor Friedman-Bernal first had found the peculiar potsherds. If her memory didn't fool her. It was there, when it was light enough tomorrow, that she would dig. In violation of Navajo law, of federal law, and of professional ethics. If her memory only had not fooled her. And now she had more evidence than just her memory.

She couldn't wait until daylight. Not now. Not this near. Her flashlight would be enough to check.

Her memory had been excellent. It took her unerringly and without a misstep on an easy climb up the talus slope and along the natural pathway to the rim. There she paused and turned her light onto the cliff. The petroglyphs were exactly as she had stored them in her mind. The spiral that might represent the *sipapu* from which humans had emerged from the womb of Mother Earth, the line of dots that might represent the clan's migrations, the wideshouldered forms that the ethnographers believed represented kachina spirits. There, too, cut through the dark desert varnish into the face of the cliff, was the shape Eddie had called Big Chief looking out from behind a red-stained shield, and a figure that seemed to have a man's body but the feet and head of a heron. It was one of her two favorites, because it seemed so totally unexplainable even by the cultural anthropologists—who could explain anything. The other was another version of Kokopelli.

Wherever you found him—and you found him everywhere these vanished people carved, and painted, their spirits into the cliffs of the Southwest—Kokopelli looked about the same. His humpbacked figure was supported by stick legs. Stick arms held a straight line to his tiny round head, making him seem to be playing a clarinet. The flute might be pointed down, or ahead. Otherwise there was little variation in how he was depicted. Except here. Here Kokopelli was lying on his back, flute pointed skyward. "At last," Eddie had said. "You have found Kokopelli's home. This is where he sleeps."

But Eleanor Friedman-Bernal hardly glanced at Kokopelli now. The Chicken Condo was just around the corner. That was what had drawn her.

The first things her eyes picked up when the beam of her flash lit the total darkness of the alcove were flecks of white where nothing white should be. She let the flash roam over the broken walls, reflect from the black surface of the seep-fed pool below them. Then she moved the beam back to that incongruous reflection. It was exactly what she had feared.

Bones. Bones scattered everywhere.

"Oh, shit!" said Eleanor Friedman-Bernal, who almost never used expletives. "Shit! Shit! Shit!"

Someone had been digging. Someone had been looting. A pot hunter. A Thief of Time. Someone had gotten here first.

She focused on the nearest white. A human shoulder bone. A child's. It lay atop a pile of loose earth just outside a place where the wall had fallen. The excavation was in the hump of earth that had been this community's trash heap. The common place for burials, and the first place experienced pot hunters dug. But the hole here was small. She felt better. Perhaps not much damage had been done. The digging looked fresh. Perhaps what she was hunting would still be here. She explored with the flash, looking for other signs of digging. She found none.

Nor was there any sign of looting elsewhere. She shined the light into the single hole dug in the midden pile. It reflected off stones, a scattering of potsherds mixed with earth and what seemed to be more human bones—part of a foot, she thought, and a vertebra. Beside the pit, on a slab of sandstone, four lower jaws had been placed in a neat row—three adult, one not much beyond infancy. She frowned at the arrangement, raised her eyebrows. Considered. Looked around her again. It hadn't rained—at least no rain had blown into this sheltered place—since this digging had been done. But then when had it rained? Not for weeks at Chaco. But Chaco was almost two hundred miles east and south.

The night was still. Behind her, she heard the odd piping of the little frogs that seemed to thrive in this canyon wherever water collected. Leopard frogs, Eddie had called them. And she heard the whistle again. The night bird. Closer now. A half-dozen notes. She frowned. A bird? What else could it be? She had seen at least three kinds of lizards on her way from the river—a whiptail, and a big collared lizard, and another she couldn't identify. They were nocturnal. Did they make some sort of mating whistle?

At the pool, her flashlight reflected scores of tiny points of light—the eyes of frogs. She stood watching them as they hopped, panicked by her huge presence, toward the safety of the black water. Then she frowned. Something was strange.

Not six feet from where she stood, one of them had fallen back in midhop. Then she noticed another one, a half-dozen others. She squatted on her heels beside the frog, inspecting it. And then another, and another, and another.

They were tethered. A whitish thread—perhaps a yucca fiber—had been tied around a back leg of each of these tiny black-green frogs and then to a twig stuck into the damp earth.

Eleanor Friedman-Bernal leaped to her feet, flashed the light frantically around the pool. Now she could see the scores of panicked frogs making those odd leaps that ended when a tether jerked them back to earth. For seconds her mind struggled to process this crazy, unnatural, irrational information. Who would . . . ? It would have to be a human act. It could have no sane purpose. When? How long could these frogs live just out of reach of the saving water? It was insane.

Just then she heard the whistle again. Just behind her. Not a night bird. No sort of reptile. It was a melody the Beatles had made popular. "Hey, Jude," the words began. But Eleanor didn't recognize it. She was too terrified by the humped shape that was coming out of the moonlight into this pool of darkness. ▪

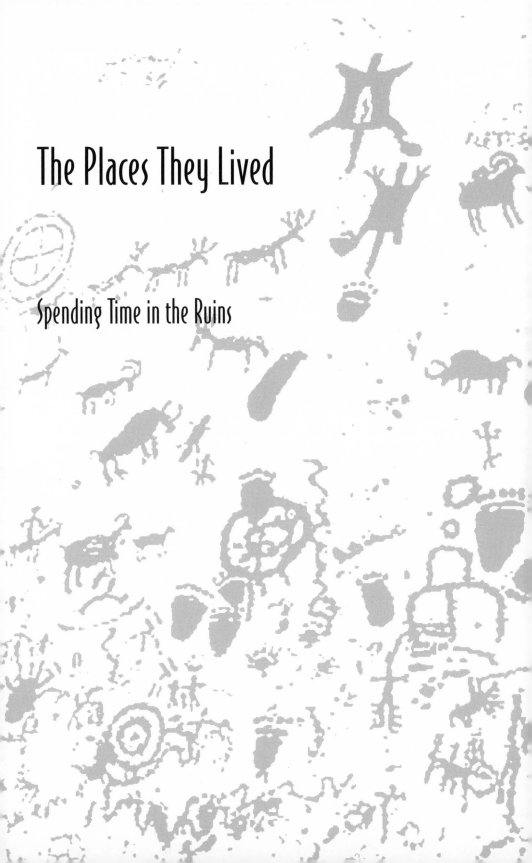

The Places They Lived

Spending Time in the Ruins

※

Compared to many other authors represented in this collection, Harry Noyes Pratt was difficult to track down. In spite of the currency his poetic work enjoyed in 1935, Pratt's is a voice that has largely been erased from modern American literature. Among the remnants that survive is "The Seventh City of Cibola," a work that records both the passage of time and the history of how the ancient Puebloans have been received, and anticipated, by the European mind. The poem is reprinted in C. W. Ceram's excellent *The First American: The Story of North American Archaeology* (1971) and quoted in an essay by Terry Tempest Williams that is included in this volume. The poem originally appeared in *Literary Digest* in 1930 and was reprinted in the anthology *Today's Literature,* published five years later. In addition to being a poet and author of *Mother of Mine and Other Verse* (1918), Pratt was the founder and director of the Crocker Art Museum in Stockton, California.

"The Seventh City of Cibola"

HARRY NOYES PRATT

Where these low walls run fast to
    desert sand
And roofs long vanished leave but
    brazen sky;
Where winds unhindered sweep a
    barren land,
A city's walls rose golden, wide-
    stepped, high.
Where now the rattler waits in his
    scant shade
Dowsing across the torrid noonday
    heat;
A living people sought long crumbled
    gates
Called by the drum's resurgent, sullen
    beat.
Here sat the weavers; here the potters
    made

Olla and urn, deft spun the patterned
      bowl;
And in the pueblo's purple, square-cut
      shade
The gamesters watched the carven
      pebbles roll.
And now the walls are worn to sand,
      and lie
Low-ridged beneath the vulture's
      lonely flight.
Silence—Only the wild, thin, far-flung
      cry
Of a coyote quavering on the desert
      night.

Although she is often associated with the
Nebraska prairie where she spent her early life and that is the setting for much of
her fiction, Willa Cather devloped a keen interest in the American Southwest when
she joined her brother for a vacation there in 1912. She visited the Grand Canyon
and Indian missions as well as Puebloan cliff dwellings. Two of her novels, *The Song
of the Lark* (1915) and *The Professor's House* (1925), draw upon these experiences.
The Professor's House includes a fictional version of the discovery of the Mesa Verde
ruins, shaped by Cather within a commentary on modern American experience.
The Song of the Lark tells the story of Swedish American Thea Kronborg, who
leaves the small Colorado town of Moonstone to pursue a successful career as an
opera singer. In the chapter "The Ancient People," Thea leaves the frenetic, largely
self-imposed pressures of her life as an artist for a sojourn to the Ottenburg Ranch
above Panther Canyon, based on Walnut Canyon outside Flagstaff, Arizona. Sleeping within the rooms of the ancient ruins below the canyon's rim and imagining the
lives of the women who had once lived there, Thea is artistically and spiritually restored, coming to understand herself bound "to a long chain of human endeavor."

f r o m

The Song of the Lark

WILLA CATHER

The San Francisco Mountain lies in northern Arizona, above Flagstaff, and its blue slopes and snowy summit entice the eye for a hundred miles across the desert. About its base lie the pine forests of the Navajos, where the great red-trunked trees live out their peaceful centuries in that sparkling air. The piñons and scrub begin only where the forest ends, where the country breaks into open, stony clearings and the surface of the earth cracks into deep canyons. The great pines stand at a considerable distance from each other. Each tree grows alone, murmurs alone, thinks alone. They do not intrude upon each other. The Navajos are not much in the habit of giving or of asking help. Their language is not a communicative one, and they never attempt an interchange of personality in speech. Over their forests there is the same inexorable reserve. Each tree has its exalted power to bear.

That was the first thing Thea Kronborg felt about the forest, as she drove through it one May morning in Henry Biltmer's democrat wagon—and it was the first great forest she had ever seen. She had got off the train at Flagstaff that morning, rolled off into the high, chill air when all the pines on the mountain were fired by sunrise, so that she seemed to fall from sleep directly into the forest.

Old Biltmer followed a faint wagon trail which ran southeast, and which, as they travelled, continually dipped lower, falling away from the high plateau on the slope of which Flagstaff sits. The white peak of the mountain, the snow gorges above the timber, now disappeared from time to time as the road dropped and dropped, and the forest closed behind the wagon. More than the mountain disappeared as the forest closed thus. Thea seemed to be taking very little through the wood with her. The personality of which she was so tired seemed to let go of her. The high, sparkling air drank it up like blotting paper. It was lost in the thrilling blue of the new sky and the song of the thin wind in the piñons. The old, fretted lines which marked one off, which defined her—made her Thea Kronborg, Bowers's accompanist, a soprano with a faulty middle voice—were all erased.

So far she had failed. Her two years in Chicago had not resulted in anything. She had failed with Harsanyi, and she had made no great progress with her voice. She had come to believe that whatever Bowers had taught her was of secondary importance, and that in the essential things she had made no advance. Her student life closed behind her, like the forest, and she doubted whether she could go back to it if she tried. Probably she would teach music in little country towns all her life. Failure was not so tragic as she would have supposed; she was tired enough not to care.

She was getting back to the earliest sources of gladness that she could remember. She had loved the sun, and the brilliant solitudes of sand and sun, long before these other things had come along to fasten themselves upon her and torment her. That night, when she clambered into her big German feather bed, she felt completely released from the enslaving desire to get on in the world. Darkness had once again the sweet wonder that it had in childhood.

II

Thea's life at the Ottenburg ranch was simple and full of light, like the days themselves. She awoke every morning when the first fierce shafts of sunlight darted through the curtainless windows of her room at the ranch house. After breakfast she took her lunch basket and went down to the canyon. Usually she did not return until sunset.

Panther Canyon was like a thousand others—one of those abrupt fissures with which the earth in the Southwest is riddled; so abrupt that you might walk over the edge of any one of them on a dark night and never know what had happened to you. This canyon headed on the Ottenburg ranch, about a mile from the ranch house, and it was accessible only at its head. The canyon walls, for the first two hundred feet below the surface, were perpendicular cliffs, striped with even-running strata of rock. From there on to the bottom the sides were less abrupt, were shelving, and lightly fringed with piñons and dwarf cedars. The effect was that of a gentler canyon within a wilder one. The dead city lay at the point where the perpendicular outer wall ceased and the V-shaped inner gorge began. There a stratum of rock, softer than those above, had been hollowed out by the action of time until it was like a deep groove running along the sides of the canyon. In this hollow (like a great fold in the rock) the Ancient People had built their houses of yellowish stone and mortar. The overhanging cliff above made a roof two hundred feet thick. The hard stratum below was an everlasting floor. The houses stood along in a row, like the buildings in a city block, or like a barracks.

In both walls of the canyon the same streak of soft rock had been washed out, and the long horizontal groove had been built up with houses. The dead city had thus two streets, one set in either cliff, facing each other across the ravine, with a river of blue air between them.

The canyon twisted and wound like a snake, and these two streets went on for four miles or more, interrupted by the abrupt turnings of the gorge, but beginning again within each turn. The canyon had a dozen of these false endings near its head. Beyond, the windings were larger and less perceptible, and it went on for a hundred miles, too narrow, precipitous, and terrible for man to follow it. The cliff dwellers liked wide canyons, where the great cliffs caught the sun. Panther Canyon had been deserted for hundreds of years when the first Spanish missionaries came into Arizona, but the masonry of the houses was still wonderfully firm; had crumbled only where a landslide or a rolling boulder had torn it.

All the houses in the canyon were clean with the cleanness of sunbaked, windswept places, and they all smelled of the tough little cedars that twisted themselves into the very doorways. One of these rock rooms Thea took for her own. Fred had told her how to make it comfortable. The day after she came, old Henry brought over on one of the pack ponies a roll of Navajo blankets that belonged to Fred, and Thea lined her cave with them. The room was not more than eight by ten feet, and she could touch the stone roof with her fingertips. This was her old idea: a nest in a high cliff, full of sun. All morning long the sun beat upon her cliff, while the ruins on the opposite side of the canyon were in shadow. In the afternoon, when she had the shade of two hundred feet of rock wall, the ruins on the other side of the gulf stood out in the blazing sunlight. Before her door ran the narrow, winding path that had been the street of the Ancient People. The yucca and niggerhead cactus grew everywhere. From her doorstep she looked out on the ochre-colored slope that ran down several hundred feet to the stream, and this hot rock was sparsely grown with dwarf trees. Their colors were so pale that the shadows of the little trees on the rock stood out sharper than the trees themselves. When Thea first came, the chokecherry bushes were in blossom, and the scent of them was almost sickeningly sweet after a shower. At the very bottom of the canyon, along the stream, there was a thread of bright, flickering, golden-green—cottonwood seedlings. They made a living, chattering screen behind which she took her bath every morning.

Thea went down to the stream by the Indian water trail. She had found a bathing pool with a sand bottom, where the creek was dammed by fallen trees. The climb back was long and steep, and when she reached her little house in the cliff, she always felt fresh delight in its comfort and inaccessibility. By the time she got there, the woolly red-and-grey blankets were saturated with sunlight, and she sometimes fell asleep as soon as she stretched her body on their warm surfaces. She used to wonder at her own inactivity. She could lie there hour after hour in the sun and listen to the strident whirr of the big locusts, and to the light, ironical laughter of the quaking asps. All her life she had been hurrying and sputtering, as if she had been born behind time and had been trying to catch up. Now, she reflected, as she drew herself out long upon the rugs, it was as if she were waiting for something to catch up with her. She had got to a place where she was out of the stream of meaningless activity and undirected effort.

Here she could lie for half a day undistracted, holding pleasant and incomplete conceptions in her mind—almost in her hands. They were scarcely clear enough to be called ideas. They had something to do with fragrance and color and sound, but almost nothing to do with words. She was singing very little now, but a song would go through her head all morning, as a spring keeps welling up, and it was like a pleasant sensation indefinitely prolonged. It was much more like a sensation than like an idea, or an act of remembering.

Music had never before come to her in that sensuous form. It had always been a thing to be struggled with, had always brought anxiety and exaltation and chagrin—never content and indolence. Thea began to wonder whether people could not utterly lose the power to work, as they can lose their voice or their memory. She had always been a little drudge, hurrying from one task to another—as if it mattered! And now her power to think seemed converted into a power of sustained sensation. She could become a mere receptacle for heat, or become a color, like the bright lizards that darted about on the hot stones outside her door; or she could become a continuous repetition of sound, like the cicadas.

III

The faculty of observation was never highly developed in Thea Kronborg. A great deal escaped her eye as she passed through the world. But the things which were for her, she saw; she experienced them physically and remembered them as if they had once been a part of herself. The roses she used to see in the florists' shops in Chicago were merely roses. But when she thought of the moonflowers that grew over Mrs.

Tellamantez's door, it was as if she had been that vine and had opened up in white flowers every night. There were memories of light on the sand hills, of masses of prickly pear blossoms she had found in the desert in early childhood, of the late afternoon sun pouring through the grape leaves and the mint bed in Mrs. Kohler's garden, which she would never lose. These recollections were a part of her mind and personality. In Chicago she had got almost nothing that went into her subconscious self and took root there. But here, in Panther Canyon, there were again things which seemed destined for her.

Panther Canyon was the home of innumerable swallows. They built nests in the wall far above the hollow groove in which Thea's own rock chamber lay. They seldom ventured above the rim of the canyon, to the flat, windswept tableland. Their world was the blue air-river between the canyon walls. In that blue gulf the arrow-shaped birds swam all day long, with only an occasional movement of the wings. The only sad thing about them was their timidity: the way in which they lived their lives between the echoing cliffs and never dared to rise out of the shadow of the canyon walls. As they swam past her door, Thea often felt how easy it would be to dream one's life out in some cleft in the world.

From the ancient dwelling there came always a dignified, unobtrusive sadness; now stronger, now fainter—like the aromatic smell which the dwarf cedars gave out in the sun—but always present, a part of the air one breathed. At night, when Thea dreamed about the canyon—or in the early morning when she hurried toward it, anticipating it—her conception of it was of yellow rocks baking in sunlight, the swallows, the cedar smell, and that peculiar sadness—a voice out of the past, not very loud, that went on saying a few simple things to the solitude eternally.

Standing up in her lodge, Thea with her thumbnail could dislodge flakes of carbon from the rock roof—the cooking smoke of the Ancient People. They were that near! A timid, nest-building folk, like the swallows. How often Thea remembered Ray Kennedy's moralizing about the cliff cities. He used to say that he never felt the hardness of the human struggle or the sadness of history as he felt it among those ruins. He used to say, too, that it made one feel an obligation to do one's best. On the first day that Thea climbed the water trail, she began to have intuitions about the women who had worn the path, and who had spent so great a part of their lives going up and down it. She found herself trying to walk as they must have walked, with a feeling in her feet and knees and loins which she had never known before—which must have come up to her out of the accustomed dust of that rocky trail. She could feel the weight of an Indian baby hanging to her back as she climbed.

The empty houses, among which she wandered in the afternoon, the blanketed one in which she lay all morning, were haunted by certain fears and desires; feelings about warmth and cold and water and physical strength. It seemed to Thea that a certain understanding of those old people came up to her out of the rock shelf on which she lay; that certain feelings were transmitted to her, suggestions that were simple, insistent, and monotonous, like the beating of Indian drums. They were not expressible in words, but seemed rather to translate themselves into attitudes of body, into degrees of muscular tension or relaxation; the naked strength of youth, sharp as the sunshafts; the crouching timorousness of age, the sullenness of women who waited for their captors. At the first turning of the canyon there was a half-ruined tower of yellow masonry, a watchtower upon which the young men used to entice eagles and snare them with nets. Sometimes for a whole morning Thea could see the coppery breast and shoulders of an Indian youth there against the sky; see him throw the net, and watch the struggle with the eagle.

Old Henry Biltmer, at the ranch, had been a great deal among the Pueblo Indians who are the descendants of the cliff dwellers. After supper he used to sit and smoke his pipe by the kitchen stove and talk to Thea about them. He had never found anyone before who was interested in his ruins. Every Sunday the old man prowled about in the canyon, and he had come to know a good deal more about it than he could account for. He had gathered up a whole chestful of cliff dweller relics which he meant to take back to Germany with him some day. He taught Thea how to find things among the ruins: grinding stones, and drills and needles made of turkey bones. There were fragments of pottery everywhere. Old Henry explained to her that the Ancient People had developed masonry and pottery far beyond any other crafts. After they had made houses for themselves, the next thing was to house the precious water. He explained to her how all their customs and ceremonies and their religion went back to water. The men provided the food, but water was the care of the women. The stupid women carried water for most of their lives; the cleverer ones made the vessels to hold it. Their pottery was their most direct appeal to water, the envelope and sheath of the precious element itself. The strongest Indian need was expressed in those graceful jars, fashioned slowly by hand, without the aid of a wheel.

When Thea took her bath at the bottom of the canyon, in the sunny pool behind the screen of cottonwoods, she sometimes felt as if the water must have sovereign qualities, from having been the object of so much service and desire. That stream was the only living thing left of the drama that had been played out in the canyon centuries ago. In the rapid, restless heart of it, flowing swifter than the rest, there was a continuity of life that reached back into the old time. The glittering thread of current had a kind of lightly worn, loosely knit personality, graceful and laughing. Thea's bath came to have a ceremonial gravity. The atmosphere of the canyon was ritualistic.

One morning, as she was standing upright in the pool, splashing water between her shoulder blades with a big sponge, something flashed through her mind that made her draw herself up and stand still until the water had quite dried upon her flushed skin. The stream and the broken pottery: what was any art but an effort to make a sheath, a mould in which to imprison for a moment the shining, elusive element which is life itself—life hurrying past us and running away, too strong to stop, too sweet to lose? The Indian women had held it in their jars. In the sculpture she had seen in the Art Institute, it had been caught in a flash of arrested motion. In singing, one made a vessel of one's throat and nostrils and held it on one's breath, caught the stream in a scale of natural intervals.

IV

Thea had a superstitious feeling about the potsherds, and liked better to leave them in the dwellings where she found them. If she took a few bits back to her own lodge and hid them under the blankets, she did it guiltily, as if she were being watched. She was a guest in these houses, and ought to behave as such. Nearly every afternoon she went to the chambers which contained the most interesting fragments of pottery, sat and looked at them for a while. Some of them were beautifully decorated. This care, expended upon vessels that could not hold food or water any better for the additional labour put upon them, made her heart go out to those ancient potters. They had not only expressed their desire, but they had expressed it as beautifully as they could. Food, fire, water, and something else—even here, in this crack in the world, so far back in the night of the past! Down here at the beginning, that painful thing was already stirring; the seed of sorrow, and of so much delight.

There were jars done in a delicate overlay, like pinecones; and there were many patterns in a low relief, like basketwork. Some of the pottery was decorated in color, red and brown, black and white, in graceful geometrical patterns. One day, on a fragment of a shallow bowl she found a crested serpent's head, painted in red on terracotta. Again she found half a bowl with a broad band of white cliff houses painted on a black ground. They were scarcely conventionalized at all; there they were in the black border, just as they stood in the rock before her. It brought her centuries nearer to these people to find that they saw their houses exactly as she saw them.

Yes, Ray Kennedy was right. All these things made one feel that one ought to do one's best, and help to fulfil some desire of the dust that slept there. A dream had been dreamed there long ago, in the night of ages, and the wind had whispered some promise to the sadness of the savage. In their own way, those people had felt the beginnings of what was to come. These potsherds were like fetters that bound one to a long chain of human endeavour.

Not only did the world seem older and richer to Thea now, but she herself seemed older. She had never been alone for so long before, or thought so much. Nothing had ever engrossed her so deeply as the daily contemplation of that line of pale yellow houses tucked into the wrinkle of the cliff. Moonstone and Chicago had become vague. Here everything was simple and definite, as things had been in childhood. Her mind was like a ragbag into which she had been frantically thrusting whatever she could grab. And here she must throw this lumber away. The things that were really hers separated themselves from the rest. Her ideas were simplified, became sharper and clearer. She felt united and strong. . . .

. . . The cliff dwellers had lengthened her past. ■

As a teenager in the 1970s, my already prodigious interest in backpacking and mountaineering was nourished by Colin Fletcher's *The Complete Walker*. In addition to this narrative guidebook, Fletcher has written *The Thousand-Mile Summer*, an account of his summerlong walk through the deserts and high country of California, and *The Man Who Walked Through Time*, the story of his 1967 solo trek through the Grand Canyon. For Fletcher, the journey "through time" is the descent through the geological strata of the canyon's rock formations. In this passage recounting his experience camping within an isolated Puebloan house deep within the canyon, he brings a sense of the present to an ancient landscape and reintroduces human nature to the long timeline.

f r o m

The Man Who Walked Through Time

C O L I N F L E T C H E R

I climbed back to my pink apartment house, unpacked, and settled in.

Of the four little rooms, one of the center pair was so small that I felt sure it had been built for a child. The other, rather less cramped, looked as though it might have done for a reasonably petite wife. The two end chambers were bigger, and the farthest offered not only the widest part of the ledge as its front porch but also a jutting section of wall that created a little alcove—the sort of useful place in which any present-day man would unhesitatingly dump his traveling bag when he had unpacked. I designated this farthest chamber the "master cubicle."

When I had first looked inside the cubicle I had thought: "What tiny people they must have been!" Yet when I crawled in through the doorway and stretched out full length I found that there was plenty of room for my hundred-and-eighty-pound bulk. The cubicle showed every sign of having been built for a man just about my size. Its floor measured three feet by seven. The roof, at the point I needed to sit up, seemed to have been chipped away to give a convenient three-foot clearance.

Once I had grown used to the gloom and a slight stuffiness, I decided that my master bedroom was a distinctly comfortable place. It offered advantages that would roll easily off any realtor's tongue. It was cool, and quite free from the usual desert dust. And its picture doorway commanded, beyond the blue-and-white river, a breath-stopping sweep of curved rock—a view that would have added thousands of dollars to the value of any house built today.*

---

*At the time I was distinctly vague about when the cliff dwellings had been built, but soon after I came out of the Canyon an anthropologist at the Museum of Northern Arizona told me that my cliff dwellers—who were apparently the same people as my house dwellers—used the Nankoweap site as recently as A.D. 1200.

The anthropologist also told me that expert opinion presently regards these cliff dwellings as having been built as storage rooms

I dwelt in my cliff dwelling for twenty-four hours. And, hour by hour—conscious of my vast ignorance, yet curiously confident—I began to focus my cave dweller more sharply.

First I pictured him building his home. I saw him chipping patiently away at the roof of the cave, so that there would be headroom when he sat up in his cubicle. (If I was right in assuming that he had built this cubicle to fit his own person—and at the time I had no doubts at all—then he was a shade shorter than I am, butt to crown, though only by a bare inch.) I saw him chipping back the footwall at an angle, so as to make room for his legs. I saw him, next, choosing with unhurried care the material for the cubicle walls. I saw him cementing each piece of rock in place with pink mud-plaster that he had probably made from pounded rock. I saw him nod with satisfaction when, after fitting several oversize pieces near the place his head would come, he lay down full length and found, sure enough, that the protrusions formed neat little ledges in exactly the right convenient place for whatever he wanted handy little ledges for. (Not pen and notebook, like me, of course; but he wanted them for something, all right.) I saw him fashioning the doorway: neatly rectangular and just big enough for him to pass through once he had learned the proper jackknife technique (which I soon did). I saw him, next, making the door lintel: peeling the bark off a stick about an inch in diameter and three feet long, smoothing off its undersurface, and squaring off one side for about nine inches at each end so that when he cemented the stick in position it could not rotate. (Like most natural sticks, it was not quite straight, and if it had been free to rotate it would not have done its job.) Finally I saw my satisfied craftsman jackknifing through the doorway to make sure that the stick was in exactly the right position to warn him, by touching his bent back, that if he straightened a half inch more he would break the stick and the rough stone above the doorway would gouge into his bare skin. I found myself wishing he could have known that thanks to his meticulous work this same stick, protected from rain and direct sunlight and practically indestructible in

---

(or granaries), though they may have been used from time to time as habitations. But I must confess that, having assumed all along that they were indeed dwellings, and having so recently seen how they appeared to have been built with considerable care to accommodate the human frame, I found this conclusion difficult to swallow. Frankly, standing foursquare on my base of open-minded ignorance, I still do. I would accept, perhaps, that my people may have lived in the cliff dwellings only in bad weather or when enemies threatened, but that is as far as I am presently willing to retreat.

such a dry climate, would also be brushing my back in timely warning, all these years further down the line.*

I slept soundly through a warm night. Then it was day again. And as the hours passed I came to feel that slowly—not through conscious effort, but merely by living as he had lived—I was coming to know a little more about this man who had preceded me. Piece by untidily added piece, I explored new sectors of the life he had led. Or at least that I confidently imagined he had led.

It seemed reasonable to assume that fear of enemies had driven him up into the cliff. No other reason, in fact, made much sense. And he had chosen a superb defensive position. His rear and flanks were impregnable. And any frontal attack would smack of suicide. In daylight, enemies could approach no closer than the foot of the talus, six hundred feet below, without being seen. And as soon as they began to scramble up the talus they became vulnerable to rolled rocks and thrown stones as well as plunging arrows. If the attackers managed to climb close enough to retaliate, the small doorways of the cubicles would protect the cowering women and children. Even the men, hurling rocks or firing arrows, would be quite well protected by the lip of the ledge. And in the final savage moments the defenders would hold every advantage as they swung their long clubs and as a last desperate resort kicked and punched at the breathless, precariously balanced invaders.

At night, the dice were hardly less loaded. Any intruder had to climb the last forty feet on small ledges he had never seen. And if he succeeded in creeping up to the first cubicle (which had a neat peephole overlooking the only approach) without awakening anyone (assuming that the family ever slept *en bloc*), he still had to make a mortal thrust through the small doorway before any kind of startled, clumsy push sent him cartwheeling back the way he had come, screaming and doomed.

Day or night, there was precious little doubt whose side I would rather be on.**

---

*At the time I had no doubt at all that this was the stick's function. I still think it was; but I am less sure. It may be that what my man made so carefully was a curtain rod. Perhaps reeds hung from the stick, or beads on some kind of string. I doubt it, though: the empty doorway was a tight enough fit, even allowing for my man's undoubtedly superior agility.

Some anthropologists apparently regard the sticks as mere supporting units for strengthening the stone-and-plaster structure. But I am afraid I simply cannot bring myself to accept this contention. The sticks are frail, and quite superficially attached. The walls are very strong.

**An obvious objection to the defensive situation I have outlined is one that frankly did not occur to me at the time: that attackers had only to sit down and wait for the defenders to

In time of danger there would naturally be fear as you waited. But there always is, in any kind of warfare. And that unoutflankable ledge did not seem too bad a place to be frightened in, especially if you were squatting there with a comfortable stock of boulders poised ready to roll, and a mound of sling-size stones, and a bow and flint-headed arrows, and, as final reserve, a long and trusty club close at hand and held fast by stones to keep it from rolling down and away. A better place to be frightened in than a World War II pillbox, certainly. An incomparably better place than somewhere deep and anonymous with the firing button of an ICBM under your metaphorical thumb as you waited, waited, waited to be told at the hundredth remove that some distant member of the same demented species had just pushed his own terrible and impersonal button.

During my stay in the cliff dwelling I also kept company with my man in a few of his peaceful leisure moments and learned some of the little, important things. I sat as he must often have sat, doing nothing in particular, outside his cubicle door. My bare butt occupied the same convenient little squatting-ledge that his must have occupied. My toes curled over the same rough lip of rock that his had curled over. My eyes saw what his had seen: river, rock, sky, space, and luminous light. My eyes heard what his had heard: silence; the roar of the river; the repetitive but liquid call of a rock wren; the tearing of air as a swift plunged past; the mewing of two hawks that had made their home in the cliff face, a hundred feet higher than his. ("Were there really hawks nesting up above in his time?" I wondered.)

By now I had picked up some other facts too. I had discovered that bare feet are remarkably safe engines to use for climbing around on loose rock. Also that my man's soles were tougher than mine. I learned that when he belched, it echoed. And when, following up this revelation, I lay in our little cubicle and called out to his wife through the partition, I confirmed that we lived—he and I—in a natural echo chamber.

There was one thing about the life of this man and his wife that I understood more clearly now than I had done in the beginning. The first time I looked inside the master cubicle I had thought not only what small people the occupants must have been but also how difficult it must be to beget children in such cramped quarters.

---

run out of water. But to my relief the anthropologist I consulted on this point did not find the objection valid. He seemed to accept that attackers would be very small bands of marauders passing through the territory. Even if these marauders wanted to lay siege to the cliff dwellings—which was not apparently the accepted pattern of things—they would have to find food to subsist on. And that would be no easy task in such inhospitable country.

After I had spent a night in the cubicle I knew better. There was plenty of room. It was a warm place too, and snugly private. You could do much worse.

Many details of my cliff dweller's domestic life still puzzled me, of course. The family no doubt tossed their garbage down the cliff. But what, I wondered, about toilet arrangements? And there was also the problem of how to keep the kids from falling downstairs.*

Many such surface details of my man's life remained a blank. But in the course of the second morning I began to feel that I was learning things of a quite different kind.

It seemed clear to me by then that my man was blessed with an insight that we modern men tend to lose, walled in as we are by our complexities (or do I mean walled *out?*). Living his simple life—eating breakfast with his wife and children on the ledge, watching the swifts plunge past and snap up their insect breakfasts, watching the hawks come mewing back to their upper-story home with breakfasts for *their* children—he could hardly help but understand, clearly and steadily, that man is an integral part of everything that goes on around him. More particularly, because the rock was a part of everything he did—sitting, seeing, hearing, cooking, fighting, making love—he understood it. Naturally, his understanding was different from mine. Even his questions were different. When he lay in our master cubicle and looked up at the chipped gray limestone above his head—at the same chip marks that I looked up at— he probably did not wonder why the rock was gray inside and red on its surface. He almost certainly did not conclude that it was stained by long ages of rainwater from the red rocks above. And yet (it seemed contradictory at first, but I don't think it really was) I felt that he knew something about the rhythm of the rocks. Not in a logical way, of course, that he could have talked about. But I had an idea that when he looked at a partly detached slab of pink rock down near the kitchen and wondered how long before it would fall, he would have known in his own way that it would still be standing partly detached when I passed by, centuries later, to take his place for a day and a night.

---

*When I raised this question with one anthropologist he said: "Oh, that's easy. Go and watch the Hopi families. They live on high mesas, and their children play quite freely close to cliff tops. Safety is a communal affair. The older children learn to keep a strict eye on the younger ones until they have learned to look after themselves. The system works."

With plenty of children, I'm sure it works. But it seems to me that my one-family—or at most, two-family—residence might have been rather lightly populated for such a neat and practical solution.

Because this man lived in a different age, the surface of his answers would clearly be different from mine. He could not ponder on the marvel and mystery of a Redwall that had been built by the remains of countless tiny organisms that are in a tenuous sense our ancestors. He would undoubtedly think in terms of some kind of a god. And his god, I felt sure, was the Spirit of the Rocks.*

Today, we no longer believe in the Spirit of the Rocks. Or if we do, we put the idea rather differently. But we all, willy-nilly and in spite of our conscious selves, have to believe in something. ▪

---

*While I lived in his cliff I was quite sure of it. Anthropologists wisely steer clear of this kind of speculation, but one of them remarked to me that as such people tend to have naturalistic religions, my assumption is in a broad sense quite reasonable.

In the long narrative poem *Martin* (1986), the narrator speaks from a point of view drawn from Jimmy Santiago Baca's own life and experience: an abandoned child, a homeless young man living the hard life of the road, a mestizo "detribalized Apache." At Quarai Ruins in New Mexico, the timeworn pueblo and mission church are the touchstones for Martin's resolve to seek out his heritage, to root himself in the land of his birth. A native of Santa Fe, chicano poet Baca's other works include *Meditations on the South Valley* (a companion piece to *Martin*), *Black Mesa Poems,* and *Immigrants in Our Own Land and Selected Early Poems.*

---

f r o m

Martin

JIMMY SANTIAGO BACA

. . . .

Dawn in the Manzano mountains.
Pine and piñon from chimneys
smoke the curving road
with resinous mist.
My black feathered heart
effortlessly glides
in the clear blue sky
above the pueblos
de Manzano, Tajique, Willard y Estancia.

At the foothills
my grandmother herded sheep
and my grandfather planted corn y chile.

I turn my motorcycle off
next to QUARAI RUINS,
and silence drops
into the canyon
sounding an ancient song of sadness,
like a distant boulder
echoing into the blue sky and stubble grass.

I step into the open rock-pit
hollowed in earth
with flat rock door facing east,
pinch red clay and chew
my teeth black with earth prayer,
 then speak with QUARAI—

O QUARAI! Shape
the grit and sediment I am,
mineral de Nuevo Mejico.

I will learn the dark red Apache words
and wind burnished chants,
the blazed red Spanish names of things
that absorb centuries of my blood.

Blow your lower-world breath
into my journey, O QUARAI!
I am ready to work,
all I ask is that I don't starve,
that I don't fail at being a good man,
that things go good for me,
that I meet a woman who will love me deeply,
that I meet strong spiritual brothers and sisters,
and that I have healthy children.

O QUARAI,
these things I promise—
to work hard and stay close to Mother Earth,
to raise my children through your eyes,
to teach them the old names of things,
and pray to the four directions.

I will not run
when You appear to me
as I did when younger, O QUARAI.
I will be strong and listen, and follow.

. . . .

As I swerved back down mountain curves,
crunching rock chippings
from finished arrowheads, piñón nuts
and pine cones, the sun rose
and embered QUARAI monument with fiery light.

I thought I saw the dark-skinned ghost
of my grandfather, on his horse, with sombrero,
waving to me from QUARAI,
and the gray-haired ghost of my grandmother,
carding sheep fur
beneath the green teepee of a pine tree,
by the arroyo.

. . . .

✷

Dick Fleck gave up being a ranger in Colorado's Rocky Mountain National Park to become a university professor some years ago, but that hasn't kept him out of the hills. He is currently dean of arts and humanities at the Community College of Denver. In addition to being a novelist and poet, Fleck has written books on John Muir and Native American literature, most recently *Critical Perspectives on Native American Fiction* (1993). He joined me in 1995 when I took a group of Hope College students into Grand Gulch for a few days of "ruining" and reading. This essay explores the experience of a nighttime visit to Perfect Kiva in Bullet Canyon in the Grand Gulch Primitive Area.

"Anasazi Depths"

RICHARD F. FLECK

People camped at the junction of Grand Gulch and Bullet Canyon warned us that water was extremely scarce in Bullet Canyon but that we might find a few springs at the Perfect Kiva Ruins. Our trail rose rapidly, and with each foot gained in altitude we enjoyed what we thought was slightly cooler air. The higher we trudged, the easier it seemed. Passing under Jail House Ruins (with jail-like bars in the windows), we knew we had but a half-mile to go to set up our campsite. We selected a high ledge of slickrock a few hundred yards from the Perfect Kiva. My son and I chose a sandy spot within the slickrock to pitch our tent and cook our meal. Others in our hiking party did the same in the waning hours of the day.

Having to break camp early the next day, some of us grabbed our flashlights for a nighttime exploration of this Anasazi site containing a perfectly preserved kiva. Stumbling along the dark and dusty trail with my flashlight, I recalled night climbers scampering up the sacred slopes of Mount Fuji in hopes of greeting the rising sun. Just a few piñons studded the nightscapes below us in a much more arid and stark landscape than the previous sites. When the last of our group arrived at the level terrace housing the Perfect Kiva, we explored these dark dwellings individually, shone lights on eerie pictographs, and eventually each of us descended the ladder into the kiva.

The world of the kiva is a world of its own. My descent into this earth's womb at nighttime on an upper ledge above Bullet Canyon brought me back even further in history—perhaps to the beginnings of mythological time. All history is mythology, wrote Thoreau. If one goes back far enough in time, human history blurs with mythological tradition. Contemporary southwestern tribal peoples believe that humans emerged from a lower spirit world in ancient times. All spirits pass through a small entrance, called a *sipapu,* to and from that spirit world. Modern-day kivas still possess *sipapus* like those dug in kiva floors during Anasazi times. For a moment or two in the darkness of this womb I imagined a stream of souls coming and going to and from this earthly life. It seemed like a clearance house, and anyone alive in bodily flesh here would have to be reminded of the transience of human existence. Do I have enough corn to eat? Are my springs plentiful? Will it rain? All these questions are put into perspective in the kiva.

Many have conjectured about the activities in a pre-Columbian kiva. One ranger-archaeologist at Mesa Verde National Park suggested to us years ago that a priest or shaman may have danced by firelight upon a foot drum made of timber boards, and he may have chanted to his listeners the story of human emergence from the lower depths. He may have preached the necessity of maintaining harmony through prayer and ceremony. Without prayer there would be no rain. Without concern for the entire village, one person may reap undue benefits from nature. *Heya, hey, hey!* I almost heard the shaman sing. Time to climb out and let others experience the world of the kiva.

Amazing to see the luminescent sandstone glowing in starlight far below. Where was I? Still on this earth? As others emerged from the kiva's depths we gradually regrouped and sat in silence, staring into space. Each of us in his or her own way had been vary far away, and each of us had to come back. One person thought he might have seen the piñon pines moving along the sandstone floor; he wasn't back from that other world yet.

After carefully picking our way downslope and getting some water from a lower spring, we were ready for sleep in the comfort of our tents. But not yet. Just as we unrolled our sleeping bags, a strange light appeared on the rimrock far above. Were we still in the kiva? What on earth was going on? Then a big arc of light rose over the canyon rim right next to the strange bright light. What we saw was the rising of the moon and

Jupiter, father of the planets. The moon gradually illuminated a semicircular sandstone cliff across from our camp as though some grand and soulful theater performance would soon take place. Moonlight emphasized each crack in the cliff, making it look like spirit rock. The Perfect Kiva attuned each of us to the nature beyond nature, and we were thankful. We slept soundly that night somewhere between here and there. ■

Ann Weiler Walka has published her poems in several of the small journals and newsletters that speak most eloquently and clearly about the social and environmental issues facing the American West today. In 1993 she was awarded a creative writing fellowship by the Arizona Commission on the Arts, and in the same year her remarkably personal and stunningly geographical book of poems and short narratives, *Waterlines: Journeys on a Desert River,* appeared and became popular among those who know the San Juan River in its largest contexts. Walka's poem reprinted here gives a sense of her experience as a boatwoman on the San Juan, floating time and again through the human and geological history of the river's deep course.

"Away from the River"

ANN WEILER WALKA

Away from the River
a column of heat
rises between the sandstone cliff
and a grove of thorn trees
The air swarms with dust motes
cicadas' shrilling
other peoples' visions

Over our heads
mazes and spirals
snakes   four-leggeds
wide-shouldered shamans
are carved into a blue-black sheen
of desert varnish

We're out of our element here
Toeing potsherds
we speculate earnestly
and ignore the smell of singed corn
a low hum   the light
tangled in our hair

One of the founders of the 1950s Beat movement, William S. Burroughs has written a score of influential books, including *Junky, The Ticket That Exploded,* and *The Last Words of Dutch Schultz.* His 1959 *Naked Lunch,* a bizarre series of seemingly hallucinatory episodes in the history of an unbalanced modern world, established Burroughs early on as a challenging and incisive writer of fiction. In his 1983 novel *The Place of Dead Roads,* a story that can be compared to Edward Dorn's epic psychedelic western poem *Gunslinger,* dime novelist and gunfighter Kim Carsons travels the West in his strange efforts to reform the planet into a saner place. In this passage, set somewhere northwest of Santa Fe, Carsons camps among abandoned mesa-top ruins and reflects on, well, the artifacts he finds there.

---

f r o m

The Place of Dead Roads

WILLIAM S. BURROUGHS

For three days Kim had camped on the mesa top, sweeping the valley with his binoculars. A cloud of dust headed south told him they figured him to ride in that direction for Mexico. He had headed north instead, into a land of sandstone formations, carved by wind and sand—a camel, a tortoise, Cambodian temples—and everywhere caves pocked into the red rock like bubbles in boiling oatmeal. Some of the caves had been lived in at one time or another: rusty tin cans, pottery shards, cartridge cases. Kim found an arrowhead six inches long, chipped from obsidian, and a smaller arrowhead of rose-colored flint.

On top of the mesa were crumbled mounds of earth that had once been houses. Slabs of stone had been crisscrossed to form an altar. *Homo sapiens* was here.

Dusk was falling and blue shadows gathered in the Sangre de Cristo Mountains to the east. Sangre de Cristo! Blood of Christ! Rivers of blood! Mountains of blood! Does Christ never get tired of bleeding? To the west the sun sets behind thunderclouds over the Jemez Mountains, and Jiménez straddles the mountains with his boots of rock and trees, a vast *charro* rising into the sky, his head a crystal skull of clouds as his guns spit from darkening battlements and thunder rattles over the valley. The evening star shines clear and green . . . "Fair as a star, when only one/Is shining in the sky." That's Wordsworth, Kim remembers. It is raining in the Jemez Mountains.

"It is raining, Anita Huffington." Last words of General Grant, spoken to his nurse, circuits in his brain flickering out like lightning in gray clouds.

Kim leaned back against stone still warm from the sun. A cool wind touched his face with the smell of rain.

Pottery shards . . . arrowheads . . . a crib . . . a rattle . . . a blue spoon . . . a sling-shot, the rubber rotted through . . . rusting fishhooks . . . tools . . . you can see there was a cabin here once . . . a hypodermic syringe glints in the sun . . . the needle has rusted into the glass, forming little sparks of brown mica . . . abandoned artifacts . . .

He holds the rose flint arrowhead in his hand. Here is the arrowhead, lovingly fashioned for a purpose. Campfires flicker on Indian faces eating the luscious dark meat of the passenger pigeon. He fondles the obsidian arrowhead, so fragile . . . did they break every time they were used, like bee stings, he wonders?

(Bison steaks roasting on a spit.)

Somebody made this arrowhead. It had a creator long ago. This arrowhead is the only proof of his existence. Living things can also be seen as artifacts, designed for a purpose. So perhaps the human artifact had a creator. Perhaps a stranded space traveler needed the human vessel to continue his journey, and he made it for that purpose? He died before he could use it? He found another escape route? This artifact, shaped to fill a forgotten need, now has no more meaning or purpose than this arrowhead without the arrow and the bow, the arm and the eye. Or perhaps the human artifact was the creator's last card, played in an old game many light-years ago. Chill of empty space.

Kim gathers wood for a fire. The stars are coming out. There's the Big Dipper. His father points to Betelgeuse in the night sky over Saint Louis . . . smell of flowers in the garden. His father's gray face on a pillow.

Helpless pieces in the game he plays
On this checkerboard of nights and days.

He picks up the obsidian arrowhead, arrow and bow of empty space. You can't see them anymore without the arm and the eye . . . the chill . . . so fragile . . . shivers and gathers wood. Can't see them anymore. Slave Gods in the firmament. He remembers his father's last words:

"Stay out of churches, son. All they got a key to is the shit house. And swear to me you will never wear a lawman's badge."

Hither and thither moves, and checks, and slays,
And one by one back in the Closet lays.

Playthings in an old game, the little toy soldiers are covered with rust, shaped to fill a forgotten empty space.

Rusty tin cans . . . pottery shards . . . cartridge cases . . . arrowheads . . . a hypodermic syringe glints in the sun. ▪

Writing for what she calls the Coyote Clan—those who know the Four Corners as more than a region drawn in lines on a map and who understand its spiritual landscapes and historical and cultural significance—Terry Tempest Williams has long been a sensitive recorder of the inner life of the plateau country and a participant in its ongoing story. She is Naturalist-in-Residence at the Utah Museum of Natural History and author of *Coyote's Canyon* (1989), and *Pieces of White Shell* (1983), one essay from which is reprinted here. Tempted to bring home an ancient potsherd, she realizes that, only if they are left in place can the fragments of a distant life continue to tell their stories.

"A Potshard and Some Corn Pollen"

TERRY TEMPEST WILLIAMS

Silence. That is time you are hearing. We are in Anasazi country. This is a place where canyon walls rise upward like praying hands. Veins of water run between them. You may choose to walk here, ankle deep in the midst of chubs and minnows. If you wish you can brace your hands flush against either side of the slickrock and fancy yourself pushing down walls. Look up. The sky is a blue ribbon. These are the canyons, cool refuges from exposed heat, dripping with red mimulus and ferns. This is the landscape that gave these people birth.

To the Navajo, Anasazi means the Ancient Ones. In prehistoric days they inhabited the Four Corners region, where Utah, Colorado, New Mexico, and Arizona share a common boundary point. There was a day in mid-November when the children of Montezuma Creek, Utah, took me by the hand and told me stories of Anasazi.

"Who are the Anasazi?" I asked as we were walking down to the river.

"They are the long-time-ago people who lived on this land. They are the relatives of the Hopi and Pueblo people. We find their baskets, sandals, and pottery but do not take them."

"Why not?"

"People say that if you take away their property and put it in your house a spirit will come and it will get you. It might even kill you. I don't know if it's true, but my grandmother told it to my sister and she threw away the pottery she had. That's why I don't take pottery. They also say that the long-time-ago people's spirit stays with their body and if you touch their bones you will have nightmares."

"Have you ever found any Anasazi bones?"

"Yes." We came to the river and sat down.

"You can find their houses around here, but we don't go in. I know where some ruins are by my aunt and uncle's place. And up from Calf Creek Wash there are one hundred and sixty-three white handprints slapped on the red face of the rock. [Anasazi applause, I thought, as goose-flesh appeared on my skin.] And then below that the rocks have waves in them and everywhere you look you can find Anasazi rocks."

"What do you mean?"

"Anasazi rocks—these . . ." I looked down to where little fingers pointed, and sure enough the children had located countless pieces of pottery, all of which I had mistaken for sandstone or shale.

You cannot travel very long through Navajoland without stubbing your toe on the Anasazi. You can feel these things the children speak of, for the wind carries voices: Every conversation, every sigh uttered by the "long-time-ago people" circulates above you. Perhaps that's why the clouds move so quickly in the Southwest.

Cerulean skies and deep vinaceous bands of sandstone become places of power. Pit houses dug in the earth and cliff dwellings hanging on ledges still house the Anasazi spirit. Listen. You may hear music inside their ancient earth architecture. I have—I think.

There have been occasions when I stood in their ruins and found tiny shriveled cobs of corn, reminders that the genius of Anasazi lay in their ability to conserve and utilize scarce water and fertile soil, creating a farm-based culture in an area unsuited for such a subsistence pattern. Crops such as maize, beans, and squash were central to their survival.

And there is their pottery: black on white and black on red. You walk through sagebrush, down arroyos, and up hillsides innocently, until an irregular rock attracts your eye. You pick it up, turn it over, and realize this is pottery. I have held in my hands pieces of coiled pots . . . once wet clay rolled into a snake, then spiraled into a vessel. I have seen Anasazi fingerprints thousands of years old pinched into this clay to ensure tightness. Whole generations pass before you as you examine this ancient, domestic chip. Who made this? What did it belong to? How long has it been here? Like an onion, layers upon layers of civilization are peeled until, finally, you face the Anasazi bare.

Now you are caught in a dilemma's web: What to do with this remnant of Anasazi life? Do you keep it? Take it home and place it on your mantel as a tangible reminder of your affinity with Desert People? ("Of course no one would appreciate it as I do.") Or do you turn this piece of clay in? Confess your findings to a local museum or nearby National Park Visitor's Center, trusting that they will find an appropriate home for it (most likely in drawer 240-B, after you have filled out USGS Form #A876-5 with your #2 lead pencil)? Or do you leave it ("But someone else will just come along and take it.") in the keeping of another thousand years to be kneaded back into desert sands?

PUBLIC—No. 209

An Act for the Preservation of American Antiquities

Be it enacted by the Senate and House of Representatives of the United States of America in Congress assembled, that any person who shall appropriate, excavate, injure, or destroy any historic or prehistoric ruin or monument, or any subject of antiquity, situated on lands owned or controlled by the Government of the United States without the permission of the Secretary of the Department of the Government having jurisdiction over the lands on which said antiquities are situated, shall upon conviction, be fined in a sum of not more than five hundred dollars or be imprisoned for a period of not more than ninety days, or shall suffer both fine and imprisonment, in the discretion of the court. . . . (Section 1)

Approved June 8, 1906 (34 Stat. L. 225)

We infer about another culture through their physical remains. The questions encircling ancient peoples' social systems could never even have been asked a few decades ago. Now we can speculate. Pottery patterns, designs, and motifs are providing clues as to whether the Anasazi were a matrilocal or a patrilocal society. If archaeologists find a continuum among pottery designs they can infer matrilineal order, with mother passing pottery motifs on to daughter as she brings her husband into the village. A hodgepodge of pottery designs suggests a patrilineal society, each man bringing in a woman with her individual design.

Stories. More stories. If these artifacts are lifted from their birthplace they cease to speak. Like a piece of coral broken from its reef, they lose their color, becoming pale and brittle. Somehow we need to acquaint ourselves with the art of letting go, for to own a piece of the past is to destroy it.

But it's a difficult thing to do. I know because I have pocketed a piece of pottery. In the context of all the desert's loveliness it became numinous. I had to possess it. Somewhere deep inside me I hoped this potshard might become a talisman, an amulet. I was wrong. What once glistened in those pastel sands collected dust on my dressing table. Its loss of dignity haunted me.

Lessons painfully learned evoke humility. I could never take a potshard now. Like Coyote's fur, I am wary of its power. It belongs to the earth and a culture which has passed through it. I remember holding a plaited Anasazi slipper, small, wide, and curled. As I carefully turned it over and over I kept thinking, "What is of value here—the sandal or the sandaled foot?"

AND NOW THE WALLS ARE WORN TO SAND,
AND LIE
LOW-RIDGED BENEATH THE VULTURES
LONELY FLIGHT.
—*Seventh City of Cibola*
HENRY NOYES PRATT

Chaco Canyon. The standing ruins have metamorphosed into standing rocks. From the sun-scorched earth they were taken, to the same soil they return. The cool breezes which run through them are the voice and spirit of Anasazi.

I have found these ruins to be as alive as I allow them to be. Sitting near the threshold of Pueblo Bonito, I rebuild these eroded walls with my imagination. Uneven skylines are immediately transformed into smooth, symmetrical pueblos. Remnants of this ancient village become a cornerstone to a thriving community. In the courtyard I see women dressed in crude tunics of handwoven muslin. Some are grinding corn with their *manos* and *metates*; some are sitting on fibrous mats weaving baskets; others are pinching clay pots, already coiled; and a few women are retrieving water, carrying pots on their heads. I hear the laughter of children. They run in and out of hidden corridors, a terra-cotta maze. Domesticated turkeys squabble about. I listen to the mumbling of elders as they speak to one another. They lean against white adobe walls. I feel the power of holy men as they meet in the giant kivas below. Corn pollen offerings are left in key-shaped doorways, the same corn pollen that can absorb a deer's spirit or bless a child. For this brief moment, the boundaries of time and space dissolve. Anasazi drums return.

Before leaving Chaco, I step inside a small pueblo room. I don't think anyone saw me; for some reason this is important. Solitude. Whitewashed walls. Handprints, streaked across the surface. Female energy. I hold my hand against hers. Cold contact. Her hand, so much smaller, more square. I shiver. I picture a young woman sitting in the corner, legs outstretched—perhaps a babe at her breast. Silence. I don't want there to be: Silence. I want to talk, listen, share, spend entire afternoons in womanly conversation about her life, mine. Somehow, I sense that a thousand years do not separate us. ▪

Newer Stories

Antiquity in the Twentieth Century

※

In 1909, at the age of twenty-two, Jesse Nusbaum rode from Greeley, Colorado, to Santa Fe on an Excelsior motorcycle, breaking, by his account, the record over the dirt-road route by three hours. His early interest in archaeology had brought him to Santa Fe to work with Edgar L. Hewlett, director of the Museum of New Mexico, then in the old Palace of the Governors, and once there Nusbaum rubbed elbows with Mabel Dodge Luhan's Taos circle of artists and writers. From Santa Fe he went on to do fieldwork with Earl Morris in Frijoles Canyon and with Alfred Kidder at Pecos and Mesa Verde. Eventually he went Back East to take a position with the Museum of the American Indian in New York. In 1921, Nusbaum was appointed superintendent of Mesa Verde National Park, then mired in mismanagement and corruption, its ancient sites inadequately protected from looting. Nusbaum describes his arrival at Mesa Verde in this passage from *Tierra Dulce: Reminiscences from the Jesse Nusbaum Papers,* collected by his wife, Rosemary, in 1980.

f r o m

Tierra Dulce: Reminiscences from the Jesse Nusbaum Papers

JESSE NUSBAUM

Armed with my appointment as Superintendent to Mesa Verde, I resigned from the Museum and arrived in Mancos in late May. At the park office I discussed the state of park affairs with the superintendent I was replacing, then for the balance of that day and the two following days with his clerk, a man of seventy years, appointed as a ranger, but not serving due to age. Since the superintendent was not in a position to do other than sign his name to a letter prepared for his signature, I discussed all matters of immediate concern to me. The clerk kept the books on the current status of appropriations and outstanding obligations for the fiscal year, which was about to end June 30th of that year.

The park entrance was then passable and I phoned the other ranger, the son-in-law of the outgoing superintendent, to drive to Mancos and take me to the park. I assumed he would be driving the recently purchased Model T Ford, a four-door enclosed car which I had been informed in Washington, cost $1,300 and would be the official car. I was surprised on his arrival to see he was driving a Model T Ford without a windshield—actually a chassis on which he had mounted a green painted delivery box in the rear and between it and the instrument board had mounted a ranch wagon seat board on which an old automobile cushion was placed. I asked him "how come?" He answered that his father-in-law and some friends had made one trip to the park in the new closed car and had to push it up most of the grade because it was underpowered, so on their return the closed body had been sold to Haller's garage for $200, the gas tank and instrument-warden switch had gone with the body and as a result he had a local rancher make a new body and had installed a new gas tank, switch and seat thereto and it was the only car available for transporting supplies to his headquarters in the park. Before leaving Mancos I informed the clerk I would establish residence in the park from the time of my arrival at the location of Spruce Tree camp and to arrange for the concessioner's accommodations there and that I hoped to start building a superintendent's residence in the fall.

Again an uproar ensued. All stated that superintendents had always resided in Mancos adjacent to the park office there, that the entrance road would be closed winter-long by deep snowfall. No white person had ever lived atop the Mesa Verde during the long winter period. My initial two hour auto trip as superintendent from the entrance of the park to Spruce Tree Camp was over the single lane buggy road on which the first superintendent Hans Randolph had started construction in 1908 and the third fellow, my predecessor had finally opened to horse drawn vehicles in 1914, which road was a major concern to me because of its excessive length. There were grades running up twenty to thirty percent or more for short stretches and a large number of successively sharp switch backs over which even a Ford had to back and fill even to get around one of them.

What I saw at the end of the road was an unholy mess. There was a grand commingling within a small area overlooking Spruce Tree Camp of concessioner's property consisting of kitchen, dining room and related facilities, including two single room framed cabins and seven floor tents. The government property was a log cabin—rangers quarters recently converted to museum purposes when a new framed cottage had been built for this purpose—with a most conspicuous automobile shed of rough board, pitched roof construction supported by high poles, barbed wire and odd tools, as well as articles of indiscriminate sorts. What I observed in the next two weeks about this commingling situation and what had to be done by the Park Service in the public interest was to establish first, sole and firm control of all activities in the park, which became my immediate and paramount concern.

The use by the ranger of the park Ford for transportation, concession supplies, and for personal purposes was prohibited. I had water piped from the park storage tank to a roadside faucet for visitors convenience, constructed two "pit" toilets screened by cedar barricades to the rear of the automobile shed, thus ending visitors dependence on two in the concessioner's backyard. Visitor registration and issuance of park permits, questions, and park pamphlets was shifted from the concessioner's main building to the park museum where a ranger or park relief employee handled these features with greater dispatch and efficiency. The practice was terminated whereby the eight-year-old son of the ranger and other boys would jump on the running boards of incoming cars and competitively solicit their services as guides to all the ruins, for a fee, on the premise that they knew all about the Mesa Verde and its archaeology. Morning and afternoon schedules of trips to the ruins were inaugurated, conducted by rangers or other employees I indoctrinated and trained for such service.

By such means ruins were protected from visitors damage, which told a related story of the Mesa Verde. When I went out to look at the ruins I had found kids climbing all over the walls and people climbing and photographing as they wished. They were picking up any and all shards and at that time there were many. I also started a large cedar-crotch pole enclosure adjacent to the museum, dug and rock-lined a shallow campfire pit, and placed long split-log benches with backrests around it so that I could begin giving regular evening campfire talks to visitors, principally on Mesa Verde archaeology and, in context explain the purposes and objectives of the Preservation of American Antiquities Act, the penalties for its violation in Mesa Verde National Park and all other federal lands.

I constructed a short access loop road, cleared a series of bordering parking and camping spaces, and installed two more "pit" toilets at the nearest suitable location apart from the park's water supply storage tank and piped water was extended with faucets for camping use. The purpose was to terminate random camping in any place that visitors could drive cars off the main entrance road and in the headquarters area due to consequent damaging and loss of natural vegetative cover and the fire hazard.

Reacting to Director Mather's order at his first inspection, the prior superintendent had had his ranger, in the spring of 1921, clear a sizeable area on the opposite side of Spruce Tree Canyon, more than two miles round-trip from the concessioner's nearest faucet, dig two pits and remove every vestage of dry wood fuel for camping purposes. No one to my knowledge ever camped there. Methods had always been directed to force all advantage toward the concession and keep the Park Service clear out of the picture. The political picture was obvious. There was hardly a directional or distance road sign in the park, so as funds became available, suitable place name signs, enameled and enduring, were placed. Visitors had long complained that Mesa Verde was practically devoid of signs for reasons requiring no explanation. If a fender hopping youngster was not retained as a guide, you did not know where to find or get to a ruin.

Confirmed by evidence, found pertinent to payroll examination, was the fact that the ranger and his helpers had been paid by the Park Service for time devoted to illegally excavating and looting park ruins of the large collection of artifacts exhibited in the park museum in the five locked cases, for which the ranger did indeed hold the keys and claim such collections were personal property. Prior to the departure of all concession personnel at the close of the park travel season October 15, 1921 for Mancos, I conferred with the concessioner who was incapable for reasons of physical and mental debilities from remaining through the winter. About seven months were spent tending his own business in Mancos and only five months per annum to the park—most unsatisfactory.

I stated that I would seize the collections as Government property, file Antiquities Act violation charges against him if he failed to turn over to me as Superintendent of Mesa Verde National Park, the collection of artifacts, the keys to the five exhibit cases and submit his resignation as ranger . . . all of which was promptly done and the atmosphere was cleared so we could get started. I was further convinced that confidential business matters were being disclosed elsewhere. There was only a telephone over which to talk with the clerk in the park office. Wires coming in to me were phoned out from the station agent at Mancos who received them. Mine were called back in. All information was spreading and when going into Mancos, I found that people knew things that had taken place and it could come over one source only: the phone. I made contact with the Colorado Mountain States Manager, Paul A. Holland, and asked for a new operator. The operator relieved turned out to be the daughter of the former superintendent and I was, and had been from the first, working against one family who held key political jobs.

Now I received a call from the senator from Colorado at the park. He had been informed by regional cronies that I had established my official residence there. When I so confirmed, he instructed me to return promptly to Mancos, where all previous superintendents had resided near the park office. I informed him I would continue to reside in the park. He then stated: "It's your responsibility to run the park and attend to republican lines in that region and let the ranger run the park." I informed him I would continue to reside in the park, that I'd pledged to administer the park in the public interest and I planned to devote full time to this responsibility and finally to terminate the commingling of concession structures and related facilities with those of the Park Service.

A loop access road was constructed by the Park Service bordering the sheer wall perimeter, of the promontory between Spruce and Spruce Tree canyons, southward of the concession's main building. After spaces were cleared bordering the road by skids and on beams and dollies, I moved all concession structures to their new locations and the water line was extended to serve this area. Only by such cooperative means could the park recover space so vacated for planned development as park headquarters.

After this, things moved along and worth noting is a visit which followed from Senator Rice Means and his wife. After spending days conducting them through the main ruins I asked them to a cool drink on the porch. Almost at once I answered a loud knocking on the rear door, the man and woman standing there introduced themselves as from Denver. He said he was a member of the K.K.K. and his wife head of the Klavern. He further informed me that Senator Means and others from the local town were assembled there by special dispensation and for $25 I would become a Klansman. He stated that after campfire that night they planned a torch light parade around the circle then take me over to Sun Temple and induct me by the light of a burning cross in the ruin. He further stated that I could then always call on local Klansmen for any help if trouble occurred in the park. I promptly told him I was not interested in his proposal, that the ranger force would handle any matter in the park, that I opposed both torchlight parade and the use of a ruin for such purpose as they were contemplating. After the Means left I tipped off the sole ranger and a half dozen other employees to assemble before the campfire program was over and be prepared to break up any torchlight parade that might develop. A bit later I went up into a near shack and when I lighted a match, I found these employees sitting on the floor with pick handles in hand to stop any possible disturbance. ▪

By his early twenties, Joseph Foster was already a successful and aggressive editorial writer in William Randolph Hearst's newspaper empire and had married the cultivated and rebellious daughter of William Gardener Hale, cofounder of the University of Chicago. Foster abandoned the Chicago fast track early on for an adobe ranch house in New Mexico. Yearning to write creatively, he associated himself with Mabel Dodge Luhan's Taos circle of artists and writers during the 1920s. It was there that Foster met D. H. Lawrence during the novelist's two visits to New Mexico, in 1922 and 1924.

In the wake of the ongoing controversy and success of Lawrence's *Sons and Lovers, The Rainbow,* and *Women in Love,* Luhan became convinced that Lawrence should write an epic novel about the Indians of New Mexico. Foster describes one of Luhan's misconceived attempts to fascinate a reluctant Lawrence with New Mexico in this excerpt from *D. H. Lawrence in Taos* (1972). Here, Luhan has persuaded Lawrence, already quite ill with tuberculosis, to take a dusty, bone-jarring four-hundred-mile drive in an open car to see the Hopi Snake Dance in Arizona. Luhan suggested a detour along the way to Chaco Canyon's Pueblo Bonito. Lawrence was not impressed. Although he never wrote his American epic, Lawrence's own observations of the Hopi Snake Dance appear in his 1927 *Mornings in Mexico.*

---

f r o m

D. H. Lawrence in Taos

JOSEPH   FOSTER

"It seemed to me," reasoned Mabel, "that if Lawrence could emancipate himself from that limitation of the known, the grip of the manifest fact and folly of mankind, he, of all men alive, could perceive the peculiar vestiges of another mode of life that had miraculously survived [in the Southwest]." She was still directing his destiny from her sun porch on the third story of her ranch.

But Lawrence did not know if he wanted to go to the Snake Dance. It was too far. There was also the problem of the Brett. Mabel didn't want her to come along. She had to be left behind.

Then there was Lawrence's throat—terribly sore. "Bring a good gargle for my throat: it hurts like billy-o! this evening."

Not a very auspicious beginning for a trek across the Great American Desert the first week in August, 1924 for Frieda, Lawrence, Mabel, and Tony in Mabel's little touring car.

Lawrence was uncomfortable in the big Harvey House for dinner in Albuquerque. He began to ridicule American food. There was a hostile atmosphere around him. He threw looks of hatred everywhere.

They pushed on into the warm desert night through Navajoland. There were red buttes jutting far forward in the darkness.

"The lonely stars," said Lawrence. "Would you like to be a star?" he asked Mabel.

"No," she said. "I would rather be just what I am: the space between the stars."

Again she had failed. It was a love gesture on Lawrence's part. She had no sensitivity of response—ever.

They traveled far into the night to a small ruined town in Arizona.

Hopiland!

Margaret and I have been there again and again. There is no experience like it.

I remember the crimson, the carmine sands, dune-ing the desert in a final compositional silence—a last emblazoned mode of life. And the sky was atmosphered in azure dust—sometimes cerulean, at others the perfect cobalt, though at night it was always a living black on which the coyotes scrawled their pitiful warnings from canyon to haunted canyon.

It did not rain. It never rains. We counted the ruined kivas of Pueblo Bonito, where the Indians had lived and died, and buried their dead, doubled knees to chin, in painted baskets ten centuries before. And we pieced together the lost designs of shards and laughed at the lilac lizards on the rocks and Margaret wondered at the brown cliffs, the brown ruins, the golden greasewood blooming. We were lost, lost in the rare red air, I thought forever, while we contemplated a lonely surge of stone scathed by the world's last sun, its ragged shadows strewn toward eternity.

Hano, Walpi, Shipaulovi, Sichomovi, Shungopovi, Mishongnovi, Oraibi, Hotevilla, Bakabi, Moenkopi are the ruined cities of stone, cliffed high above the intoning silence. The desert does not satisfy, nor does love. Dust into dust—but spirit into spirit as well. It is madness to deprive oneself of what the red wastes are offering. . . .

But Lawrence did not really like the desert. "One wonders what one came for. The Hopi country is hideous," he wrote to Spud Johnson. "Death-grey mesas sticking up like broken pieces of ancient grey bread.

"Three thousand people. . . . There were Americans of all sorts, wild west and tame west, American women in pants, an extraordinary assortment of female breeches: at least two women in skirts, relics of the last era. There were Navajo women in full skirts and velvet bodices: there were Hopi women in bright shawls: various half breeds: and all the men to match.

"And what had they all come to see—come so far, over so weary a way? Men with snakes in their mouths, like a circus? Nice clean snakes, all washed and cold-creamed by the priests (so-called). Like pale wet silk stockings. Snakes with little bird-like heads, that bit nobody, but looked more harmless than doves? And funny men with blackened faces and whitened jaws, like a corpse band?

"Just a show! The Southwest is the great playground of the white American. The desert isn't good for anything else."

So Lawrence wasn't going to write an epic about the Indian for Mabel. ▨

Well known for a dozen novels set in New Mexico and Colorado, including *The Man Who Killed the Deer, People of the Valley,* and *The Woman at Otowi Crossing,* Frank Waters has been a central figure in western American literature since the 1970s. Part Native American himself, Waters has also authored *Masked Gods: Navaho and Pueblo Ceremonialism* and the widely read but controversial *Book of the Hopi,* each of which blends popular anthropology with Waters's interest in philosophical dualism.

His 1966 novel *The Woman at Otowi Crossing* is based on the life of Edith Warner, who ran a tearoom at Otowi Crossing, just down the mesa from Los Alamos, during the period of the development of the atomic bomb. The book focuses on the character of Helen Chambers, who when diagnosed with cancer finds spiritual peace in the sense of universal connectedness with place, people, and all creation that Waters sees at the heart of Native American culture. Meanwhile, Helen's daughter Emily, an aspiring anthropologist writing her dissertation on the relationship between the Aztecs and the ancient Puebloans of New Mexico, begins a relationship with Edmund Gaylord, a Los Alamos scientist. In this excerpt, Gaylord is stricken by dual yearnings, one toward science and the other toward more fundamental connections to humanity. The scene is one of many in the novel that stress the contrast between the modernity and menace of Los Alamos and the antiquity of the nearby ruins. Love is one of the things that happens among the ruins.

from

The Woman at Otowi Crossing

FRANK WATERS

Gaylord found a chair in back and sat down with proper modesty at being present in such distinguished company. Around him, almost anonymous in sweat-stained shirts and wrinkled trousers, there sat and lounged talking in the aisles physicists, chemists, metallurgists, mathematicians, engineers and technicians drawn from universities, laboratories, industrial plants and hospitals throughout the United States. Among them he recognized several men for whom he had worked on the Chicago pile including Enrico Fermi, who travelled under the name of "Eugene Farmer," and Dr. Arthur Compton, known as "Mr. Comstock." Others had fled from Europe to escape Nazi persecution or capture. Sitting down next to Dr. Breslau was the great Danish physicist and pioneer explorer of the structure of the atom, Niels Bohr, whose pseudonym was "Nicholas Baker." Off to the left sat a delegation from Great Britain headed by Sir James Chadwick. Still more whom Gaylord could not identify kept coming in. Undoubtedly he was looking at the most extraordinary galaxy of scientific stars ever gathered under one roof.

As he sat there waiting for the room to fill and quiet, Gaylord knew that he had been lucky from the day he had been picked to work on the Chicago pile. That brief preliminary landing on the New World already seemed remotely far behind him. The New World he had glimpsed then had been no more than an entrancing, deceptively inviting shoreline. Now he saw it for what it was—a dark, unknown and forbidding continent which threw up unknown obstacles, unguessed problems to hinder every foot of advance.

Gaylord had prided himself on his new doctorate. Now, dwarfed by an imposing staff of Nobel Prize winners and world-famous scientists, he sweated night and day over problems that seemed insignificant when they were assigned to him, but which seemed hopeless when he confronted them. Yet he persisted with methodical thoroughness. Gaylord, in fact, was an extremely capable young physicist; and at this early period of his career it was precisely his lack of imagination and his meticulous attention to detail that made him valuable. He prided himself, with the little personal vanity he had, that he never let his emotions get the best of him—emotions that he did not yet know he possessed in the periodic table of his own elemental personality.

The room by now had filled and quieted. A subdued feeling of excitement washed over him when General Leslie R. Groves, in over-all charge of the Project for the Manhattan Engineer District, stood up for one of his infrequent appearances. Heavy-set, his impeccable uniform in odd contrast to the sloppy shirts and pants of the scientists, Groves seemed to Gaylord to have the air of a bulldog worrying a bone. Chewing away, he assured every one of the 100 university-employed scientists present that twelve men had been brought in to help him. There were now, he said, nearly 1200 military personnel, civilian Government employees, and construction workers who were doing their best to provide living accommodations. Housing was still short, however. Until more space was made available, he had taken over Frijoles Lodge in Bandelier National Monument fourteen miles south. He hoped that the men assigned there would understand why.

Gaylord groaned to himself; he already had been transferred and had to commute the exorbitant distance over a lonely mountain road each day.

The next speaker was a Security officer whom Gaylord could not identify, but whom he resented instantly for his repetition of familiar facts. The speaker cautioned him not to give his address when writing letters. "Post Office Box 1663, Santa Fe, New Mexico, is all that is allowed. As you gentlemen know, it is the largest post office box in the world. To it are addressed boxcars of equipment, truckloads of supplies. Our children are born in it. We dwell in Box 1663." This was an old joke already. Nobody smiled.

Gaylord began to squirm uneasily in his seat. Despite the urgency, exhilaration and pervading air of excitement as the work got underway, he had felt irked from the start by the strict secrecy. Now he was shaken by a sense of alarm as the speaker commenced reading from a new handbook on Security.

> Do not establish or maintain social relations with residents of nearby communities. It is expected, as a condition of employment, that project employees will break normal social relations with the outside world.
>
> Do not arrange for visits with friends or relations in nearby communities without special permission from the Director.

To emphasize the importance of these restrictions, the speaker now read a new memorandum issued by the Security committee:

> Under no circumstances must any project employee go to parties or dances in nearby communities or maintain any other social relations except for quiet visits with their families.
>
> Make only very occasional visits with your families and get special permission in each case to do so.

Gaylord's resentment flared. He had no real cause for frustration, being without a family to visit, and detesting parties and dances for which he never had had time in school. Yet the memorandum touched the quick of his secret longing. There jumped at him the vision of Emily excitedly talking at a gay party, swirling away in a dance . . . .

He pushed it away as a thin, shy and ascetic looking man with a crew haircut eased up on the platform. It was J. Robert Oppenheimer, the Director. As always, he commanded Gaylord's instant attention and complete admiration.

"Things are getting underway," the Director said simply. "The conferences on procedures began about the middle of April. On the 14th we began laying the bottom pole piece of the cyclotron magnet. Material is coming in. The cyclotron from Harvard, two Van de Graaff electrostatic accelerators from the University of Wisconsin, the Cockcroft-Walton from Illinois, chemical and cryogenic equipment from the University of California. New facilities are shaping up. Next month—early in July, the first experiment will be performed. I think you know all the work that lies ahead of us."

Experimental work of all kinds. Differential experiments for determining the cross section for fission of specific isotopes, and integral experiments for determining the average scattering of fission neutrons from actual tampers. Perfection of the use of the Van de Graaff. Measurements of nuclear constants of U-235, U-238 and plutonium over a wide range, and final purification of the enriched fissionable materials.

". . . hard work, long hours, the utmost concentration," Oppenheimer was saying. "I do not have to remind you what it means to so many. But from one whom you all know, I have received this letter—"

And suddenly, almost miraculously, a great, laughing President wielding a long cigarette holder like a sword and a scepter began speaking directly to Gaylord in the rousing, resonant voice of all America, and with the invincible hope of the whole free world:

I know that you and your colleagues are working on a hazardous matter under unusual circumstances. The fact that the outcome of your labors is of such great significance to the Nation requires that this program be even more drastically guarded than other highly secret war developments. . . . You are fully aware of the reasons why your own endeavors and those of your associates must be circumscribed by very special restrictions. Nevertheless, I wish you would express to the scientists assembled with you my deep appreciation of their willingness to undertake the tasks which lie before them in spite of the dangers and the personal sacrifices. . . . Whatever the enemy may be planning, American science will be equal to the challenge. With this thought in mind, I send this note of confidence and appreciation. . . . While this letter is secret, the contents of it may be disclosed to your associates under a pledge of secrecy.

No, resolved Gaylord striding out from the meeting, nothing should swerve him from this task to which he had dedicated the highest hopes of his unspent youth. Nothing! This exaggerated exhilaration swept him to his car, carried him to the edge of the high mesa. Showing his pass, he was cleared through the guard gate, and dropped swiftly down the tortuously winding canyon road. At the junction below he stopped and looked back. Up above, the Tech Area complex of laboratories and shops stood out on the edge of the sheer, high cliff. Flooded with spotlights, white and shining against dark sky and black mountain walls, it gleamed with all the romantic unreality of a medieval castle, an isolated monastery in mysterious Tibet. A queer tingle raced up his spine. For the first time he realized why it was beginning to be called "Shangri-La, the Forbidden City of Atomic Research."

He drove on now through the dark and untouched mountain wilderness. A deer bounded out of the piñons. A porcupine waddled across the road and stopped, blinded by the headlights. Soon the rough dirt road narrowed. Dizzy drops and horseshoe curves leapt at him from the darkness. His high mood ebbed; wearily he reached Frijoles and climbed into bed.

When he got up next morning he was merely a rundown machine, a fish out of water, a man with a day off and nothing to do. The isolated stone Lodge always acted on Gaylord like this. It cut him off psychologically as well as geographically from Los Alamos, marooning him in a world with which he had no contact. It sat in a deep, narrow valley flanked on each side by sheer, high cliffs of pink and buff tufa, down which trickled El Rito de Los Frijoles, the Little River of the Beans. The Lodge was run by homey Mrs. Frey, who offered comfortable rooms and good meals. It was now utilized, as explained at the Security lecture, by the Project to temporarily house staff members without permanent quarters on the Hill.

Unaccountably irritable, Gaylord walked up the canyon in front of caves pecked into the cliffs, and past the crumbled walls of rude talus-slope house groups. He came then to the excavated ruins of ancient Tyuoni, once a circular walled city five stories high, with two large kivas sunk in its enclosed court. Allegedly famous, it didn't interest Gaylord. How Emily could be so devoted to such jumbled old ruins was a mystery. What was the good of them now, littering these sunless canyons?

A mile farther, he glimpsed a huge cave high in the cliff wall. From its floor protruded the tip of a ladder leading down into another of those everpresent kivas. Another ladder led up to the cave itself. On a sudden impulse he climbed up it.

Here he saw her sitting on the rim of the kiva. It was as if she had been patiently waiting for him, staring dreamily out across the wide blue distance that stretched unheeded far below. Her little red beret lay in her lap. The wind touseled her soft brown hair.

She turned to see him and smiling, lifted her hand in greeting. The gesture was so natural, casual and unaffected that it erased immediately the time and distance between them; dismissed as inconsequential the prehistoric past in which generations here had lived and bred and died forgotten, and all the nebulous hopes and fears of a future yet unborn. The time was now, complete and self-sufficient. Gaylord felt like a vacuum suddenly filled with a rush of life.

"Emily!"

He ran forward, caught her as she rose, and clung eagerly to her warm and living softness that bent and gave to something within him that he had never dreamed existed . . .

Their meetings on companionable procedure had begun in April. Now it was late June, and his first experiment in the simply mystery of living had begun—the only true science of mankind. ▪

※

Essayist and poet Reg Saner writes about the American West with an insight and vitality that come from his love of its rugged landscapes. He is the author of *Climbing into the Roots, Essays on Air, Red Letters,* and *So This is the Map.* Saner has lived in Colorado for many years and teaches at the University of Colorado. In this passage from the essay "Technically Sweet," part of *The Four-Cornered Falcon: Essays on the Interior West and the Natural Scene* (1993), Saner mingles his own experience of climbing into a kiva in Frijoles Canyon in Bandelier National Monument, his sense of Puebloan antiquity, and the dangerous modernity of the nuclear age, which began, as Frank Waters emphasizes in the excerpt from *The Woman at Otowi Crossing* included in this volume, just up the road in Los Alamos.

f r o m

"Technically Sweet"

REG SANER

Weeks before Little Boy and Fat Man are scheduled to fall through bomber doors toward cities where even a newborn is old enough to die, Kenneth Bainbridge, in charge of the Trinity test, looks at the world's first pillar of lethally radioactive cloud still rolling, ascending, and says to Oppenheimer, "Well, now we're all sons of bitches."

In Cañon de los Frijoles I descend the sapling ladder into an Anasazi kiva. The imperfect circle of its freestone interior seems made of ocher dust, which any image I try to summon partakes of. A tribal male squats, putting a live coal to dust in a pipestone bowl. Arthritic and toothless oldsters half doze in the midst of their own stories, whose tongues are dust. Nobody sits weaving yucca twine into square-toed sandals, or discussing the crescent moon's cue for bean sprout rituals. Over the dusty floor nobody outlines a world with pinches of cornmeal, powdered charcoal, pine pollen.

Through the roof hole come shafts of sunlight made visible by the dust I stir up looking for the kiva's *sipapu*.

Surely there once was one: a symbolic, navellike dimple in the dirt floor. I've seen dozens in kivas elsewhere—*sipapuni,* some Hopi call them—because pueblos along the Rio Grande Valley and pueblos of the Hopi in Arizona still use kivas surprisingly like Anasazi versions abandoned in the twelfth and thirteenth centuries. Through that hole all humankind escaped a sin-struck nether cosmos turned chaotic; the so-called Third World. From it they fled upward into a fresh chance—this one we now live in, the Fourth World.

The Third World had fallen into corrupt ways, the Hopi believe, because people forgot "the meaning of life." A faithful few remembered. In their songs they asked, "Who are we? Where do we come from? Why are we here?" Their answers reminded them: they had been created by Tawa, the sun. They had come through many worlds. Evil in the human heart had brought each to ruin. So they rose into the Fourth World, leaving evil behind. They were to roam, seeking other Hopi, seeking the place where all scattered and migrating Hopi would meet again.

Up rungs of peeled juniper I climb from kiva-gloom, emerge blinking at the day-light. Hopi myth suggests I ought to feel the significance of being born again into it. But I don't, not a bit. So much for the spot my topographical map marks "Ceremonial Cave."

Or maybe my kiva reemergence into the hard sunlight of this Fourth World means, "It's all to do again, everything, every time. Daily you have to pump gods back into the scenery; so you can breathe. You can't breathe just scrub woodlands and yucca and cactus and rock." I'm weary, thirsty. Those last Anasazis who climbed out of this kiva must've taken the gods with them. ▪

Bruce Hucko is an independent photogra-pher and art educator who is the photographer for the Wetherill–Grand Gulch Re-search Project (WGG). The project applies the principle of "reverse archaeology" by working to locate and document the primary collections of artifacts removed from the Grand Gulch and Cedar Mesa region beginning in the late 1880s. The process includes locating and mapping historic canyon inscriptions, locating historic jour-nals, cooperating with museums in the search for missing collections, repho-tographing historic photos, conducting research trips to eastern museums to document collections, photographing sites, and assembling all related materials. This excerpt, revised from an essay by Hucko in the WGG *Anasazi Basketmaker: Pa-*

pers from the 1990 Wetherill–Grand Gulch Symposium, reflects the experience of
working with Puebloan sites and how, for many of us, that experience can make our
contemporary contexts seem strangely unfamiliar.

f   r   o   m

"Cave to Cave—
Canyon to
Canyon"

BRUCE HUCKO

Having spent years roaming the realm of the Anasazi in the
rugged and beautiful canyons of Cedar Mesa in Southeastern Utah, it was an ironic pleasure to be on an eastbound
train following their trail again. As the photographer for
the Wetherill–Grand Gulch Research Project, I was charged
with aesthetically photographing hundreds of objects removed from their ancient home nearly one hundred years
ago and now residing in the canyon alcoves of our nation's
leading museums. . . .

After day-long sessions in the museum, usually beginning at sunrise and ending with us getting a brief glimpse
of sunset, we would walk the towns
looking for other forms of "cultural"
education, food and entertainment, before retiring to our
rooms for evening research sessions. Fixed as we were on
the Anasazi, it was easy to confuse where we were.

Leaving the American Museum of Natural History one
night and walking Broadway back to our flat, we came
upon a scene reminiscent of an earlier age. It is purely spec-
ulative, but there on the sidewalk beneath the sun-rimmed
deep city walls and amidst the refuse of a dying culture, a
ragged man of undeterminable descent sharpened a knife
on the curb. Surrounded by the "rock art" graffiti of his age,
he steadily honed the blade, oblivious to passersby. Was this
act done for protection, a weapon, or for hunting? Would
there be a victim or merely a full belly for the first time in
days? Only once did he look up and there, in his bloodshot
eyes, one could see the longing and despair that may have
come to the Anasazi in the waning years of their time on
Cedar Mesa. I had to shake my head to gather my senses

and to focus on old brownstones and sirens where for an instant there had been desert varnished walls and the canyon wren.

The city, especially New York, offers a cold and harsh analogy for what may have met the Anasazi. There is tension. People are afraid. No one talks to strangers. Subsistence food and shelter are scarce. People beg and eat from garbage piles. Buildings deteriorate along with spirit. Yet through it all one street musician can be heard singing his song, the Kokopelli of Manhattan.

There were lighter musings in this land of parallels as well. Again in New York, for several nights we would return to Miss Pringle's Parlor for late night cheesecake and tea. The dessert choices were endless, necessitating repeat visits. And I wondered, what did the Anasazi do for dessert? What was their Miss Pringle's?

During our stay in New York, I flew to Seattle for my sister's wedding. My flight out was at night, but the return was in daylight. As we ascended over the Cascades, I looked down upon hillside after hillside of slopes clear-cut for their timber. Traversed back and forth by logging roads, the hills were deeply scarred and patterned. All I could think of were pottery designs. Beginning there, the entire flight was an aerial Anasazi visual feast of basket weaves made of farmland plowing, river ways drawn out like rock art, and cloud patterns resembling rock forms. I wondered if they had ever flown?

These distant musings scattered throughout our experience served to bind me further to our work. In the aerial design of our abuse of the land, I saw another pattern, that of the continuum of human expression upon the land. We had come to the eastern shore of our continent in search of the Anasazi. In both distance and time we were a long way from our and their home, yet that distance now seemed not so far. ▪

Poet and scholar Wendy Rose, born in Oakland, California, in 1948, is of Hopi, Chowchilla, Miwok, Scottish, and Irish descent. Growing up in the Bay Area during the 1950s, the so-called termination era when the federal government sought to "get out of the Indian business" by relocating Native Americans from reservations to urban areas, Rose had ample occasion to reflect on the situation of Native Americans in a contemporary urban society largely unhinged from any significant sense of origin and community. After receiving her master's degree in anthropology from the University of California at Berkeley, Rose taught at Berkeley, Fresno State University, and Fresno City College. Her poetry has appeared in several volumes, beginning with *Hopi Roadrunner Dancing* (1973), and including *Long Division: A Tribal History* (1976), *Academic Squaw: Reports to the World from the Ivory Tower* (1977), *Lost Copper* (1980), and *Halfbreed Chronicles* (1985). In 1994, the anthology *Bone Dance* compiled selections from her previous collections and included her most recent work.

Militant and uncompromising about both her mixed ethnic identity and her gender, Rose lodges within her poetry both a personal voice and a broad dimension to the complexity and beauty of Native American survival in the face of cultural conquest. Although Rose has written that she will "never be able to live on the earth as a Hopi woman on Hopi land," in exploring her identity as a mixed-blood Hopi she considers the ancient Puebloans a vital part of her heritage.

"To Some Few Hopi Ancestors"

WENDY ROSE

No longer the drifting
and falling of wind,
your songs have changed;
they have become
thin willow whispers
that take us by the ankle
and tangle us up
with red mesa stone,
that keep us turned
to the round sky,
that follow us down
to Winslow, to Sherman,
to Oakland, to all the spokes
that leave Earth's middle.
You have engraved yourself
with holy signs, encased yourself
in pumice, hammered on my bones
till you could no longer hear
the howl of the missions
slipping screams through your silence,
dropping dreams from your wings.
        Is this why

you made me
sing and weep
for you?
Like butterflies
made to grow another way
this woman is chiseled
on the face of your world.
The badger-claw of her father
shows slightly in the stone
burrowed from her sight,
facing west from home.

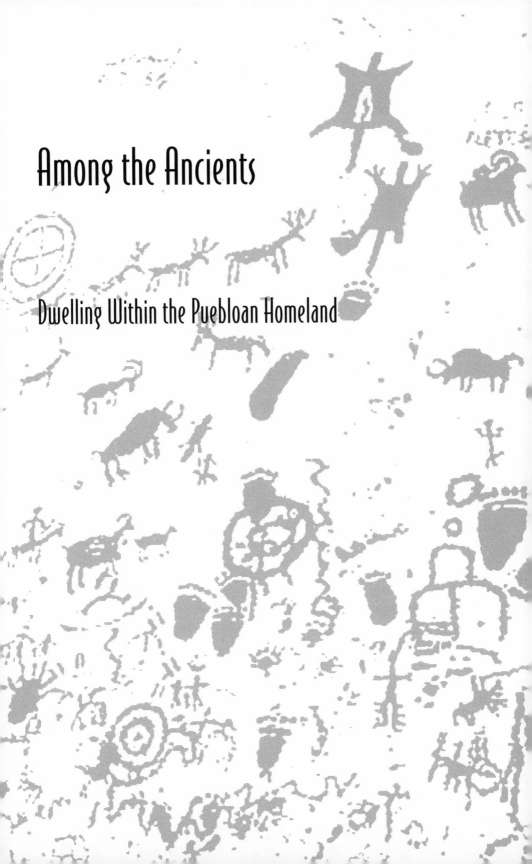

Among the Ancients

Dwelling Within the Puebloan Homeland

❁

Albert Yava, a Hopi-Tewa, was born in 1888 and grew up in the village of Hano on First Mesa, now on the Hopi reservation in northeastern Arizona. Like thousands of Native American children across the country at the time, Yava attended a government school as part of the forced assimilation policies of the era. But his memoirs, recorded by folklorist Harold Courlander in the 1978 autobiography *Big Falling Snow,* reveal that Yava retained his traditional Hopi heritage.

Today the book is highly regarded by many Hopi. Yava speaks with great conviction about his own life as well as about Hopi traditions and interactions with non–Native Americans. What might be misinterpreted as humility in Yava's reluctance to emphasize his own individual experiences and perceptions actually suggests his participation in the sense of collective experience that lies close to the heart of traditional Hopi culture. At the same time, he succeeds in illustrating the great variety that exists in the thinking of the Hopi, undermining old stereotypes that deny Native Americans individuality.

In this brief excerpt, his discussion of the "Anasazi," Yava clearly establishes the Hopi sense of the inappropriateness of the name and the dangers that lie behind it. He reveals how, for the Hopi, issues associated with "Hopi ruins" and attributed to "ancient enemies" are a complex weave of cultural, historical, and political realities.

---

f r o m

Big Falling Snow

ALBERT YAVA

From the Hopi point of view, the Navajos were not good neighbors because they were aggressive and warlike whenever they needed something. They not only took food in their raids, but women and children too. You can say that they believed aggressive action was the way to survive, in contrast to the Hopi concept of hard work and restrained behavior. Even after the Navajos were more or less settled on their reservation, they still had that aggressiveness in them. They stopped being a wandering people, but we Hopis were outsiders to them and fair game if they needed something we had. Horses, for example. It was as if the Navajo men were pretending it was still the old days, when a brave went out and got a horse wherever he could find it.

When the white people started coming in around here they found Hopi ruins all through this region. They asked the Navajos who the ruins belonged to, and the Navajos said Anasazi. Well, the white people wanted to know, who were the Anasazi? And the Navajos said, "It means the Old Ones, or the Ancient People." They never acknowledged that these ruins were left by Hopi clans in the old days, because they didn't want the Hopis to have any claim to land the Navajos wanted to use. I heard from someone who seems to know what he is talking about that the word Anasazi properly translated really means Old Enemy. One thing is certain, that practically up to the present time the Navajos have thought of Hopis as the offspring of Old Enemy. When Hopis see Navajos occupying land that is traditional Hopi land, some of it designated by the Government as Hopi territory, they can't help but feel that the Navajos still have that old predatory attitude.

Still, quite a few Hopis have Navajo friends, and some have intermarried. You will find some pretty conservative Hopi families here and there whose sons or daughters are married to Navajos. That could be a trend of the future, when all our hard feelings will be washed out. I myself have been welcomed into Navajo hogans as a clan relative. Even someone I didn't know might ask me, "What clan are you?" And I would say, "Spruce Clan, related to Bear and Spider." He'd say, "You are my clan brother. I am Bear Clan." I can count many times that I have eaten and slept in a Navajo hogan. ■

Clyde Benally is a Navajo, a ranger at Mesa Verde National Park, a writer, and a thoughtful and personable man. When he took a group of my Hope College students through Balcony House in 1995, I told him we were more interested in the human experience of its ancient inhabitants than we were in how many meters across the kivas were. That seems to be what he had in mind anyway. That night around the campfire, Benally made the ancient culture come alive in ways we could all understand. He suggested that, like us, the ancient people saw a powerful beauty in the natural landscape of Mesa Verde and that their whole way of life reflected that experience of reverence and wonder.

Together with Andrew Wiget, John Alley, and Garry Blake, Benally is the author of *Dinéjí Nákéé Nááhané: A Utah Navajo History,* a remarkable history book written from the Navajo point of view and used in the public schools around the Four Corners. Although the migration of the Navajo to the Southwest is often cited as a possible cause of the abandonment of the ancient pueblos, and though the Navajo are often represented as the antagonists of contemporary Puebloans, particularly of the Hopi, Benally focuses here on the affinity and mutual influence of the two cultures.

---

f r o m

Dinéjí Nákéé Náahané

C L Y D E   B E N A L L Y

The Navajos emerged from the lower worlds onto an island in the middle of a lake surrounded by tall and beautiful mountains. That lake, say the stories, lies somewhere in the north. And modern science has agreed, at least in part, with this Navajo tradition. In 1852, it was shown that the Navajos speak an Athabascan language. Athabascan is the name given to a group or "family" of related languages found mostly in Canada and Alaska. With that discovery, scholars began to accept the idea that the People came from the north.

Navajo tradition gives a number of clues to this northern origin. Many Navajo stories do not resemble those of the Pueblos who surround the modern Navajos. But similar stories can be found among tribes in Canada, Washington, Idaho, and the Northern Plains. Even the Navajo origin story is different from those of other southwestern peoples. Of all such stories, only that of the Navajo admits that the People were not the first to live in the land they now occupy. Instead it says that the Pueblos, or Kiis'ánii, were there to greet the People when they came out.

But when and how the Navajos and Apaches came from Canada to the Southwest is not certain. Some scientists say that the Navajos moved through the High Plains and entered the Southwest about A.D. 1525. These scientists think that the Navajos were hunters who followed the buffalo down from Canada. Evidence from some ancient sites in the western Plains tends to support this point of view. These old camps, called the Dismal River Sites, seem to have been used by Athabascans. The people who made these camps lived in earth lodges, made a special kind of pottery, and hunted buffalo.

Other scientists disagree. They think the People may have come to Dinétah, the southwest Navajo homeland, much earlier than A.D. 1525 and that they could have followed an intermountain route. These scholars point out that pottery like that found at the Dismal River site is also found throughout an area from eastern Colorado to Promontory, Utah, near the Great Salt Lake. Athabascans, these scholars argue, seem to have favored mountain sites. Because of that, the mountain trails would have caused few problems for the People, who might even have preferred them to the Plains routes. Also, the People would not have needed to stay on the Plains to hunt buffalo. As late as the beginning of the last [19th] century, buffalo roamed across Colorado and into northern Utah.

An early arrival of the People could answer other puzzles, too. As more than one scientist has pointed out, the complex Navajo religion could only have come about through long contact between the People and the Pueblos. If the People did not arrive until A.D. 1525, there would not have been enough time for such a complex religion to develop. Also, during the twelfth and thirteenth centuries, the Anasazi peoples of the Southwest built dwellings that came to look more and more like forts. Then, about A.D. 1300, the Anasazi left these homes. Pressure from Athabascan neighbors might help to explain these things. But most scholars have not accepted this intermountain route. They point out that there were many reasons why the Anasazi moved out of the Four Corners area. Of those, the scholars argue, pressure from a competing culture was perhaps the least important.

Recently some scholars have suggested a third explanation. The Navajos, they say, could have reached the Southwest as early as A.D. 1000, traveling over a number of routes. George Hyde was the first to suggest this idea. He believed that a large group of migrating Athabascans split up somewhere in central Wyoming. Then, he stated, the Navajos traveled through the area near the Great Salt Lake. From there they crossed the Wasatch Mountains and went south through eastern Utah. The Jicarilla Apaches went around the eastern edge of the Uinta Mountains and then traveled across central Colorado into northern New Mexico. The Dismal River Apaches, ancestors of the Lipan Apaches, came down through the High Plains.

Of the three explanations, Hyde's seems the most reasonable. There is support for it in both Navajo tradition and recent studies of the Fremont Culture of Utah and Colorado. Between A.D. 400 and A.D. 1300, changes began to appear in the Fremont Culture. Most important, some Fremont peoples began to make a new kind of pottery. It has been found throughout eastern Utah and southwestern Colorado, near regions through which the Navajos might have traveled. The new pottery was made with calcite and decorated as pottery on the Plains was. In some ways, it is much like older Navajo pottery. So perhaps the Athabascan peoples brought this way of making pots to the Fremont peoples they met on their journey. And there are other changes that could have come about as a result of contact between the two groups. Such things as barbed bone points and arrowheads, ground slate knives and pendants, and a Mexican type of corn also suggest a northern or Plains influence on local Fremont groups.

Navajo stories contain some clues that also tend to support this idea of an early arrival. In the 1890s, Hataałii Nez said that the Navajos reached the Southwest when Kin Ntéél was being built. One of the clans, he added, joined the People later, when Kin Ntéél was in ruins. Kin Ntéél has been identified as Chetro Ketl, a ruin in Chaco Canyon, New Mexico. It was built about A.D. 1000 and abandoned by A.D. 1300. Other Navajos have identified the Home of the Flints as the Sun Temple at Mesa Verde, Colorado. This was built about the same time as Chetro Ketl. These clan and chantway stories suggest that the People came to the Southwest early, perhaps as early as A.D. 1000. ■

Three novels, *Go in Beauty* (1956), *The Bronc People* (1958), and *Portrait of an Artist with Twenty-Six Horses* (1963), established William Eastlake as nothing short of one of the American West's finest twentieth-century novelists. The best known of these, *The Bronc People,* celebrates the natural landscape of the West in an episodic account of the friendship of Little Sant Bowman and Alistair Benjamin, one white and the other black, as they grow up on a southwestern ranch and find their own identities against the backdrop of racial differences and stereotypes of cowboys and Indians. Eastlake's characteristic comic satire is clearly at play in the scene excerpted here. As the young men scale a cliff to visit an ancient pueblo, they keep up a running dialogue, as do their "contemporaries," who observe their climb from below. Eastlake's Native Americans are very much of the present, and their involvement in this excursion to a ruin site makes that very clear.

f r o m

The Bronc People

WILLIAM EASTLAKE

When they had got the horses swinging easily and together in a nice lope through the mouth of the wide Baca Arroyo and were approaching the narrow neck of Wetherill Canyon, big, towering, orange and clean up to the sky on both sides, Alastair Benjamin looked up at the slit of hard blue above.

"You still going to be a bronc man when you get grown up?"

"I'm grown up."

"I mean when you get paid for being grown up."

"When I get paid for grown up—yes sir!"

"How much will you charge for a bronc show?"

"Forty hundred dollars or so. I don't know."

"Them movie cowboys aren't really cowboys."

"No sir!"

"They shoot sixty shots from a six-shooter."

"Yeah."

"And they ride through brush country without chaps. That would tear a cowboy's clothes all off."

"Yessir."

"They say Tom Mix and Zane Grey were real cowboys."

"That's because they're dead."

"Is Zane Grey dead?"

"I think he is."

They were moving deep into the dark canyon now. The bright walls all became gray on the shadow side. They moved easily at the bottom of the long crack that led even deeper into the heart of the wild mountain.

"You take an Indian," Alastair Benjamin said. Alastair Benjamin ran his arm along the neck of his white horse to reassure the animal against the darkness of the canyon. "You take an Indian," Alastair Benjamin repeated, his soft voice knocked back sharp from the close rock. "Why won't an Indian join our outfit?"

"It's a white outfit," Sant said.

"Will the Indians always be our enemies?"

"I guess so."

"Why?"

"Well, what would there be to do for example if they weren't?"

"Yeah."

"Indians are just naturally Indians."

"And there wouldn't be nobody to fight if they weren't. For example, there'd be nothing to do."

"That's right. I wonder what they do in the city, where there are no Indians."

"Nothing I guess."

"Oh they probably do something."

"I guess they do."

Now the canyon began to widen and let in more of the sky, which allowed the rock to resume its varicolors again, still towering but vivid now and visible, shone upon and shining back, greeted and greeting back, all lighted and lighting in pyrotechnic reds to the abrupt sky.

"You like this better?" Alastair Benjamin asked his horse.

Sant began to work his eye along the sheer face of the left canyon wall to pick up the geological fault that, as they rode on, would become wider. It would always remain about two hundred feet up but soon the slipping formation beneath would become a narrow ledge that a man could walk on, then it would become so wide you could set down a house, which the Old People had done before the white man came. Even before the Navajos came. Alastair Benjamin had been the first white man to see it and Sant had been the first to climb up to it. Climbing up to it was quite a trick. The Old People had used handholds and yucca fiber ropes that they pulled up after them at night or when being chased by the people who must have finally caught them.

"There she is," Sant said, pointing. They both pulled in their horses and their eyes followed the great distance up the side of the wall to where the secret house sat on a secret ledge. Actually part of the house was in a natural cave, but even that part had a roof and wall and window openings, and part of the house was a tower like those that the same people had built in the flat open country. In other words, it seemed as though these people didn't give up a style easily. When they built in the cliff they built the same way they had always built. They weren't going to give up something simply because they were hiding.

"Who you think they were hiding from?" Alastair Benjamin said.

Sant looked away from the house and to the top of the cliff two hundred feet above.

"New people, I guess."

"But what did the new people have against these people?"

"They was here."

"That's all?"

"I guess that was plenty," Sant said and he moved his pinto horse down the gentle slope, and Alastair Benjamin followed on his all-white.

After going up a steep path they arrived now at the spot where they made the two-hundred-foot climb straight up the face of the cliff. The Old People had chipped handholds in the flat rock most of the way up but the earth from the bottom of the cliff had eroded down ten feet since then, or they had used their yucca fiber ropes at the bottom. Anyway there were no handholds on the first ten feet of the climb, so it was necessary for Sant to stand tiptoe on the pommel of his saddle to begin his climb. As soon as Sant's weight left the saddle the pinto moved forward and began to graze, and Alastair Benjamin moved his horse in and followed Sant.

They worked their way up and up the flat burning face of the cliff. They could have waited until the sun left the cliff but then it would have been in shadow—more comfortable but more dangerous—much easier then to mistake a weathering on the face for a true handhold. Shadows hide and they deceive too. But, most of all, shadows come before the darkness of a fall. So they sweated and burned upward in the sun, rapidly like quick monkeys against the moving of the sun. Before the dangerous arrival of the shadows on the sheer face, they went upward like quick monkeys moving fast.

"There," Sant said. "Look down there."

Alastair Benjamin turned his head cautiously downward and saw two Indian boys leading away their horses.

"Now, why would they do that?"

"Because we're here," Sant said between his teeth, and clinging.

They reached a ledge soon where they could sit down. Above them the handholds ceased and they would have to use a rope—the lasso that Sant had carried around his neck.

"Yeah," Alastair said, sitting and watching down, "I been cogitating."

"You been thinking too," Little Sant said.

"Yeah," Alastair said watching the Indians move down canyon with their horses. "I been thinking that the universe is not moral, that things fall upon the just and the unjust equally almost."

"That's what my dad says, but Ma doesn't agree."

"Yeah."

"What does it mean?"

"Big Sant says it covers everything," Alastair said.

"Does it cover us ambushers being ambushed?"

"I guess it does."

"What else do you know?"

"We come a fur piece."

"I know where you got that. From the movie cowboys."

"Yeah."

"Like us, they got a secret language too."

"Yeah, I guess they have."

They had reached the point now in the climb where they had to cross a wide fissure in the rocks. It was about ten feet across. When the Old People built the house the crack might not have been there, or they had used the yucca ropes. Anyway now it was a ten-foot gap with almost one hundred feet of nothing beneath to the floor of the canyon. Sant rose, uncoiled his rope, adjusted the loop, and began swinging it around his head. There was not too much room and it was difficult. He kept his eye on a pinnacle of rock twenty feet above. The thing was to lasso this pinnacle, which was part of a formation that, up there, hung over the middle of the void. You lassoed this and then swung over the ten-foot gap. Sant caught the pinnacle on his first try and winked back at Alastair Benjamin.

"Lemaitre," Alastair Benjamin said.

Sant moved to the edge of the gap now, pulling in the loose rope and coiling it around his wrist.

"Okay," Sant said. "Shove me off."

Alastair Benjamin moved in behind him and gave him a push. Sant swung out over the void and when he reached the other ledge he touched it with his foot and pushed back hard with his leg. Back he came across the gap almost into the arms of Alastair Benjamin. Alastair Benjamin gave him another push, sending him again out over space, and this time he had enough momentum to drop off on the other side. He held the rope. He made a coil of the loose rope now and shot it back to Alastair Benjamin. Alastair Benjamin caught the rope and advanced to the edge of the big drop, coiling the slack rope and tensing himself to jump.

"Be nonchalant," Sant shouted.

Alastair Benjamin wiped the sweat off his forehead and said, "I'm coming." Then he came. Sant was ready for him and shot him back across the gap. The second time he came back he still did not think he had the momentum to land safely.

"Again," he said, and Sant gave him another shove out over space. "Again," Alastair Benjamin said when he came back.

"Land this time," Sant said.

"Landing," Alastair Benjamin said and he landed on top of Sant and they both went down.

"There," Sant said from the scramble and looking down below. "There go the Indians with our horses."

"The ambushers been ambushed," Alastair Benjamin said.

"The bushwhackers been bushwhacked," Sant agreed.

"We can't go back down."

"So we got to go up."

"Who was it stole our horses, can you see?"

"Indians."

"But what Indians?"

"Bad Indians."

"But what's their names?"

"Including the middle name their names is Awful Bad Indians."

"I think one of them is Afraid Of His Own Horses. He's wearing a red baseball cap this season."

"And instead of stealing second an Indian steals horses."

"That's not a very good joke, Santo."

Sant looked up at the cliff above and back down the void where they had come. "I guess it's not too funny," Sant said.

"Afraid Of His Own Horses always hangs out with The Other Indian."

"The Other Indian's a pretty good guy. Are you saying he'd try to break up our outfit?"

"Yeah."

"Yeah, I guess he would all right."

"Shall we get started up?"

"Yeah, I guess we better get started up."

The old handholds resumed again now and Alastair Benjamin went first. They had left the lasso rope dangling. They would retrieve it when they reached the pinnacle twenty feet above.

"I got a feeling," Alastair Benjamin said, "that the shadows are coming on."

"Keep going, Alley," Sant said.

"I don't know whether the next one's a handhold or not."

"Keep moving, Alley."

Well, that one was.

"They've got to be. We can't back, we've come too far and we can't get caught on the face now. We would be lost in five minutes. The only way now is up."

"I don't know—what do you think about this next one?"

"Just keep moving, Alley."

The next one was okay, but what now?

"Just up, Alley. Always up. We stop and it's all over."

"I think I'll rest."

"You can't rest here, Alley."

"You should have gone first, again."

"I can't pass you now, Alley."

"I guess I'm finished, Santo. My hands have gone dead."

Sant looked at his own hands and realized he could not feel them or control them at all.

"Alley?"

"Yes, Santo."

Sant was quiet long moments and then he said from the now-lengthening shadows, "Alley, I've got hold of a mountain mahogany bush. I've moved over to the right and have got hold of a mountain bush. If you keep moving up I can see the handholds get much larger. If you fall you'll just land in the bush. Get started up, Alley."

He heard Alley move up above him in the shadows. He could not move himself; he would have to hang here and think of another trick to get himself moving, but he could think of nothing, only feel the pain in his deadening arms.

What does a bronc man do? What does a real bronc man do?

Now he felt something brush his face. It was a rope. A bronc man has friends in high places.

Above, when Alastair Benjamin had made it over the ledge, he got the rope and dropped it down to Sant. Now he gave the final heave that pulled Sant up on the ledge too.

"Not that you needed any help," Alastair Benjamin said.

"No. I was okay," Sant said.

They sat a long time resting and recovering and finally trying to capsulize all the wisdom of the ages into one good sentence that might last. The best they could do was: In this country it never rains in June and almost never in August with the exception, anyway as far as last August is concerned, of last year and maybe the year before that. They couldn't remember.

"Anyway, Santo," Alastair Benjamin said standing, "let's get moving."

"*Cómo no?*" Sant said. "Why not?"

It was easy going now along the wide ledge that ran to the cliff house. When they got to the cliff house the first thing they did was go in and see if the gold was okay—iron pyrites they had dug off the side of the ledge that looked more like gold than gold did.

"The gold is okay, Santo," Alastair said.

"Yeah," Sant said, running his hands through it. "It sure is handy to have a lot of gold if you ever want to run away or something."

"Yeah," Alastair said. "Like the trader, Mr. Peersall, says, it sure gives you a lot of mobility."

"What does that mean?"

"It covers about everything, I guess."

"I bet it does. I bet gold covers about everything, I guess. Alley, let's speak our secret language."

They spoke the secret language now, the one that Alastair had invented.

"Santo," Alastair said finally in English. "Let's get out of here."

"Yeah, but how?"

"The easy way."

"You want to take the easy way?"

"Don't you think we've had enough of the hard way for one day?"

"Yeah, I guess we have."

First they checked the house thoroughly to make sure that everything was okay. The house was divided into apartments with woven willow reeds over cedar logs for the roofs. To get from one apartment to the next you had to go through the low doors in a stooping position, so the Old People could dispose of you quickly if you didn't belong. Also you always had to go through another apartment to get to your own, which must have made for interesting living. The whole thing was built in about the tenth century, when the Old People had been pressured off the flat country to down here in the middle of cliffs to make a final stand. There was a cesspool-like hole in the front of the building, called a kiva, where the religious rites were held and restricted to men. They must have gathered down there every evening to ask for something they thought important, but the New People finally got everything anyway.

"They sure built nice buildings," Alastair Benjamin said, staring up at it.

The house was made of flat rectangular stones the Old People had gathered above on the top of the mesa and lowered down here. They were mortared with adobe, but the fact that they were worked perfectly and fitted exactly accounted for the building still standing after one thousand years. Around the building were scattered large pieces of pottery with abstract colored pictures, painted with freedom, which signified nothing except maybe that a thing called art is a deeper part of us than we suspect.

"Well, I guess we better get moving before we get attacked."

Alastair Benjamin allowed his eye to climb above the shallow cave where the building lay and to go all the way up, which was about another twenty feet, to the top of the cliff.

"You think they're going to attack us from up there?"

"Well, you know Indians."

"Yeah."

"Indians never miss a chance."

"Why are Indians that way?"

"Because they're Indians."

"It's not because we're white men?"

"Oh, it's that all right."

"Before you said it's because we're here."

"Well, I guess it's a little of both, but we better get started up."

They followed the ledge until a deer path branched off that led quickly to the top of the mesa—that is, it always had. Now they came to a cutback and the path was gone.

"Indians," Sant said.

"Yeah."

Here the sandy bank was very steep and below fell off abruptly at the stone cliff. The sharp, small hard feet of deer had begun, and maintained by continuous use, a path here; but now someone with a sharp instrument had destroyed it, and to try to walk it would send you sliding and then falling to the canyon floor three hundred feet below.

"Indians."

"Well, I guess we better get started back down."

"Yeah."

When they got back to the Old People's building they sat down next to the hole where the men who lived there used to think, and that's what they did too.

"I wonder," Alastair Benjamin said, "what the women did while the men thought."

"Made these pots," Sant said.

"I guess so. Have you thought of anything yet?"

"Yeah," Sant said. "From here we got to throw a lasso over the top and climb up that way."

"We've done it before."

"But not with Indians up there."

"That's true."

"You think when we got started up they would unhook the lasso?"

"Well, you know Indians as well as I do."

"I'm afraid I do."

Alastair Benjamin looked all the way to the top, shading his eyes. "What makes you think the Indians are up there?"

Sant thought a while and then he said, "Well, I know Indians. I may not know nothing else but I think by this time I should know a little about Indians."

Alastair Benjamin rubbed his nose and tried to think of an interesting way he could contradict Sant. And then a rock fell.

"I guess you do," he said.

They retreated back into the part of the cave that overhung the building but the rocks continued to rain down anyway.

"Just to show us they're there," Sant said. "Just to show us how smart an Indian is. And an Indian's awful smart."

"If they was smart they'd pretend they weren't there and when we started up they'd unhook our lasso."

"Well, an Indian ain't that smart."

"I wonder if this is the way they killed off the people that lived here."

"Maybe not killed them. Maybe just got them out of here. This same kind of pots"—Sant touched a pile with his foot—"I've seen at the pueblos where people live right now."

"But why didn't they kill them all off before they got away?"

"I just don't know."

"You mean you don't know everything, Santo?"

"Yeah. Not everything, I guess I don't."

"Now the rocks have stopped raining. You think they gave up?"

"Yeah. The Indians don't stay with an attack very long."

"You sure it's safe now to throw up the lasso?"

"Yeah," Sant said, uncoiling the rope. "Maybe I don't know everything but I should know Indians by now."

"I hope you do," Alastair Benjamin said.

Above, the two Indian boys sat near four horses under some piñon scrub, waiting for the rope to come up. They were giggling. Sant's mother had said that Indians, especially Navajos, were the gigglingest people she had ever met.

"You think they'll be fools enough to throw up that rope?"

"Well," The Other Indian said, "if they don't I don't know my whites. And if I don't know my whites I don't know anything."

"Well," Afraid Of His Own Horses said, "there is a bunch who claim you don't know any—" A rope landed near them. "And another bunch who claims you do."

Before they could grab the rope and make the boys below think they had caught something solid the rope was dragged below again.

"You want me to try this time?" Alastair Benjamin said.

"Yeah. Okay. Try to make her land flat and hook one of those tree stumps we've seen up there."

Alastair Benjamin whirled the rope twelve times around his head before he let her fly.

"That puts mojo on it," he said, but it didn't do any good. The rope fell back.

"This way," Sant said, twirling and pumping the loop with a snap. "Like Lemaitre. It puts style into it." He flung the loop with quick grace. "Style," Sant said.

Now he pulled the slack in and the rope went taut.

"I think I've caught something solid," he said. "You want to feel?"

Alastair took the rope and pulled. "It's okay."

"You sure we haven't caught an Indian?"

"Yeah."

"How can you be sure?"

"By the feel."

"How does an Indian feel?"

"With his hands."

"Boy, you're in lousy shape today. I better go first."

Sant took a good grip on the rope, and The Other Indian above dropped the loop on the saddle horn of the horse they had stolen below.

"Something happened," Sant said.

"Yeah, you lost your nerve."

"No, something happened."

"Yeah, you lost your nerve."

"All right," Sant said and he started up. When he got up a way, Alastair Benjamin started up too. Sant turned his head and looked back.

"Don't you feel it's kind of giving?"

"Yeah. Like the tree is bending."

"It feels funny."

"You sure we didn't catch an Indian?"

"Pretty sure."

"Now it's only pretty sure."

"Well, as sure as a man can be. Anyway it's something bigger than an Indian."

"Is it bigger than the both of us?"

"It's funnier than you," Sant said and he began to climb again rapidly now to get it over with.

Above, Afraid Of His Own Horses watched the stolen horse brace himself.

"You think he can hold them?" The Other Indian said.

"That's what we're going to find out."

"Maybe we should back the horse up a bit closer to the edge. Make it more interesting."

"Why not?" The Other Indian said.

Sant looked back down. "The rope seems to be stretching."

"If it don't stretch it breaks. You learned that in school."

"We should have stayed there," Sant said and he climbed hard trying to make up for the stretch.

"Well," Afraid Of His Own Horses said, "we can't back the horse any farther without it going over the edge."

"Is that bad?"

"It sure is. Then we couldn't steal the horse again."

"Then why don't you try running the horse forward?"

"Why didn't I think of that?"

"Well, you're not very smart," The Other Indian said.

"Does it strike you that the rope is getting shorter?" Alastair Benjamin said.

"Yeah," Sant said. "What they say about that in school?"

"Indians. We roped an Indian," Alastair Benjamin said, and they both held on as they flew upward fast.

Sant and Alastair Benjamin ended up all in one heap on top of the mesa alongside the tree that they were trying to rope and beneath two of the "gigglingest people"—even for Navajos—that ever lived.

Sant unwound himself to a sitting position and looked carefully at Afraid Of His Own Horses.

"You crazy Indians. Don't you know you almost—?"

"We didn't though, because—well, because—" Afraid Of His Own Horses looked at The Other Indian.

"Because, why, because," The Other Indian said, "if we did that—"

"Let you fall," Afraid Of His Own Horses said.

"Yes. If we did that there wouldn't be anybody left to fight."

"We had that figured out all the time," Alastair Benjamin said.

Sant looked down on the building of the Old People below and then on down to the far canyon floor beneath, blue with distance. Then he removed his small finger from his nose and examined it.

"Yes, that stopped us a lot of times too," Sant said. ■

Nineteenth-century literature depicted Mormons, or the Church of Jesus Christ of Latter-day Saints, in internationally popular and sensational anti-Mormon novels that emphasized the perils of Mormonism and the moral turpitude of polygamy. Beginning in 1898 with the work of Nephi Anderson, Mormon fiction writers began to respond. The 1939 *Children of God* by Vardis Fisher, himself raised as a nominal Mormon, is still regarded as the definitive historical novel about the Saints and their mid–nineteenth century settlement of Utah.

In recent years Levi Peterson, along with Terry Tempest Williams, has emerged as one of the most persuasive and talented writers dealing with Mormon subjects. If the tradition of fiction about the Mormons has been either openly hostile or defensive, Peterson successfully avoids both shortcomings, crafting psychologically realistic representations of contemporary Mormon experience. In the title story of his 1982 collection *Canyons of Grace*, Peterson relates the excavation of a southern Utah Puebloan site to the evolving relationships of his central character with her family, her religion, and her emerging sexuality.

f r o m

"Canyons of Grace"

LEVI PETERSON

One summer Arabella Gurney worked as a member of an excavation team at an Anasazi site in the canyon country of Utah. The dig was situated on a small promontory half-encircled by the meandering wash of a broad canyon. To the north were high ridges and the blue Abajo Mountains. South and west the canyon country opened. Its chopped, tilted plains, marked by the red rock of buttes, monoliths, and mesas, ran to the distant rim of the world. In this benign wilderness Arabella found a growing courage for translating her seditious thoughts into an irreversible act. She could remember that, hardly five years earlier, she had thought God loved to bless his children; now she believed his subtle purpose was to demean them.

Arabella was in the kiva on a Saturday morning, working carefully with a tiny pick and brush to unearth a ceremonial dish. Looking up, she saw Franklin's feet dangling against the masonry of the kiva wall. He sat at the edge of the excavation, smiling down like a satyr, his curly hair matted with dust and his bare chest marked by muddy rivulets of sweat.

"I'm coming down," he said, eyeing the ladder.

"There isn't any room," Arabella said. She stood and put a hand on his boot. "Your feet are too big."

He lifted his leg and examined his ponderous boot. "Well, you come up here and sit by me."

When she had seated herself on the rim of the kiva, she reached out and scraped a fingernail along his muddy shoulder. "Utter dirt. You have the hygienic habits of a ground squirrel."

"That dirt," he said proudly, "is the result of a single morning of trenching." He stretched his arm into a right angle and flexed a muscle. "The essence of the male. You may feel it if you want to. Once only."

She pinched his arm vigorously. "Your muscle gives. Maybe it's just water and fat."

"My strength is marvelous, considering what we're getting to eat lately," he said. "The others can't cook worth a damn. The only decent food this camp has had was during the week you and I did the cooking."

"Chiefly me, as I recall."

"Well, yes. I made policy, you carried it out."

"Which means you sat in a camp chair and popped a dishtowel at my behind while I cooked the sausages and eggs."

"I was engaged in creative thought," Franklin said, scratching his head. "I keep wondering where I'd be now if I had minded my old father and had kept out of this pauper's field of anthropology. I have a talent for engineering. I have in mind a project for making alcohol from the juniper berries out there in all those canyons."

"Have you thought of harnessing buzzard power?" Arabella asked, looking up toward a bird floating in the distant sky.

Disdaining her comment, he went on. "I'm looking for a dissertation topic, but there isn't a good one around here. I want to cause an upheaval in anthropology. Maybe I could show that *Homo sapiens* evolved in the Americas."

"Yes, and maybe you could show that Anasazi mythology was piped in on cable TV."

"Lord, you don't take me seriously," Franklin protested. "That's what comes of a fellow being the camp wit and trying to keep everybody's spirits up. When it's time for serious talk, nobody believes him."

Then abruptly, before Arabella could say more, he added, "How come you and me don't set up my little tent across the wash and sleep together?"

A minor tremor of triumph ran through Arabella. She had intuited this moment, had willed it, from the day she had recognized that Franklin was honoring her with the lion's share of his banter. Unmarried and thirty, she had a flat belly and trim thighs; she wore the standard camp dress of boots, jeans, and halter; each morning she combed her hair into a long tail and tied it at the nape of her neck. She found herself extraordinarily attracted to Franklin's black, curly hair, undisciplined even after combing, his ruddy cheeks and chin, his perpetual smile of satiric good humor. Franklin was garrulous, inveterately drawn to any incongruity, and abounding in appetites. He seemed to be limitlessly educated. He was an unquestioning believer in science and had, in Arabella's judgment, a kind of secular innocence, an enviable ability to suppose that whatever he did was good.

Three ancient cottonwoods spread over the tents and tables of the camp. Directly across the wash from the camp was a hillock covered by sagebrush where Arabella supposed Franklin meant to pitch his tent. It seemed an excessively public place. She had imagined that making love with him would be an occasional matter, something done spontaneously and passionately in the privacy of a remote ravine. Despite an abundance of irreverent talk in the camp, she had seen no pairing off among the graduate students. As for Dr. Muhlestein, he seemed asexual; he puffed stolidly on his pipe, completely absorbed in the plotting and cataloging of the dig and its artifacts. Sleeping in Franklin's tent struck Arabella, on this first consideration, as a too casual, too public declaration of her concupiscence; yet the offer was not something she could let slip by.

"How about it?" Franklin said. "Let's bust out of the dorm tents. Jack snores anyhow."

"Look what courting has come to!" Arabella said. "All you have in mind is getting away from Jack's snoring."

"You want romance? OK, here's a poem: Arabella, Arabella, I'm sure glad you ain't a fella."

"That stinks."

"Arabello, Arabello, you have turned my heart to Jell-O."

"Knock it off."

Franklin stretched out his hand, opened his mouth pretentiously, and bellowed out lines from *La Traviata*. When he stopped, he said, "That was dedicated to my new tentmate."

"Whom you have just killed with an overdose of decibels."

"I continue with a catalog of your charms. You are healthy, you have pearly white teeth, you are descended from sturdy pioneer stock. It would be an honor to go to bed with a daughter of the Utah pioneers."

"And you," she retorted, "are descended from the prince of darkness. You are the very essence of perversity."

A gratified smile came over Franklin's face. "An apt description. But let's not digress from praises of your splendid person. There is about you a mathematical perfection which demonstrates that the human gene has a passion for geometry. I draw lines from here to here to here"—his finger traced imaginary lines between her navel and the points where her halter covered her nipples—"and, voilà, we find a perfect equilateral triangle. A marvel of nature!" He leaned back and squinted to get perspective, then made as if to measure the triangle with the span of his hand.

"Keep your lewd hands off me."

"Lewd! Reverent would be a better word. Besides, lubricity and lasciviousness are the oil of the living engine: they keep society renewed. The next generation does not come from a cabbage patch, as you may have thought."

He placed his hand over her mouth to stifle her reply. "Stop, cease, desist!" he said. "The camp jester is herewith banished; it is Franklin speaking to you. I knew from the first time I saw you that it would be easy to fall in love with you."

Arabella eyed him dubiously. "I would rather not hear things like that."

"What do you want to hear?"

"Love is a word that doesn't clarify anything."

"OK, no more about it," he agreed. "Is it all right, then? Shall I set up my tent tonight?"

"Not tonight. Next week."

"Next week! Let's compromise. Tomorrow."

"Wednesday."

"Day after tomorrow."

"OK," she said. "Day after tomorrow."

Franklin shook his head in perplexity. "The whims of the female sex!" He elevated his eyes. "O Heaven, observe my patience in the face of ignoble treatment."

"You'll be struck down for blasphemy," she said.

When Franklin left, Arabella returned to her work on the floor of the kiva. She bent again over the emerging ceremonial dish. Ordinarily, as she pried at the resisting soil and brushed away its loosened particles, she fell into a harmony with the artifact; she round a rhythm, an unthinking cooperation of her attentive eyes, her accurate hands, her tenacious will. In certain mystical moments she became a creator, a sculptor who from the melded mass of soil and buried artifact declared the original shape of the past and returned it to the dawning moment of the present. But on this day, her mind taken up by Franklin's proposition, she could not find the rhythm of her work. She circled about the fact of her courage: it was incredible that she had held steady, had been calm, a little coy, and able to parry his banter. Fragments of passionate fantasy jostled in her mind. She saw herself with Franklin. They stood in the middle of the wash late at night, watched by the bright stars. He embraced her, unfastened her halter and fondled her breasts, as men were pleased to do.

"I have this book," she said to him. "It says that when a bride and groom go to bed for the first time . . ."

"Who's a bride and groom?" Franklin protested.

"According to this book, which I bought last spring in Salt Lake City, and which, really, you might want to read—"

"Hell, Arabella," Franklin groaned, "this isn't any time to be talking about a book. I know what to do."

"I mean that when a woman has had no experience, the man is cautioned to go easy. The first time."

"God, you're a virgin," Franklin said with reverence for the gift she was giving him.

Abandoning her reserve, she drove her fantasy to lush intensity. They lay naked on top of sleeping bags in Franklin's tent. They explored each other completely and ardently, and then, making love, they triumphed.

In the floor of the kiva near where Arabella squatted was a small, rock-lined excavation. It was a *sipapu,* a representation of the passage through which, in Anasazi creation myths, the first human beings had passed into the light of day from the dark, gestating caverns of the earth's womb. It was, as Dr. Muhlestein had said one evening at supper, an Anasazi fertility symbol, a celebration of the human vagina. Arabella was both attracted and repelled by the *sipapu.* It looked like no part of the female body, yet at times, as she had worked in the kiva, it had served as an aphrodisiac, impelling her erotic fantasies. Hidden away in this ancient place of pagan worship, connected to the inscrutable earth in wild holiness, it seemed to warrant rebellious desire. But at other times the sacred *sipapu* was a reproach, and now, as Arabella's mood shifted, she remembered grimly that her ovaries, her womb, her vagina were not hers to dispose of in pleasure; they belonged to God, a sacred territory which Arabella held in virginal stewardship.

She remembered a night in May less than a month before she had come to the canyon country. She had been home from the university for the weekend. Her mother had called her into the kitchen for milk and cookies. Her father was there, too, and the three of them, dressed in bathrobes, talked aimlessly. After a while her father turned off the kitchen lights to show the moonlight in the backyard. Through the screen of the patio door they saw, washed in white, the lawn, the flower borders, the oak thicket, the tangle of rose and pyracantha bushes at the edge of the property.

In an apologetic tone her mother said, "It seems like a mother shouldn't be asking for promises when her daughter is thirty."

"Promises?"

"Smell those plum blossoms from up the way," her mother said. "We used to walk up to Jorey's orchard with you kids. That stopped when they built the subdivision above us. We ought to drive around sometime and see the trees, I guess."

"They're relics," her father said. "Jorey doesn't cultivate his trees anymore. They just grow wild."

"What kind of promises?" Arabella insisted.

Her mother reached across the table and stroked the back of her hand. "Forgive me for being so fearful. Please promise me that you will never be with a man until you have prayed to see if it is all right."

"To be with a man?"

"I mean to have an intimacy."

"To have sex," Arabella said belligerently.

"Yes," her mother said. "Because if it is right, you will know it after you have prayed."

"That seems like an odd thing to say to me," Arabella said. "I'm not thinking of getting married."

"I wish you liked somebody enough to get married," her mother said. "That Jerald Henson was a nice man."

"Gol, Mom, let's not go into that again. I wouldn't want him under any circumstance."

"Well, never mind. What I wanted to say is that, with the loose way things are in the world, anybody needs protection. If you pray about it, you won't fall."

Arabella's mother went to the refrigerator, returning with a container. She set her husband's glass into the strip of moonlight on the table and poured him more milk. An accusation had been made, Arabella saw; yet she could not maintain the indignation she had felt when her mother had first spoken. She was frightened to acknowledge the uncanny precision with which her parents had intuited her intention.

"Chastity is a serious thing," her mother said.

"I know."

"Even married people have to be careful. I mean with each other. You have to have a consideration for each other in the way you dress, and you shouldn't do things that will provoke each other before the Spirit tells you it is proper to make love."

Arabella held the lip of the ceremonial dish with firm fingers while she pried a pebble from its underside; then she paused to trowel the gathered detritus into a bucket. Caught in the mood of that May night, she had worked in the kiva with a mechanical inattention. She recognized now that the cookies and milk had not been coincidental; her parents, usually reticent, had been coerced into an extreme action. She had not thought of them for days in this hot, sun-filled wilderness, but now, in the aftermath of Franklin's proposition, she again felt their drastic pull. She recognized that they had believed her to be on the edge of disaster: the unprecedented allusion to their own intimate life and the embarrassing presence of her father were evidence of that. Arabella could not remember having ever heard from either of them the slightest admission that they knew each other sexually, though the fact was visible enough in their ten children. Her father and mother were amazingly alike: reverent in the extreme, scrupulous in keeping the commandments, and doubtful of their salvation. Arabella loathed them for their subservience, yet she also loved them, needed their approval, and understood perfectly that God was to be feared. She sat back for a moment on the floor of the kiva to relieve the ache of her squatting legs. She remembered the grieving good-by which had hung in the air of the moon-spotted kitchen. Again she wavered, had second thoughts, and wondered whether she could reconcile herself to God's will. And again she marveled at her unrelenting, desperate compulsion to persist in her freedom—to the point of perdition, if necessary. ▪

Born in Durango, Colorado, in 1924, H. Jackson Clark grew up on the Colorado Plateau, where he worked as a trader for over forty years among Navajo artisans. As a child, he came to know such colorful southwestern figures as John and Louisa Wetherill, Mike Goulding, Jesse Nusbaum, and archaeologist Earl Morris. Later in life he befriended western novelist Louis L'Amour. In 1993, he recorded his experiences of living a life of "stark contrasts" in *The Owl in Monument Canyon and Other Stories from Indian Country.* In this loving account of an excursion with his father to a ruin on the Ute Mountain Reservation southwest of Durango, Clark describes the sense of care and respect all visitors should have for the ancient places of the Southwest.

f r o m

The Owl in Monument Canyon

H . J A C K S O N C L A R K

My dad and I walked single file through the sagebrush and scrub juniper trees until we came to the canyon rim. One moment we couldn't see the canyon for the underbrush, and the next instant we were on the edge of a three- or four-hundred-foot vertical cliff. I moved close to him and brushed against his leg. Heights scared me. I felt as though some unseen hand was about to reach up from the canyon to drag me over the side.

Dad touched my shoulder reassuringly. "It's okay. You'll just have to learn to trust your senses and your footing. Plant your feet solidly on the rock, and don't lean too far over. You're not going to fall and we are not going to do anything dangerous."

Before we had left home that morning my mother had warned me, "Now, you know how Dad is. He'll want to climb the cliffs and get down in that canyon. I worry that you might fall. Watch out for rattlesnakes, too." Mother was a worrier, especially if she wasn't leading the group. If she'd been along on this day she'd have urged me on. I'd heard her encourage me many times. "Come on. You can do it."

I was eleven years old on this bright Sunday morning in the fall of 1935. The two of us were out on the Mountain Ute Indian Reservation about twenty miles south of Mesa Verde National Park. We had crossed into the reservation through a gate in the barbed wire fence that separated Indian land from private land and hadn't seen a single car or human being since. It was always like this. Nobody ever went to this remote area. It seemed like we had the whole place to ourselves. I could almost feel the silence it was so calm. Dead calm.

Dad and I stood and talked for a few moments. He said, "I think it is so strange that most people in Durango don't even know about this canyon country. If you tell your friends about it, don't let on where it is. Let's keep it as our secret." I agreed. It was nice to have a secret place, and both of us wanted to keep it that way.

The lead gray peaks of the La Plata Mountains stood out like sentries silhouetted against the blue sky. They dominated the landscape far to the north of us. We could see tinges of autumn gold on the aspen trees high on the mountains. An early snowstorm had dusted the peaks with a sprinkling of white powder like sugar on a cake. The weather was warm and I wore only a long-sleeved cotton shirt. Dad wore a hat, gray gabardine slacks, a jacket with big, baggy pockets, a Pendleton shirt, and necktie.

He always wore a tie, even when he worked in the yard at home. He was a very proper Dude, a gentleman, a city man who understood the outdoors, equally at ease in a fancy restaurant or the wilderness. I don't think I appreciated his versatility until it was too late and he was gone.

We perched on a slab of sandstone. Dad used his binoculars to scan the canyon wall on the north side of the canyon. It must have been more than a half mile from where we were to the north rim. He looked up and down the canyon for several minutes and then handed them to me. "Here, take the field glasses. Now, look over there. Do you see those two good-sized ruins high in the cliff, right under the La Platas? It looks like there are ten to fifteen windows in the one on the left, and a few more in the ruin on the right. Do you see them?"

I spotted the ruins in the glasses. They loomed large and mysterious against the backdrop of the cliff, an ancient city hanging on a steep wall as though it had been pasted there.

"How did the cliff dwellers get up there? I don't see any trails, do you?" Dad took the glasses from me and looked toward the ruins.

"I think that the trail, handholds and all, has broken off and fallen into the canyon. You can see the big trees down there in the bottom. There's a spring there. That was probably their water supply. Let's get the map out and see if we can locate the ruins on the map."

Dad always thought that we might be able to spot a certain large ruin, but as on previous days we hadn't found it. A cattle rancher had told him that in the head of Johnson, Weber, or Mancos canyon there was a huge ruin not shown on the map. There are always rumors of "lost cities," but we never found one.

We walked away from the canyon rim and decided to explore a small canyon branch that lay a short distance to the west. The little canyon came to a distinct V, and a large stand of evergreen trees grew alongside the cliff. Dad stopped and looked down into the canyon, then he said, almost in a whisper, "Look! Down there! There's a pretty little ruin almost hidden in the trees."

Sure enough, there it was, a ruin with about ten doors or windows facing southwest, perched on a ledge in this canyon. Dad was excited. "Gosh, we have been by here several times and I didn't see it until now."

We decided we'd try to get a closer look and after a while found a precarious trail down the watercourse at the head of the small canyon. We scrambled over the rocks, slid down the talus, and made our way to the base of the cliff directly below the ruin. Then it was at least twenty feet above us. We looked for handholds or some means of access, but found none. A slender dead spruce tree leaned against the canyon wall near the ruin.

Dad looked at me and asked, "Do you think you could shinny up that dead tree and get in the ruin? I'll make sure it won't slip." Mother's words came ringing back in my ears, "You know how your Dad is. . . ."

"Yeah, I can do it, if you watch me."

"I'll watch you. Just take your time. Here, use my gloves, and I'll steady the tree." Actually, I wasn't at all sure, but after a few deep breaths I started up. It was surprisingly easy. The tree was solid, the stubs of branches provided handholds and footholds. In a few minutes I stood on the ledge next to the ruin. But when I looked down I got queasy. It was a long, long way down.

Dad cupped his hands around his mouth and shouted, "You're doing fine. Take your time and get a firm footing. You're probably the first human being to go in that ruin in five hundred years." I edged my way around the ledge. I tried to stand but I felt safer crawling on my hands and knees. I poked my head into a room. It was dark as a coal mine. I couldn't see a thing. The entire ruin was still in the morning shadow.

I called down to Dad, "It's dark in there. We should have brought a flashlight."

"Well, I just happen to have my little penlight." I might have known. He was always prepared.

"I've got a ball of string in my camera bag," he shouted. "I'll tie it onto a rock and toss it up to you. Then I'll tie the penlight to it and you can pull it up." A perfect solution.

In a few minutes I had the penlight and crawled back toward the dark, deserted room. It was spooky. I hoped that I would not look into the leering face of a skeleton, or find a lurking wild animal.

"What do you see? Are there any pots or baskets in there?"

I looked around and saw only a few Anasazi corn cobs and rat droppings.

"The room's empty, and it doesn't look like anyone has been here before."

He was thrilled. "How does it feel being the first person in that room for hundreds of years?" Before I had a chance to answer, the tiny beam from my penlight hit a mark on the back wall of the cave.

"It feels good, but I'm not the first person to be here. There's a smoked marking on the back wall, like someone had a torch. It's hard to read, but I think it says, 'J.W.N.Y. Oct 1910.'" Someone had been there twenty-five years before.

I looked in all the other rooms, maybe five or six in number, and then climbed down the tree. We had a good laugh about the whole episode. Dad said, "It's getting harder and harder to be the first person anywhere. But at least you are one of the first. I wonder who J.W. was and if N.Y. means New York. J.W. may be John Wetherill. He and his family explored most of these canyons after they discovered the ruins in Mesa Verde. I'd like to know." I don't know any more now than I did then, nor have I been back to what we named "J.W. House."

Anasazi ruins fascinated my father. He loved to spot "mounds" that disclosed where surface structures had been. Quite often as we drove or hiked through the desert country, we'd find a site that could be confirmed by pottery sherds. We never missed an opportunity to visit a new "discovery" and learn as much as we could.

Jesse Nusbaum, who was superintendent of Mesa Verde National Park for two tours of duty during the 1930s, was a special friend of my parents. We spent many wonderful days exploring hidden canyons in the park. After he was transferred to Santa Fe we visited him many times. I'm sure that Nusbaum sparked Dad's interest in Chaco Canyon, particularly the magnificent Pueblo Bonito and some of the lesser ruins that Nusbaum felt had great ceremonial significance.

He also told us to be sure to see the large slab of rock that had detached from the cliff behind Pueblo Bonito. Centuries before white men first saw Chaco Canyon, the inhabitants of the Pueblo had attempted to shore up the one-hundred-thousand-ton rock that threatened to smash the pueblo. It was called Threatening Rock. Throughout Navajoland Pueblo Bonito was known as Tse-biya hani ahi, Place of the Braced-Up Cliff. The National Park Service did what little they could to stabilize the monstrous rock by attaching cables to the rock and anchoring them into the cliff at the top. I suppose the theory was that if it slid away from the bottom it would do much less damage than if it toppled over.

All efforts to stabilize Threatening Rock ended on the afternoon of January 22, 1941, when it buckled and fell, crushing a portion of lovely Pueblo Bonito to smithereens.

A group of Navajos who were working on ruin stabilization witnessed the event. According to accounts, many feared that the end of the world was near because the rock had fallen. Sacred corn pollen and turquoise were scattered in a semicircle around Pueblo Bonito in an attempt to placate the Great Spirit who had allowed Tse-biya hani ahi to fall. The collapse of Threatening Rock also had a profound effect on my father, enough that he sent me a Western Union telegram in care of New Mexico Military Institute, where I was in school. The event was well covered in the newspapers, but he didn't want me to miss hearing about it.

Dad knew most of the Park Service people, who often told him about large, unexcavated ruins. Many of the traders on the reservation shared his enthusiasm. We often stopped at reservation stores to get directions to some remote canyon. We always carried a shovel in the trunk of the car to dig ourselves out of an arroyo or mudhole. One day I suggested that we dig for pottery in a large surface ruin near Mancos Canyon.

"I don't mind searching for ruins," Dad replied, "and it's okay to pick up pieces of broken pottery and to look for arrowheads, but I don't want to dig. I don't know anything about it. If we dig down into a pot we'd break it. Let's leave that type of thing to the archaeologists. If we found a pot, what would we do with it?"

Today there is a great public outcry against pothunters in the Southwest. Many priceless prehistoric pieces have been found and carried off to be sold for astronomical prices. It is a major threat to many archaeological sites. I'm proud of my father, who recognized his lack of knowledge and refused to dig, way back in the 1930s. ▪

✳

Poet and short story writer Simon Ortiz is a member of the Acoma Pueblo community. He was educated first in reservation schools and later at the University of New Mexico. Among his several books, *Woven Stone* (1992), from which the poems reprinted here are taken, is a powerful compendium of his interests and work. Ortiz emphasizes in his poetry the impact and integrity of the oral tradition and the deeply felt relationship to place and heritage that must form the basis for sound and healthy human experience. In these poems he affirms the continuity between contemporary Pueblos and their ancestors—those often misnamed the Anasazi—whose artifacts and even bodily remains have often been treated like museum commodities by mainstream American society. Ortiz may finally be suggesting that only a profound alienation from the land and from history could account for the creation of a "National Sacrifice Area."

"A Designated National Park"

SIMON   ORTIZ

Montezuma Castle in the Verde Valley, Arizona.

DESIGNATED FEDERAL RECREATION FEE AREA
ENTREE FEES
$1.00 FOR 1 DAY PERMIT
MONTEZUMA CASTLE ONLY INCLUDES PURCHASER
OR OTHERS WITH HIM IN PRIVATE NON-COMMERCIAL
VEHICLE
$0.50 FOR 1 DAY PERMIT
MONTEZUMA CASTLE ONLY INCLUDES PURCHASER
IN COMMERCIAL VEHICLE

AUTHORIZED
BY THE LAND AND WATER CONSERVATION FUND
ACT OF 1965

This morning
I have to buy a permit to get back home.

Birds,
they must have been,
these people.
"Thank you for letting me come to see you."
I tell them that.

Secreted in my cave,
look at the sun.
Shadows on sycamore
a strange bird and a familiar bird.
River, hear the river.
What it must be,
that pigeon sound.

Hear
in my cave, sacred song.
Morning feeling, sacred song.
We shall plant today.

PRESS BUTTON

(on a wooden booth)
            "For a glimpse into the lives
            of these people who lived here."

Pressing the button, I find
painted sticks and cloth fragments
in a child's hand,
her eyelashes still intact.
Girl, my daughter, my mother,
softly asleep.
They have unearthed you.

59TH CONGRESS OF THE UNITED STATES OF AMERICA
AT THE FIRST SESSION,
BEGUN AND HELD AT THE CITY OF WASHINGTON

ON MONDAY, THE FOURTH DAY OF DECEMBER,
ONE THOUSAND, NINE HUNDRED AND FIVE.
AN ACT
FOR THE PRESERVATION OF AMERICAN ANTIQUITIES.

And a last sign post quote:

BUILT SOMETIME BETWEEN
1200 AD AND 1350 AD
ABANDONED BY AD 1450.

s/The Sinagua Indians

SEE MUSEUM FOR MORE INFORMATION

f r o m

"Our Homeland, A National Sacrifice Area"

. . .

Pueblo Bonito in Chaco Canyon
is maintained by the U.S. Park Service.
Northwards, 65 miles away,
is Aztec National Monument.
To the northwest, another 85 miles,
is Mesa Verde National Park.
The park service has guided tours,
printed brochures, clean rest rooms,
and the staff is friendly, polite,
and very helpful.
You couldn't find a better example
of Americanhood anywhere.
The monuments, or ruins
as they are called, are very well kept
by the latest technology
in preserving antiquity.

At Mesa Verde, not long ago,
they had Esther in a glass case.
She was a child, born

from a woman, 1000 years ago.
The U.S. Park Service
was reluctant to let her go
when some Indian people
demanded her freedom.
Government bureaucrats
said Indians were insensitive
to U.S. heritage.
    For years, they sold
postcards of Esther.
Maybe they still do.
By pushing buttons, thousands
of yearly tourists to these places
can get an audio-taped narration.

See Museum For More Information.
. . .

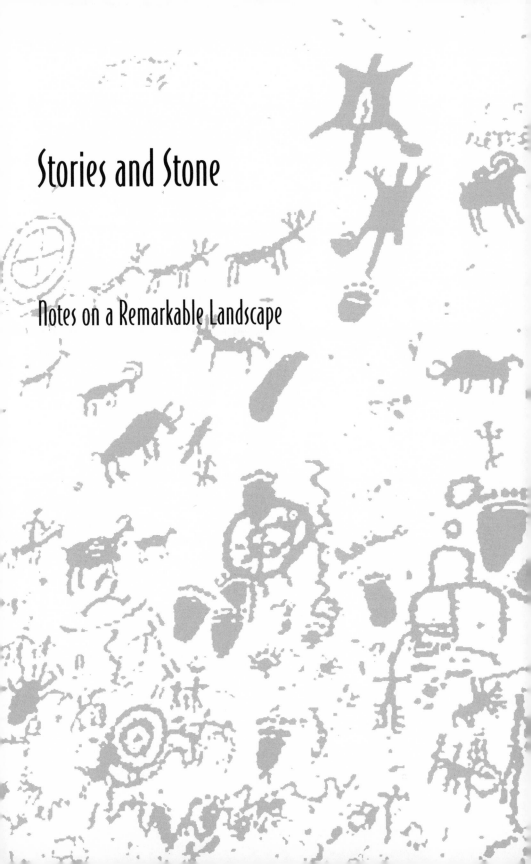

Stories and Stone

Notes on a Remarkable Landscape

No anthology of Southwestern writing is complete without Edward Abbey. *Desert Solitaire* (1968), a collection of integrated essays narrating Abbey's experiences as a ranger in southern Utah's Arches National Park, is loosely modeled on Thoreau's *Walden*. The book quickly became a classic of American nature writing and established Abbey as both a careful observer of the desert landscape and a forceful advocate for its preservation. Other Abbey essays are collected in *The Journey Home: Some Words in Defense of the American West* (1977) and *Abbey's Road* (1979), and he has written a half dozen novels, the most influential of which is *The Monkey Wrench Gang* (1975), a sprawling and wildly comic novel about a lovable and unruly group of environmental anarchists bent on blowing up Glen Canyon Dam in Arizona and freeing the Colorado River. Within the often improbable humor of *The Monkey Wrench Gang* lies Abbey's central vision, the prophetic conviction that technology, development, and unrestrained population growth is on the verge of destroying western wilderness and the freedom of individuals.

The essay "The Great American Desert" is representative of Abbey's often ironic style. Although he advises inexperienced readers that the Great American Desert "is an awful place," filled with lurking snakes, terrifying insects, poisoned water, and a host of other gruesome dangers, he speaks eloquently of his own love for that "grim ground." Why go to such a place? The close of the essay, included here, provides Abbey's answer. As he scans the spare landscape, he realizes again that the desert is a place less defined by human landmarks—even ancient ruins—than it is by the vast spaces and transcendent silence of wilderness.

---

f r o m

"The Great American Desert"

EDWARD ABBEY

Well then, why indeed go walking into the desert, that grim ground, that bleak and lonesome land where, as Genghis Khan said of India, "the heat is bad and the water makes men sick"?

Why the desert, when you could be strolling along the golden beaches of California? Camping by a stream of pure Rocky Mountain spring water in colorful Colorado? Loafing through a laurel slick in the misty hills of North Carolina? Or getting your head mashed in the greasy alley behind the Elysium Bar and Grill in Hoboken, New Jersey? Why the desert, given a world of such splendor and variety?

A friend and I took a walk around the base of a mountain up beyond Coconino County, Arizona. This was a mountain we'd been planning to circumambulate for years. Finally we put on our walking shoes and did it. About halfway around this mountain, on the third or fourth day, we paused for a while—two days—by the side of a stream, which the Navajos call Nasja because of the amber color of the water. (Caused perhaps by juniper roots—the water seems safe enough to drink.) On our second day there I walked down the stream, alone, to look at the canyon beyond. I entered the canyon and followed it for half the afternoon, for three or four miles, maybe, until it became a gorge so deep, narrow and dark, full of water and the inevitable quagmires of quicksand, that I turned around and looked for a way out. A route other than the way I'd come, which was crooked and uncomfortable and buried—I wanted to see what was up on top of this world. I found a sort of chimney flue on the east wall, which looked plausible, and sweated and cursed my way up through that until I reached a point where I could walk upright, like a human being. Another 300 feet of scrambling brought me to the rim of the canyon. No one, I felt certain, had ever before departed Nasja Canyon by that route.

But someone had. Near the summit I found an arrow sign, three feet long, formed of stones and pointing off into the north toward those same old purple vistas, so grand, immense, and mysterious, of more canyons, more mesas and plateaus, more mountains, more cloud-dappled sun-spangled leagues of desert sand and desert rock, under the same old wide and aching sky.

The arrow pointed into the north. But what was it pointing *at?* I looked at the sign closely and saw that those dark, desert-varnished stones had been in place for a long, long, time; they rested in compacted dust. They must have been there for a century at least. I followed the direction indicated and came promptly to the rim of another canyon and a drop-off straight down of a good 500 feet. Not that way, surely. Across this canyon was nothing of any unusual interest that I could see—only the familiar sun-blasted sandstone, a few scrubby clumps of blackbrush and prickly pear, a few acres of nothing where only a lizard could graze, surrounded by a few square miles of more nothingness interesting chiefly to horned toads. I returned to the arrow and checked again, this time with field glasses, looking away for as far as my aided eyes could see toward the north, for ten, twenty, forty miles into the distance. I studied the scene with care, looking for an ancient Indian ruin, a significant cairn, perhaps an abandoned mine, a hidden treasure of some inconceivable wealth, the mother of all mother lodes. . . .

But there was nothing out there. Nothing at all. Nothing but the desert. Nothing but the silent world.

That's why.

⁕

The remarkable writing career of Wallace Stegner, which spanned some fifty years beginning with his first novel in 1937, brought deserved national recognition, such as the Pulitzer Prize for fiction for *Angle of Repose* in 1971, and established Stegner as a genuinely wise and inspirational voice within western regional literature and thinking. His call for a "society to match the scenery" speaks to everyone who loves the West.

Stegner's most significant work of nonfiction, *Beyond the Hundredth Meridian* (1954) is a far-reaching examination of the human, conceptual challenges of the West. The book focuses on the life of John Wesley Powell, who for Stegner embodies a western ethos. It is characteristic of Stegner that in his discussion of the ancient people of the Southwest, he places their culture in the largest possible historical and philosophical context.

f r o m

Beyond the Hundredth Meridian

WALLACE STEGNER

It is the Plateau Province, comprising all of eastern and southern Utah, part of western Colorado, and part of northern New Mexico and Arizona, that concerns us, since it is what primarily concerned Powell. Its boundaries are precise on the north and west, less certain on east and south. Essentially the province follows an ancient shoreline of Mesozoic times, when the Great Basin, the Wasatch, and part of what is now Arizona were islands or parts of the mainland, and what is now the Plateau Province was a great loop of sea. The region of plateaus with which the Powell Survey was chiefly concerned reaches from the Uinta Mountains southwestward to the Colorado River. It is mainly in Utah but includes the slice of Arizona north of the Grand Canyon, and it laps over on the east into Colorado and on the west into Nevada. It is scenically the most spectacular and humanly the least usable of all our regions.

Here geological and human history have at least a poetic similarity. Here the earth has had a slow, regular pulse. It rose and fell for millions of years under Carboniferous, Permian, Triassic oceans, under Cretaceous seas, under the fresh-water lakes of the Eocene, before it was heaved up and exposed to rain and frost and running water and the sandblast winds. Mountains were carved out of its great tables and domes, river systems cut into it and formed canyons, elevations were weathered and carried away. What had accumulated pebble by pebble and grain by grain, cemented with lime and silica, folding into itself the shells of sea life, scales of fishes, the compacted houses of corals, began to disintegrate again. Vast cyclic changes have left only traces. Though the geological record in the Plateau Province is probably as clear as it is anywhere on earth, the boundary between ignorance and knowledge, between speculation and certainty, is often no more than a line of ancient fracture almost obliterated, or an enigmatic unconformity between two layers of rock, or a slight but significant change from salt water to brackish water fossils.

Human history in that country is almost as tentative, and to our foreshortening eyes nearly as long. A vague sort of knowledge, with plenty of speculation to accompany it, reaches back to that all-but-Eozoic time when the Ho-ho-kam in the southwestern desert and the Anasazi among the plateaus built their mortared houses and granaries, and lived for certain years whose remoteness is measurable by the fading radioactivity of their dead campfires, and were driven out by certain causes including drouths known to us by the starved growth rings of ancient trees. Gradually, over several generations, we have sorted out a kind of stratigraphy of the plateau peoples: Basket-Maker I, Basket-Maker II, Post-Basket-Maker, Pre-Pueblo, Pueblo I, II, or III. We can distinguish among their artifacts and compare what we know of them with what we know of their cultural heirs, the Pueblos, including the Hopi and Zuñi. We can mark the unconformities between strata of human history, and knowledge broadens down, not quite from precedent to precedent, but from inference to inference, toward historical time. By the same sort of taxonomy that classifies and groups and separates fossils, we classify and group and separate peoples and their leavings, and read history of a kind from them. Though we may be often and for long periods on solid ground, we are never quite out of sight of the half-effaced shorelines of speculation. Knowledge extends in promontories and bays; or to put it vertically rather than horizontally, the strata from remote to recent never lie so unbroken that we cannot find some line of unconformity where the imagination must make a leap. There are so many horizons, geological and human, where the evidence is missing or incomplete. ■

Imagine a wild and uneven band of Anishinabeg Indian "clowns" from the upper Midwest traveling across a ravaged and postapocalyptic North America stalled by environmental destruction and the depletion of fossil fuels. Along the way they find cultural fraud and brutality. They come face to face with the "terminal creeds" of Euro-American culture that deny adaptation and change and undermine indigenous oral tradition. They end up in New Mexico, at Pueblo Bonito in Chaco Canyon.

Gerald Vizenor's darkly comic—and by some accounts postmodern—novel *Bearheart: The Heirship Chronicles,* was first published in 1978. It makes *Road Warrior* look derivative. Vizenor's characters—Proude Cedarfair, Rosina, and Inawa Biwide—move freely between ordinary and mythic time, seeking Pueblo Bonito as a doorway into the Fourth World where, as mythic Vision Bears, they are released from terminal creeds forever within the infinite variety of ever-changing storytelling. Originally from Minnesota, Vizenor is an enrolled member of the White Earth Anishinabeg (Ojibwa). He has published more than twenty-five books and teaches at the University of California at Berkeley. Vizenor understands that storytelling creates community. Included here is *Bearheart*'s redemptive close.

f r o m

Bearheart: The Heirship Chronicles

GERALD VIZENOR

Their collective vision came from the mountains near the mission ruins. The two had walked in silence there for several weeks and then one afternoon while sleeping in the sun under the junipers a giant bear came to them and told them to follow their vision of him to the ancient ruins of the pueblos. Dreaming together the two pilgrims traveled in magical flight over the mountains and across rivers and the divide. At Pueblo Bonito the vision bear told the two pilgrims to enter the fourth world as bears. When their bodies changed shapes and began to float through the corner window toward the rising winter solstice sun the crows chirred and hopped through the stone frame. The shadows of the clown crows awakened the two from their bear vision.

"There is the vision window," said Inawa Biwide, pointing toward the southeast face of the pueblo. His words echoed between the massive sandstone mesas and returned to his ear stubs as his bear voice.

The crows swooped through the pueblo window while the two pilgrims passed from room to room to the window on the winter solstice. There the two waited for the first morning of the winter solstice when the sun reaches the most southern point and rises in the center of the window. The two dreamed and traveled in magical flight over and over with the vision bears from the mission ruins.

Rosina and Sister Eternal Flame visited with their new friend at the Walatowa Pueblo before leaving the mission ruins. The two women visited too long and were given blankets to keep them warm on the winter desert. The two traveled on the same course as the men. The women followed the voices of animals and birds. Listening for bobcats and desert cottontails, hognose skunks and cactus mice to lead them through the parched mountains and mesas across the desert. The two praised the living on the trail. The exotic saltcedar tamarisk and cottonwoods in the washes responded to their touch and voices. Rosina and Sister Eternal Flame spoke to grama grass and greasewood and rabbitbrush. The two dreamed during the cold nights about roaring bears ha ha ha haaa from the mountains.

Near White Horse the two women encountered three tribal medicine men who had been singing in a ritual hogan. It was the last morning of a ceremonial chant to balance the world with humor and spiritual harmonies. Evil had been turned under with the sunrise and their sacred voices. The good power of the dawn was attracted to their rituals. The first breath of dawn was inhaled to balance the world. While the old men were inhaling the dawn, the two women emerged from the desert. The men laughed and laughed knowing the power of their voices had restored good humor to the suffering tribes. Changing women was coming over the desert with the sun.

Near Chaco Canyon the clown crows flew out to meet them on the trail. Rosina was ecstatic, "the crows are here, the crows are here," she repeated while she waved her arms at them in flight. The crows swooped and flapped and landed on the shoulders and heads of the two women. The old men laughed and laughed and inhaled the dawn again. Perfect Crow nudged Rosina on the cheek while she walked. The women followed the wash to Pueblo Bonito where Pure Gumption was waiting. The two cuddled the animal and the birds and then followed the crows through the small sandstone rooms in the pueblo. In the corner room the two found cedar incense, a medicine bundle, a tribaltime watch and clothing.

That morning when the old men were inhaling the dawn and laughing during the first winter solstice sunrise, Proude Cedarfair and Inawa Biwide flew with vision bears ha ha ha haaa from the window on the perfect light into the fourth world.

Rosina touched the small white otter medicine bundle. The skin was tied with red and blue ribbons. When Sister Eternal Flame reached to open the bundle she was cautioned not to touch or look upon the contents. "His medicine has too much power to know without ceremonies . . . Proude will tell us when to open the bundle," said Rosina.

"But he is gone now now now," said Sister Flame. She leaned out the solstice window and watched the crows dropping like black hawks from the mesa rims.

"The crows know where they have gone."

"Pure Gumption will tell . . ."

"Tell us little gumption . . . Tell us where have they gone now?" Rosina asked as she cradled the animal in her arms. The small room was filled with a pale light from the golden aura.

The sun was setting over the mesas. Bright red and orange colors wheeled across the horizon. The desert turned cold. Jackrabbits and kangaroo rats leaped through their enormous shadows. Animal voices echoed down the mesas. The orange turned dark blue. The women built a small fire near the solstice window and waited for Proude and Inawa Biwide to return. The window loomed like one star in the constellations of sacred hunters and bears.

During the night while Rosina was sleeping, Sister Eternal Flame untied the red and blue ribbons on the white otter skin and opened the medicine bundle. She examined the contents. Two carved cedar figures. The deep eyes on the carved faces were glowing when she held them over the fire near the solstice window. Next she removed a rattle and wing bones from an eagle and white and blue plumes . . . The claws from a giant bear . . . Cedar incense and small fur pouches filled with herbal medicines and last she examined three cloth knots. One knot was filled with the ashes of the bishop. Sister Eternal Flame leaned closer to the fire to examine the cedar figures again. Their leer burned her vision.

Rosina awakened before sunrise. The clown crows were huddled in the corner of the room. Near the fire she saw the two cedar spirit figures and the contents of the medicine bundle. Staring out the solstice window she closed the bundle with the figures inside. Then she began to weep until the low winter sun burst in her vision through the center of the window.

Rosina heard the bears roaring ha ha ha haaa. She watched the sun chase shadows over the mesas. The bears roared from the rim of the mesa in the west ha ha ha haaaa. Then seconds later she heard the same roaring from the mesa in the east ha ha ha haaaa. Then the sound of the bears moved to the south and north in timeless flight. The bears were over time in the four directions.

"What is it? Roaring bears?" asked Sister Eternal Flame. Her vision was so weakened from the leering cedar figures that she could stare into the flaming sunrise without blinking.

Rosina took the mammoth parawoman into her small arms. The old men laughed and laughed on the sunrise with humor and tribal harmonies.

Late in the morning the two women were still holding each other in front of the corner winter solstice window. The clown crows flew to the rims of the mesas around the ancient pueblo. Pure Gumption was climbing the ancient stone stairs to the top of the north mesa where the sacred road led to rainbows and the sunrise.

On the third and last morning of the winter solstice sunrise through the pueblo window the two women heard the bears roaring again ha ha ha haaaa. In seconds, faster than birds could soar, the bears roared from the four directions ha ha ha haaaa. When the bears roared from the north there was a pause and then one final roar ha ha ha haaaa that echoed down the mesas and doubled backward through the corner window into the solstice room. The shadows of the two women trembled. Then the roaring trailed into the distance. That night several inches of snow covered the pueblo and surrounding mesas.

In the morning, Rosina found bear tracks in the snow. She followed the solstice bears from the pueblo up the sandstone stairs to the rim of the mesa. During the winter the old men laughed and laughed and told stories about changing woman and vision bears. ■

Along with N. Scott Momaday's *House Made of Dawn,* Leslie Marmon Silko's novel *Ceremony* (1977) ushered in the so-called Native American renaissance in American literature. *Ceremony* narrates the experience of a young Native American struggling to reintegrate himself into his culture after the traumatic and disorienting experience of World War II. Silko grew up at the Laguna Pueblo, attended a Bureau of Indian Affairs school, went on to the University of New Mexico, and began law school before turning full-time to writing and teaching. Like *Ceremony*, her montage collection *Storyteller* (1981) focuses on Native American experience in the Southwest. Her fascinating correspondence with author James Wright is recorded in *The Delicacy and Strength of Lace* (1986). Her most recent novel, *Almanac of the Dead*, a challenging and encyclopedic narrative about the breakdown of Euro-American civilization in the Americas and the revival of tribal cultures, perpetuates her reputation as the most influential Native American woman writer living today. Her 1986 essay "Landscape, History, and the Pueblo Imagination" suggests that the environment within which the ancient Puebloans lived was a simultaneously physical and spiritual place. Anyone who has been struck by the almost inexpressible beauty of the places in which the ancient ones chose to live will better understand their own feelings by reading Silko.

---

f r o m   From a High Arid Plateau in New Mexico

"Landscape, History, and the Pueblo Imagination"

LESLIE MARMON SILKO

You see that after a thing is dead, it dries up. It might take weeks or years, but eventually if you touch the thing, it crumbles under your fingers. It goes back to dust. The soul of the thing has long since departed. With the plants and wild game the soul may have already been borne back into bones and blood or thick green stalk and leaves. Nothing is wasted. What cannot be eaten by people or in some way used must then be left where other living creatures may benefit. What domestic animals or wild scavengers can't eat will be fed to the plants. The plants feed on the dust of these few remains.

The ancient Pueblo people buried the dead in vacant rooms or partially collapsed rooms adjacent to the main living quarters. Sand and clay used to construct the roof make layers many inches deep once the roof has collapsed. The layers of sand and clay make for easy gravedigging. The vacant room fills with cast-off objects and debris.

When a vacant room has filled deep enough, a shallow but adequate grave can be scooped in a far corner. Archaeologists have remarked over formal burials complete with elaborate funerary objects excavated in trash middens of abandoned rooms. But the rocks and adobe mortar of collapsed walls were valued by the ancient people. Because each rock had been carefully selected for size and shape, then chiseled to an even face. Even the pink clay adobe melting with each rainstorm had to be prayed over, then dug and carried some distance. Corn cobs and husks, the rinds and stalks and animal bones were not regarded by the ancient people as filth or garbage. The remains were merely resting at a mid-point in their journey back to dust. Human remains are not so different. They should rest with the bones and rinds where they all may benefit living creatures—small rodents and insects—until their return is completed. The remains of things—animals and plants, the clay and the stones—were treated with respect. Because for the ancient people all these things had spirit and being. The antelope merely consents to return home with the hunter. All phases of the hunt are conducted with love. The love the hunter and the people have for the Antelope People. And the love of the antelope who agree to give up their meat and blood so that human beings will not starve. Waste of meat or even the thoughtless handling of bones cooked bare will offend the antelope spirits. Next year the hunters will vainly search the dry plains for antelope. Thus it is necessary to return carefully the bones and hair, and the stalks and leaves to the earth who first created them. The spirits remain close by. They do not leave us.

The dead become dust, and in this becoming they are once more joined with the Mother. The ancient Pueblo People called the earth the Mother Creator of all things in this world. Her sister, the Corn Mother, occasionally merges with her because all succulent green life rises out of the depths of the earth.

Rocks and clay are part of the Mother. They emerge in various forms, but at some time before, they were smaller particles or great boulders. At a later time they may again become what they once were. Dust.

A rock shares this fate with us and with animals and plants as well. A rock has being or spirit, although we may not understand it. The spirit may differ from the spirit we know in animals or plants or in ourselves. In the end we all originate from the depths of the earth. Perhaps this is how all beings share in the spirit of the Creator. We do not know. ■

☼

I've been told that if you take Ann Zwinger's essays on Grand Gulch as a guidebook, you'll end up walking off a cliff accidently. Of course, the collection is not a guidebook but a graceful shaping of anthropology, the natural environment, and personal experience, richly illustrated by Zwinger's own meticulous drawings. Author of *Beyond the Aspen Grove, Run River Run,* and *A Desert Country Near the Sea,* Zwinger begins her 1978 *Wind in the Rock: The Canyonlands of Southeastern Utah* with a detailed and intricate description of Grand Gulch and reflections on its early inhabitants. "Before it all fell apart," she writes, "there must have been good living here." But be careful if you go.

f r o m

"Upper Grand Gulch"

ANN ZWINGER

High, high up on the walls at Junction Ruin are mud splats, which occur frequently at these sites, daubs of mud the size of a fifty-cent piece or so, obviously flipped with considerable force. Were they made by children playing, seeing who could get the highest? Or by someone practicing his aim, someone whose food supply depended upon the accurate coordination of eye and hand? There are also handprints, and they appear so often on the canyon walls that sometimes they seem more than innocent glee—a temporal notation? An indication of how many people lived here?

Lower, petroglyphs are chiseled into the wall surface, and in spite of a certain stiffness engendered by the technique, they frequently have great spirit and vitality. A coyote streaks across the sandstone, tail streaming out behind. Two mountain sheep, one above the other, face in opposite directions and seem just to have turned their heads. Some are more geometric: an elaborate yucca design is chipped into the shallow of a boulder, fitting into the irregular confines of the space. Many of these petroglyphs are faint, difficult to see; only in shadow, where the difference in depth can be seen, do they show off well. Full sun obliterates their borders and they are, for this reason, quite difficult to photograph; a flash simply washes out what are at best minimal contours. The alternative of chalking in the contours is an abomination and fortunately has only been done once or twice in Grand Gulch.

To the right, pecked into a dark varnished panel, are human figures, facing each other, dancing to the flute playing of Kokopelli, the priapic humpbacked flute player. Except in this instance (as often in Grand Gulch portrayals) he has no hump, but the flute playing is unmistakable and the dancing figures are lively. Kokopelli is a familiar figure in Anasazi art and a striking one. Associated with fertility as well as the hunt, he is sometimes represented as a locust, Locust being the musical and curing patron of present-day Hopi flute societies, and clan symbol for the Spider Clan.

Elsewhere in Grand Gulch Kokopelli appears as a combination Pied Piper and St. Francis of the canyons; he stands facing a mountain sheep that looks at him intently—mountain sheep are notoriously curious and I can well imagine one enticed to the sound of Kokopelli's flute. Perhaps Kokopelli enchants him, rendering him easier to kill. On another panel, far down the canyon, a butterfly-like shape takes flight near two atlatls while Kokopelli plays: a charm so that the atlatls would fly (as Pete suggests) "like a butterfly," their aim true, the hunting good?

Kokopelli's popularity is documented on countless walls, beginning in Basket-maker times, but the iconography most surely goes back to sources far to the south. Various medical reasons have been suggested to explain Kokopelli's distinctive attributes, such as bone tuberculosis, which could have caused both his hump and constant erection, a symptom of spinal irritation, but no reason seems as reasonable or as realistic as the postulation of an ancient ancestor, blanket full of belongings or trade goods slung over his shoulder, flute to his lips, wandering between villages like a medieval minstrel, likely a glamorous figure bringing news from exotic places, seducing a nubile female or two along the way. One anthropologist suggests that, in just such a pack as Kokopelli's, corn might have been carried from Mesoamerica.

Kokopelli is also a katchina—a deified ancestor—to the Hopi, and the ceremonies attached to his presence are to say the least ribald, emphasizing his sexual prowess. Such ceremonies are rarely performed now because their bawdy choreography was offensive to early white observers.

But the original Kokopelli still dances on the walls of Grand Gulch in full panoply. Panels with Kokopelli have an enchanting animation, a vivacity, that the hieratic figures lack. I can almost hear the music of his flute, a trifle reedy in sound, but chuckling and full of delightful phrasing, irreverent and rollickingly suggestive.

Other representations are painted on the walls: rabbit tracks, like big exclamation points, hop up the wall; ducks swim in the air, separated by vertical lines; figures, likely male, with hair bobs and necklaces, face the spectator—men wore their hair in bobs like two short pony tails sticking out to the sides, while Anasazi women often wore theirs short, trimming it to use in weaving.

But always the enigma: are they doodles? messages? The keen observation of natural forms indicates a far from primitive drawing ability, but the haphazard arrangement leaves the modern left-to-right mind at sea. Is there a connection between the dwelling site and the rock art, or were they done separately with no temporal connotations at all?

What I do sense in my own head, is that some cool morning, when there was time, an early resident took stone in hand and chipped out a record of something important—perhaps the visit of a trader from the South, or a ceremony, or the ducks he saw yesterday, or a dance—and left the figures for all to see. And then went on about his business. . . .

Shortly after 1300 the Anasazi were gone from these dwellings, leaving their maize in many of the granaries as if they were coming back. They were gone from the Cedar Mesa and the Grand Gulch Plateau, from the whole Four Corners area, having moved south to the drainage of the Little Colorado River or southeastward to the Rio Grande, where there was reliable water and where the Spaniards, looking for the mythical Seven Cities of Cibola, found their descendants nearly three centuries later in the pueblos we know today.

The fortified sites have been pointed to as evidence of invasion from the outside such as occasional raids by nomadic Athabascans coveting food crops of the Anasazi. Current evidence suggests that Athabascans did not reach the Southwest until the 1400s or 1500s. There is little evidence of warfare, and when the Anasazi moved, they went to open valleys in less defensible locations. The answer to the question of why they left does not lie in simplistic single factors but in a web of circumstances, complex and interwoven, psychological and sociological as well as environmental.

What seems the more likely reason for fortified dwellings and obscure granaries is internal squabbling and crop failure. Tree-ring evidence documents a deteriorating environment in the thirteenth century. The regular summer rains of Pueblo II times were less reliable. Pollen studies of granaries show a decrease in domestic pollens and an increase in wild food pollens. Crop failures must have become more prevalent, and corn fulfilled less and less of a role in diet, decreasing harvests implying lower nutrition.

At the beginning of such a period some "permanent borrowing" might easily have occurred in the interests of not starving, and with it a general air of mistrust; fortification-like entry walls would have protected both dwelling and granary. And many solitary granaries turn up on incredible ledges that must have required the agility of a spider to get to. Who knows what psychological stresses accompanied the diminution of nutrition, what distress followed the discovery that one's food was only as safe as the caching of it.

An emphatic change in effective moisture patterns had already occurred around A.D. 1150, and tree rings are much narrowed for the period between 1276 and 1299. Although tree rings generally are most responsive to lowered winter moisture, refined studies are beginning to show that other moisture was lacking also. Germination of seeds and young growth that depended more on stored soil moisture than spring rains were hampered by drier winters. When summer precipitation was abnormally low, crop failure resulted; when abnormally high, arroyo cutting took out alluvial flats and other near-stream acreage. Without winter moisture, springs and seeps would have been affected. Repeated flooding and/or overirrigation could have deposited so much alkali that the soil was no longer amenable to crops.

When the beneficent rains of summer came no more, a whole way of life was profoundly affected. And for twenty-three years, from 1276 to 1299, they endured devastating drought. But there had been droughts years before, some more severe than these, and one has to ask why this one destroyed such a resilient and resourceful population. Perhaps overpopulation and climate change worked together to defeat the tenacious Anasazi. The major population increase that began in Pueblo II times provided a larger labor force for agriculture and the time for specialized duties. But with limited acreages for farming, and more people farming, the less the return for each individual. The population became too large for the carrying capacity of the land under anything but optimal conditions—conditions which may well have existed in earlier Pueblo times. With a period of greater moisture such as that between 1000 and 1150 when summer rains were particularly beneficial, the Anasazi had spread far out into the marginal farmlands (some of which appear to have been abandoned some five hundred years previously because of insufficient moisture).

When population exceeds the carrying capacity of the land, there tends to be an increase in both the mortality rate and migration outward. One by one, family by family, people began to abandon outlying areas and drift southward and eastward. Without sufficient manpower to carry out all the previous functions of the settlement, those remaining were also forced to migrate. As a military wife who moved many times, I wonder if they left this canyon with reluctance, pausing, hand on doorway, for one last look inside, or if they simply went without a backward glance, leaving metate and mano, bowl and jug, point and chopper, thinking they would return.

Some may have joined larger settlements like Mesa Verde, where the environment remained favorable a little longer. But such a large site tolled its own death knell: the concentration of population could have come close to exhausting local resources, or, at the very least, put a heavy strain on them. Cutting massive numbers of trees for ever-increasing housing left bare ground open to erosion. With the removal of plant cover, small game would also have moved out of the area. Although the Anasazi utilized wild foods, replacing natural ground cover with a single crop, maize, opened that ground to more rapid erosion when that crop failed. Irrigation works would have been of little use without the water to supply them. Closer living conditions and meager sanitation could promote disease and sickness, and increase contact with disease-carrying animals such as rats and their plague fleas. By 1400 even the large population centers had disbanded. The Anasazi were no more.

And no one came here for nearly five hundred years to break the silence of the stones, to shadow the doorways that looked like empty eyes out on empty canyons, to sift the midden heaps drifted over with the silt of centuries or to peruse the petroglyphs staring down blindly from high walls—the time of comings and goings, all gone.

Yet, before it all fell apart, there must have been good living here, before the mistrust, the hunger, the fear, the bad times. Living in these sunshine-streaked canyons must have been infinitely preferable to being a serf in rainy, cold, miserable England!

My favorite site, up a close-walled side canyon, gives me just that feeling of time in the sun. Nothing here has been excavated, stabilized, or much rearranged. Very large pieces of pottery suggest that this site is still comparatively unvisited, and I sit here with a sense of time uninterrupted between then and now. There are no peephole walls here, no inaccessible ledges, no sense of threat or uneasiness, no attempt to prevent entrance, but just a low, sloping rock pavement for children to run on, a bench to sit on, a place to make pottery, a wall on which to cut petroglyphs, and perhaps, even a place to dream.

To reach this site we contour up a gentle sandstone slope at whose foot is a permanent spring. The sandstone, richly crossbedded, curves up to floor a wide, generous ledge. A V in the rock forms a trough across which remnants of a small check dam remain. If it was built up to the lip of the pour-off, a considerable reservoir of water would have been impounded, right on the doorstep.

Rising above this terrace is a sheer sandstone wall, a lovely warm beige. Within it is a small overhang. At the dripline of the overhang a strawberry cactus blooms, flowers a rich, velvety red, petals gilded with pollen, forecasting sweet-tasting "pitayas," the fruit that tastes like strawberries. A small conical granary is cosseted against the back wall. The imprint of the slab door still shows in the mudded door frame, which is spun with shining cobwebs that shimmer at my breath. Another small masonry room is still partially roofed, half-filled with a pack rat's nest. It is attached to a slab granary, constructed with big flat stones laid on edge, characteristic of Basketmaker construction. It must have been difficult to get them balanced this way, but it was done and done well. The topmost flagstone leans against a jag in the rock roof that holds it solid.

Where the floor of the overhang slopes downward, a low ledge of rock provides a comfortable place to sit, even and level. Seated here, beneath the overhang, I look out to the terrace—full of piñon and juniper, bluegrass stems shining in the morning breeze, daisies in bloom among yellow parsley, big frowzy bushes of sagebrush, narrow-leafed yucca, buffaloberry; yellow evening primroses as big as teacups, brilliant scarlet paintbrush and rice grass and Mormon tea—a lovely warm crescent filled with glorious blooming, and beyond, the green treetops of the draw below. Oriented to the sun, this terrace is an April garden. Here, more than anywhere else, I have the feeling of an open, warm, peaceful world, of sunlit living that was industrious and useful and satisfying to those who lived here.

The flagstone granary and the gray pottery sherds, of a type known as Chapin Gray, indicate this overhang was occupied early; the masonry, that it was occupied for a long time. A sherd sits heavy in my hand, a good quarter inch thick, only crudely smoothed. Because the temper was coarse, irregular pieces were dragged across the surface during smoothing, leaving tiny triangular troughs. I hold the sherd flat in one hand and rub the surface, feeling what an ancient potter knew.

Sitting on this low bench, legs out straight, sun warm on ankles and knees, I too dream. I think probably I would have been a potmaker had I lived then, grinding the clay, winnowing the clay particles in this reliable breeze, pulverizing the temper, mixing it all with water until it felt just right to the hand, letting it age, then this morning, a good morning to make a jar, waiting for the sunshine to creep closer to warm my hands so I could work more easily. While I wait, I go down to the spring and fill my gourd dipper with water. While waiting one works. I waste nothing. Not even time.

I would take up the basket my mother made, of such fine weaving, in which I once gathered plants and carried them home, but now so worn. So worn. Good now only for holding the beginning pot. I don't even know how to make as fine a basket anymore. I set it firmly on the ground, in a little depression, and pat out a disk to fit in the center.

Next I fashion a coil, not too thick, not too thin, rolling it to evenness between my palms. As my mother taught me. It fits around the base and I pinch it on carefully, being sure the joining is firm. I form another coil and add it, in a ring, pinching it carefully and neatly. As my mother taught me. When it is hand deep, I take my mother's piece of gourd and, holding one hand against the outer wall, scrape the inside wall smooth. I dampen my fingers and rub them over the concave interior. I want it to be very smooth, this pot. To be even. To go on the fire and not crack. Then the outside—but no, the jar says no, wait.

I feel the satisfaction of the form taking shape between my hands. I look out over the terrace, everything visible, everything lucid. My world within these comforting walls, behind this screen of juniper. I pinch the last coil on. Again I take the piece of gourd my mother used to finish the smoothing. Then something in the pot speaks to me. Speaks to my hands. Along each coil I press the clay between thumb and forefinger, making a crimp, and another, until I have gone around once, and then another row, and another, trying to align each tiny pointed scallop with the one below, winding it upward, filling the whole surface with a fine-shadowed crosshatching. Such a pleasure in the doing.

And I feel joy. I might have no word for "joy" but that is what I know. Contentment. The pot will be good and useful. Easy to hold on to, firm in the hands. Good to look at. I set it aside to dry.

The day is beautiful. There is a little clay left. I waste nothing. With happiness in my fingers, I begin another bowl, a tiny one. As my mother taught me. ■

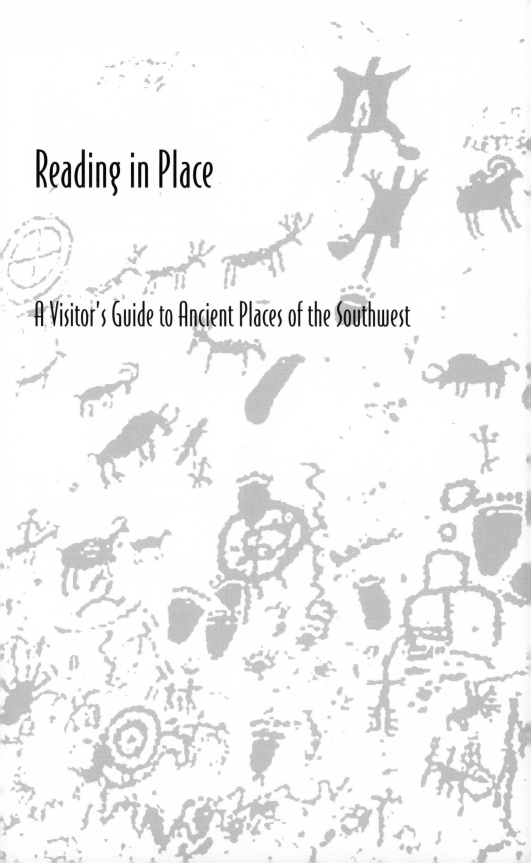

Reading in Place

A Visitor's Guide to Ancient Places of the Southwest

Visiting with Respect

Ed Abbey's advice, in *The Journey Home,* about visiting the desert is simple and to the point. "Stay out of there," he suggests. "Don't go. Stay home and read a good book, this one for example." I understand his point. It defines the dilemma of anyone committed to the preservation of wilderness: Should I simply discourage people from discovering the wilderness and keep at least *their* feet off the land, or should I encourage people to go in the hope that the experience will nurture their love and care for wild places?

The same hard choice faces anyone writing about the delicate and sacred sites of the ancestral Puebloans. I clearly have made my decision, but doing so I place a trust with you, the reader. A visit to an ancient ruin can be an educational and personally enriching experience, but it can also be potentially destructive. The way you walk, the way you behave, can be of crucial importance. I'm not suggesting some sort of artificial display of reverence here but rather simple care. At an ancient site, every step you take invites soil erosion. A human step can accelerate the effects of gravity, the force that finally brings down all structures built by men and women. I believe that if you keep in mind the guidelines I suggest here, your visit to ancient sites will be more rewarding to you because you will be participating in their ongoing life.

1. *Know the context.* Remember that you are walking on the land and in the homeland of indigenous people who consider the broken walls of ruins and the artifacts of their ancestors spiritually alive. Consider yourself a guest.

2. *Learn.* If the ancient sites of the Southwest are new to you, take the time to understand their significance. Visit the more carefully protected sites first—places like Mesa Verde, Navajo National Monument, Hovenweep, and Chaco. Go with a ranger on a guided tour. Supplement your experience with reading.

3. *Consider your approach.* As you enter a ruin site, stay on the trails that have already been established. Many alcove and cliff sites are entered through their most fragile areas, the middens, or talus-covered trash heaps, just downhill from the buildings. Middens contain valuable evidence of the daily life of the indigenous inhabitants. In many cases they are burial places for the dead. Avoid middens if possible, or at least follow the most obvious trails of those who have visited before you.

4. *Look at the walls.* Leaning, standing, or sitting on walls inevitably hastens their deterioration and literal fall.

5. *Leave artifacts where you find them.* These objects belong to the living ancestors of the men and women who made them. They are not free for the taking. Furthermore, displacing a piece of pottery or a flaked scrap of stone makes it unintelligible to those who study the site from a scientific perspective. Do not add to the arrangements of artifacts placed on "museum rocks" by previous visitors.

6. *Camp somewhere else.* Don't camp within the ruins. Sure, you have read about people doing it, but we know better. The activity of camp life erodes these fragile sites. Smoke from a modern campfire can destroy the possibility of scientists radiocarbon-dating a site. Established camping spots outside the ruins are available.

7. *Look at the rock art.* There is a good reason why the *Mona Lisa* remains behind a protective shield. The same reason applies to the pictographs and petroglyphs at ancient sites. Don't touch them, don't chalk them, and don't make rubbings of them. The oils from human skin encourage erosion of petroglyphs and degrade the pigments of pictographs.

8. *Document and preserve historic inscriptions.* The names and dates left in bullet lead and charcoal by early explorers and scientists are often the only means of retracing the routes of early expeditions and hence of matching artifacts housed in museums with their original locations.

9. *Be aware of the actions of others.* Encourage other visitors to have the same respect for ancient sites that you have. Don't hesitate to report acts of vandalism to the appropriate land management agency as soon as you witness them. Vandalism is a serious and widespread crime—the problem is severe enough that you should pay attention to names, faces, and license plate numbers if you suspect something criminal is going on.

10. *Become involved.* Government agencies are always making important decisions involving the preservation of ancient sites and are often required by law to seek public response. In this era of shrinking government, there are opportunities for volunteer work in the interest of preservation. Consider contacting such public advocacy groups as the Southern Utah Wilderness Association and the Grand Canyon Trust, both of which work toward the preservation of Puebloan sites.

Visit with respect.

Sites Mentioned
in *Stories and Stone*

Several of the writers included in this collection refer to the ancient Puebloans of the Southwest in a general cultural sense or otherwise do not make reference to specific, identifiable sites. Those sites that are mentioned by name are listed here, along with the writers in whose work the sites appear. An author index follows.

Bandelier National Monument
(Austin, Bandelier, Lummis, Ortiz, Saner, Waters)
Located in the Jemez Mountains near Los Alamos, New Mexico, Bandelier is forty-six miles west of Santa Fe. To reach Bandelier from Santa Fe, drive north on U.S. 285 to Pojoaque, then west on New Mexico 502 across the Rio Grande River toward Los Alamos to the junction with New Mexico 4. Proceed south on New Mexico 4 for twenty-four miles to the monument entrance. You will quickly drop down into Frijoles Canyon, and Tyuonyi Ruins is a quick stroll from the Visitor's Center. Camping is available in the monument. Permits are required for backcountry travel. For information, call (505) 672-3861.

Barrier Canyon Pictographs (Momaday)
You almost can't get there from here. Barrier Canyon, more frequently called Horseshoe Canyon, is located in a remote district of Canyonlands National Park in southeastern Utah. To reach the canyon, leave Interstate 70 at exit 147, west of Green River, Utah. Travel south on Utah 24 approximately twenty-three miles to a marked turnoff. Proceed east on rough dirt roads to the rim of the canyon. The Great Gallery, described by Momaday, is a vigorous hike down into (and back up again) the canyon from the end of the road. Camping is not allowed in the canyon. Be sure to consult Canyonlands National Park for more specific information: (801) 259-7164.

Bright Angel Pueblo (Powell)
See Grand Canyon National Park.

Cañon (Rita) de los Frijoles (Austin, Bandelier, Lummis, Saner, Waters)
See Bandelier National Monument.

Canyon de Chelly National Monument (Morris)
Canyon de Chelly is located in northeastern Arizona, on the Navajo Indian Reservation east of the town of Chinle. To reach the monument from Interstate 40, leave the Interstate at Chambers and follow U.S. 191 north approximately seventy-five miles to Chinle. Follow the signs to the entrance. For information, call (520) 674-5436.

Casa Grande Ruins National Monument (Kino)
Casa Grande is located east of Interstate 10 about halfway between Phoenix and Tucson and one mile north of the town of Coolidge. To reach Casa Grande from Tucson, drive north on Interstate 40 to Exit 211 and north on Arizona 87 through Coolidge to the monument. To reach Casa Grande from Phoenix, take Interstate 10 south to Exit 185, follow Arizona 187 six miles to the junction with Arizona 87, and proceed eleven miles to the monument entrance. For information, call (520) 723-3172.

Casas Grandes (Casteneda)
These ruins lie just outside the town of Nuevo Casas Grandes in Chihuahua, Mexico, a 180-mile drive south of the international border at El Paso and Ciudad Juarez. To reach Casas Grandes, take the Mexican "Christopher Columbus" Federal Highway 45 south to Mexico 2. Follow Mexico 2 west to the junction with Highway 10, and drive south on Highway 10 to the ruins.

Chaco Culture National Historical Park
(Benally, Foster, Gregg, Simpson, Vizenor, Williams)
West of the Jemez Mountains in northwestern New Mexico, Chaco lies north of Interstate 40 and south of New Mexico 44 on New Mexico 57. To reach Chaco from Interstate 40, turn north on New Mexico 57 at Thoreau and drive sixty-four miles to the park entrance. To reach Chaco from New Mexico 44, turn south at Blanco Trading Post on New Mexico 57 and follow the signs for twenty-three miles. From both directions most of New Mexico 57 is graded dirt, and conditions can vary from dusty washboard to muddy and slick depending on the season. There is no lodging in the park. Camping space is limited during the busy spring season. For information, call (505) 786-7014.

Chetro Ketl (Benally)
See Chaco Culture National Historical Park.

Chinle Wash (Hillerman, Walka)
Chinle Wash is a seasonal tributary of the San Juan River in southeastern Utah and enters the river between Bluff and Mexican Hat, Utah. The wash is on Navajo land on the south side of the river and is accessible only from the river. It is best to enter in the company of professional river guides, who stay current on access policies. For information, call Wild Rivers Expeditions: (800) 422-7654.

Grand Canyon National Park (Fletcher, Powell)
Following the Colorado River in northwestern Arizona, the park can be reached from the south by taking Interstate 40 west of Flagstaff to Arizona 64 at Williams. Follow Arizona 64 north to Grand Canyon Village. To reach the park from the north, take U.S. 89 south from Page to Alternate U.S. 89. Follow Alternate U.S. 89 west to Arizona 67 and drive south to the North Rim. The North Rim is closed from about mid-October to mid May. The Bright Angel Ruins are several thousand feet below the North Rim and accessible only by foot, horseback, or the river. Bright Angel Pueblo lies at the bottom of the canyon close to the Kaibab Trail and the Kaibab Footbridge over the river. Limited camping and overnight accommodations are available at Phantom Ranch, less than a mile away. Reservations are required. The Nankoweap site described by Fletcher is very remote and accessible from the river or the Tonto Trail. Contact park headquarters for information: (520) 638-7888.

Grand Gulch Primitive Area (Fleck, Hucko, M. Wetherill, Zwinger)
Grand Gulch lies south of Natural Bridges National Monument and north of Monument Valley in southeastern Utah. To reach Grand Gulch, drive west on Utah 95 from Blanding or north on Utah 261 from Mexican Hat to the Kane Gulch Ranger Station on Utah 261, six miles south of the junction of Utah 261 and Utah 95. Grand Gulch is a designated Primitive Area and is accessible by foot via trailheads at Kane Gulch and nearby Bullet Canyon. Register and obtain information about weather conditions at the Kane Gulch Ranger Station. Advanced reservations may be required for larger groups. Junction Ruin, at the confluence of Kane and Grand Gulches, is about a four-mile hike from the ranger station. Perfect Kiva is eighteen miles from the Kane Gulch trailhead, four and a half miles from the Bullet Canyon trailhead. For information, call (801) 587-2141.

Fitzmaurice Ruin (Barnett)

Fitzmaurice Ruin is located six miles east of Prescott, Arizona, on the south bank of Lynx Creek in Agua Fria Canyon. It is on private property currently owned by the Fain Cattle and Land Company, and as of the time of this writing public access is not encouraged in the interest of preservation. Plans by the Fain family are currently underway, however, to deed the ruin and surrounding area to the city of Prescott as a park, and an on-site museum is planned.

Hopi Mesas Area (Yava)

There are several ruin sites located on the Hopi Indian Reservation in northeastern Arizona, including Kawaikuh, Sikyatki, and Kokopnyama, but they are not necessarily accessible to the public. For more information, contact the Hopi Cultural Preservation Office at (520) 734-2244.

Hovenweep National Monument (Austin)

Hovenweep lies along the Utah-Colorado state line west of Cortez, Colorado. To reach the monument headquarters at the Square Tower Group, leave U.S. 191 eleven miles south of Blanding and follow Utah 262 generally east, leaving the highway to follow signs toward Hatch Trading Post and to the monument some ten miles beyond. Much of the road is unpaved. Because there is no telephone at the headquarters, for information call Mesa Verde National Park at (970) 529-4461.

Mesa Verde National Park
(Austin, Chapin, Ingersoll, McNitt, Nordenskiold, Nusbaum, R. Wetherill)

Close to the Four Corners in the southwestern part of Colorado, Mesa Verde National Park is on U.S. 160 ten miles east of Cortez, Colorado, and thirty-six miles west of Durango. From the park entrance at the base of the mesa, proceed twenty-one miles south on a winding road to the park headquarters and museum. Camping is available within the park at Morefield Campground (reservations recommended). For information, call (970) 529-4461 or (970) 529-4475.

Montezuma Castle National Monument (Austin)

This highly accessible site is located in central Arizona just east of Interstate 17, and about fifty miles south of Flagstaff. To reach Montezuma Castle, leave the interstate at Exit 289 and follow the signs to the entrance. For information, call (520) 567-5276.

Navajo National Monument (Judd)

The monument is located in northeastern Arizona near the town of Kayenta. To reach it, follow U.S. 160 west from Kayenta to Arizona 564. If traveling from the west, follow U.S. 160 east from Tuba City, Arizona. From U.S. 160, take Arizona 564 about nine miles to the entrance on the rim of Tsegi Canyon. The major ruins of Betatakin and Kiet Siel are accessible only by foot, and access to Kiet Siel is carefully controlled. Betatakin is visible across Tsegi Canyon at the end of a short trail leading from the Visitor's Center. Camping is available in the monument. For information, call (520) 672-2366.

Perfect Kiva (Fleck, Zwinger)
See Grand Gulch.

Pueblo Bonito (Foster, Gregg, Vizenor, Williams)
See Chaco Culture National Historical Park.

Quarai Ruins (Baca)

The Quarai Unit of the Salinas Pueblo Missions National Monument is located east of the Manzano Mountains and east of Interstate 25, south of Albuquerque, New Mexico. To reach the ruins, leave the interstate at Exit 175 and travel east on U.S. 60 to Mountainair. Turn north on New Mexico 55 and drive eight miles to the ruins. For information, call (505) 847-2290.

Tyuonyi (Lummis)
See Bandelier National Monument.

Ute Mountain Tribal Park (Clark)

The park, on the Ute Mountain Indian Reservation in southwestern Colorado, lies south of Cortez near Mesa Verde National Park. Access to the ruins in the park is by guided tour only. Tours leave from the town of Towaoc, twelve miles south of Cortez on U.S. 666. Advance reservations are recommended. For information, call (970) 565-3751, ext. 282.

Village of the Great Kivas (Alvarado, Cushing)

Village of the Great Kivas is located on the Zuni Indian Reservation in west-central New Mexico, thirty-five miles south of Interstate 40. Permission to visit the site must be obtained from the Zuni Tribal Office. Call in advance: (505) 782-4481 or (505) 782-4814.

Walnut Canyon National Monument (Cather)

Walnut Canyon is located seven miles east of Flagstaff, Arizona, just off Interstate 40. To reach the monument, leave the interstate at Exit 204 and drive three miles south to the entrance. Most of the accessible ruin sites are found along a short trail that drops down into the canyon from the Visitor's Center. For information, call (520) 526-3367.

An Index to Sites by Author

Powell:	Grand Canyon National Park
Saner:	Bandelier National Monument
Vizenor:	Chaco Culture National Historical Park
Walka:	Chinle Wash
Waters:	Bandelier National Monument
Wetherill, M.:	Grand Gulch Primitive Area
Wetherill, R.	Mesa Verde National Park
Williams:	Chaco Culture National Historical Park
Yava:	Hopi Mesas Area
Zwinger:	Grand Gulch Primitive Area

References

Bakeless, John. *America as Seen By Its First Explorers.* New York: Dover, 1961.

Boas, Franz. Quoted in Mordecai Specktor. Review of *The Book of Medicines,* by Linda Hogan, *Blood Thirsty Savages,* by Adrian Louis, and *Battlefields and Burial Grounds: The Indian Struggle to Protect Ancestral Graves in the United States,* by Roger C. Echo-Hawk and Walter R. Echo-Hawk. *The Circle* 15 (November 1994).

Chavez, Martin. Quoted in "Petroglyphs Hold Up Highway." *Wind River News* 18 (February 1995).

Cook-Lynn, Elizabeth. "Who Gets to Tell the Stories?" *Wicazo Sa Review* 9.1 (1993).

Echo-Hawk, Roger C., and Walter R. Echo-Hawk. Quoted in Mordecai Specktor. Review of *The Book of Medicines,* by Linda Hogan, *Blood Thirsty Savages,* by Adrian Louis, and *Battlefields and Burial Grounds: The Indian Struggle to Protect Ancestral Graves in the United States,* by Roger C. Echo-Hawk and Walter R. Echo-Hawk. *The Circle* 15 (November 1994).

Hucko, Bruce. "What's in a Name?" Unpublished essay, n.d.

Jameson, Frederic. Introduction to *The Historical Novel,* by George Lukacs. Lincoln: University of Nebraska Press, 1983.

Miller, Henry. *Big Sur and the Oranges of Hieronymus Bosch.* New York: New Directions, 1957.

Naranjo, Tessie. Interview by author. 23 December 1995.

Waters, Frank. "Crucible of Conflict." *New Mexico Quarterly Review* 18.3 (1948).

Wetherill, Benjamin Alfred. *The Wetherills of the Mesa Verde: The Autobiography of Benjamin Alfred Wetherill.* Edited by Maurine S. Fletcher. Cranberry, N.J.: Associated University Press, 1977.

Williams, Terry Tempest. *Pieces of White Shell.* New York: Scribners, 1983.

White, Richard. *It's Your Misfortune and None of My Own: A New History of the American West.* Norman: University of Oklahoma Press, 1991.

A Selected Bibliography of Primary Anasazi References

Abbey, Edward. "The Great American Desert." In *The Journey Home*. New York: Dutton, 1977.

Alvarado, Hernando de. "Relacion de lo que Hernando de Alvarado y Fray Joan de Padilla descubrieron en demanda de la Mar del Sur, agosto de 1540." Translated by George Parker Winship. In *Coronado: Knight of Pueblos and Plains*, by Herbert E. Bolton. Albuquerque: University of New Mexico Press, 1949.

Austin, Mary. "The Days of Our Ancients." *Survey* 53 (1924): 33–59.

———. "The Indivisible Utility." *Survey* 55 (1925–1926): 301–306; 327.

Baca, Jimmy Santiago. *Martin and Meditations on the South Valley*. New York: New Directions, 1986.

Baldwin, Gordon C. *The Ancient Ones: Basketmakers and Cliff Dwellers of the Southwest*. New York: Norton, 1963.

Bandelier, Adolf. *The Southwestern Journals of Adolph F. Bandelier, 1883–1884*. Albuquerque: University of New Mexico Press, 1970.

———. *The Delight Makers: A Novel of Prehistoric Pueblo Indians*. 1890. Reprint, San Diego: Harcourt, 1971.

Barnett, Franklin. *Crooked Arrow: A Novel of Southwestern Prehistoric Indians of the 13th. Century*. Tempe, Ariz.: Beaumaris Books, 1977.

Benally, Clyde, et al. *Dinéjí Nákéé Nááhané: A Utah Navajo History*. Monticello, Utah: San Juan School District, 1982.

Bickford, F. T. "Prehistoric Cave-Dwellings." *Century Magazine* 40 (October 1890).

Bird, Leonard. "The Wall." In *River of Lost Souls*. Guadalapita, N. Mex.: Tooth of Time Press, n.d.

Brandi, John. "At Mesa Verde." In *That Back Road*. N.p.: Wingbow Press, n.d.

Burroughs, William S. *The Place of Dead Roads*. New York: Holt, 1983.

Castaneda, Pedro de. *The Coronado Expedition, 1540–1542*. Translated by George Parker Winship. Chicago: Rio Grande, 1964.

Cather, Willa. *The Professor's House*. New York: Knopf, 1927.

———. *The Song of the Lark*. 1915. Boston: Houghton Mifflin, 1983.

Chapin, Frederick. *The Land of the Cliff Dwellers*. 1892. Tucson: University of Arizona Press, 1988.

Clark, H. Jackson. *The Owl in Monument Canyon and Other Stories from Indian Country*. Salt Lake City: University of Utah Press, 1993.

Cummings, Byron and Louisa Wade Wetherill. "A Navajo Folk Tale of Pueblo Bonito." *Art and Archaeology* 14 (1922).

Cushing, Frank Hamilton. *Zuni: Selected Writings of Frank Hamilton Cushing*. Lincoln: University of Nebraska Press, 1979.

Davis, Larry. "Sounds." In *Coyote's Canyon*, by Terry Tempest Williams. Salt Lake City: Gibbs M. Smith, 1989.

Dellenbaugh, Frederick S. *A Canyon Voyage*. 1908. Reprint, New Haven: Yale University Press, 1962.

Deuel, Leo. *Conquistadores Without Swords: Archaeologists in the Americas*. New York: St. Martin's, 1967.

Dobie, Frank J. *Coronado's Children: Tales of Lost Mines and Buried Treasures of the Southwest*. New York: Grossett and Dunlap, 1930.

The Dominguez-Escalante Journal. Edited by Ted J. Warner. Translated by Fray Angelico Chavez. Provo, Utah: Brigham Young University Press, 1976.

Eastlake, William. *The Bronc People*. Albuquerque: University of New Mexico Press, 1957.

Edgerton, Clyde. *Redeye: A Western*. Chapel Hill, N.C.: Algonquin Books, 1995.

Emory, William H. *Notes of a Military Reconnaissance from Fort Leavenworth in Missouri to San Diego in California, etc.* U.S. Senate Document 7, 30th Cong., 1848.

Estabrook, Emma Franklin. *Ancient Lovers of Peace*. Boston: privately printed, 1959.

Fletcher, Colin. *The Man who Walked Through Time*. New York: Knopf, 1968.

Font, Pedro. *Font's Complete Diary. A Chronicle of the Founding of San Francisco*. Edited and translated by Herbert E. Bolton. Berkeley: University of California Press, 1933.

Foster, Joseph. *D. H. Lawrence in Taos*. Albuquerque: University of New Mexico Press, 1972.

Fergusson, Edna. *Dancing Gods: Indian Ceremonials of New Mexico and Arizona*. 1931. Reprint, Albuquerque: University of New Mexico Press, 1970.

Frost, Robert. "A Missive Missile." In *The Complete Poems of Robert Frost*. New York: Holt, 1936.

Gregg, Josiah. *The Commerce of the Prairies*. 1844. Edited by Max L. Moorhead. Reprint, Norman: University of Oklahoma Press, 1954.

Hewett, Edgar L. *The Chaco Canyon and Its Monuments*. Albuquerque: University of New Mexico Press, 1936.

Hillerman, Tony. *A Thief of Time*. New York: Harper, 1988.

Hogan, Linda. "Ruins." In *Eclipse*. Los Angeles: American Indian Studies Center, 1983.

Howe, Sherman. *My Story of the Aztec Ruins*. Farmington, N. Mex.: Times Hustler Press, 1947.

Hucko, Bruce. "Cave to Cave—Canyon to Canyon: Photographing the Wetherill–Grand Gulch Research Project." In *Anasazi Basketmaker: Papers from the 1990 Wetherill–Grand Gulch Symposium*, edited by Victoria M. Atkins. Salt Lake City: U.S. Department of the Interior, Bureau of Land Management, 1993.

Ingersoll, Ernest. *The Crest of the Continent*. Chicago: R. R. Donnelley, 1995.

Jackson, William Henry. *Time Exposure: The Autobiography of William Henry Jackson*. New York: G. P. Putnam's Sons, 1940.

Judd, Neil M. *Men Met Along the Trail: Adventures in Archaeology*. Norman: University of Oklahoma Press, 1968.

Kino, Eusebio Francisco. *Kino's Historical Memoir of Pimeria Alta*. Edited and translated by Herbert E. Bolton. Cleveland: Arthur H. Clark, 1919.

Krutch, Joseph Wood. *Grand Canyon: Today and All Its Yesterdays*. New York: William Sloane, 1958.

La Farge, Oliver. *Laughing Boy*. 1929. Cambridge: Houghton Mifflin, 1957.

L'Amour, Louis. *The Haunted Mesa*. Toronto: Bantam, 1988.

Lomatewama, Ramson. "They Told Stories." In *Drifting Through Ancestor Dreams: New and Selected Poems*. Flagstaff, Ariz.: Entrada Books, 1993.

Lopez, Barry. "The Blue Mound People." In *Desert Notes: Reflections in the Eye of a Raven*. New York: Avon, 1976.

Lummis, Charles F. *Some Strange Corners of Our Country*. New York: Century, 1892.

———. *The Land of Poco Tiempo*. 1893. Reprint, Albuquerque: University of New Mexico Press, 1966.

McNickle, D'Arcy. *Runner in the Sun: A Story of Indian Maize*. 1954. Reprint, Albuquerque: University of New Mexico Press, 1987.

McNitt, Frank. *Richard Wetherill—Anasazi: Pioneer Explorer of Southwestern Ruins*. Albuquerque: University of New Mexico Press, 1957.

Momaday, N. Scott. *House Made of Dawn*. New York: Harper and Row, 1968.

———. "The Native Voice." In *Columbia Literary History of the United States*, edited by Emory Elliott. New York: Columbia University Press, 1988.

Morris, Ann Axtell. *Digging in the Southwest*. New York: Doubleday, Doran, 1940.

Morris, Earl H. "An Unexplored Area of the Southwest." *Natural History* (November–December 1922).

Nordenskiöld, Gustaf. *Letters of Gustaf Nordenskiöld*. Edited by Irving L. Diamond and Daniel M. Olson. Mesa Verde National Park, Colorado: Mesa Verde Museum Association, 1991.

Nusbaum, Jesse. *Tierra Dulce: Reminiscences from the Jesse Nusbaum Papers*. Edited by Rosemary Nusbaum. Santa Fe, N. Mex.: Sunstone, 1980.

Ortiz, Simon. *Woven Stone*. Tucson: University of Arizona Press, 1992.

Peterson, Levi S. "The Canyons of Grace." In *Canyons of Grace*. Urbana: University of Illinois Press, 1982.

Powell, John Wesley. *The Exploration of the Colorado River and its Canyons*. 1895. Reprint, New York: Dover, 1961.

Pratt, Harry Noyce. "The Seven Cities of Cibola." *Literary Digest* 106 (July 1930): 34.

Priestley, J. B., and Jacquetta Hawkes. *Journey Down a Rainbow*. New York: Harper and Brothers, 1955.

Prudden, Mitchell T. "An Elder Brother to the Cliff Dwellers." *Harper's New Monthly Magazine* (June 1987): 56–62.

Reisner, Marc. *Cadillac Desert: The American West and Its Disappearing Water*. New York: Penguin, 1986.

Rollins-Griffin, Ramona. *Chaco Canyon Ruins: Ancient Spirits Were Our Neighbors*. Flagstaff, Ariz.: Northland, 1971.

Rose, Wendy. *Bone Dance*. Tucson: University of Arizona Press, 1994.

Saner, Reg. *The Four-Cornered Falcon: Essays on the Interior West and the Natural Scene*. Baltimore: Johns Hopkins University Press, 1993.

Silko, Leslie Marmon. "Landscape, History, and the Pueblo Imagination." *Antaeus* 57 (1986).

Simpson, James H. *Journal of a Military Reconnaissance from Santa Fe, New Mexico to the Navajo Country*. 1849. Reprint, Norman: University of Oklahoma Press, 1964.

Snyder, Gary. *Turtle Island*. New York: New Directions, 1974.

Stegner, Wallace. *Beyond the Hundredth Meridian: John Wesley Powell and the Second Opening of the West*. Lincoln: University of Nebraska Press, 1982.

Vizenor, Gerald. *Bearheart: The Heirship Chronicles*. Minneapolis: University of Minnesota Press, 1990.

Walka, Ann Weiler. *Waterlines: Journeys on a Desert River*. Flagstaff, Ariz.: Red Lake Books, 1993.

Waters, Frank. *The Woman at Otowi Crossing*. Chicago: Sage-Swallow, 1966.

————. *The Book of the Hopi.* 1963. New York: Penguin, 1977.

Watson, Don. *Indians of Mesa Verde.* Mesa Verde National Park: Mesa Verde Museum Association, 1961.

Wetherill, Benjamin A. *The Wetherills of Mesa Verde: Autobiography of Benjamin Alfred Wetherill.* Edited by Maurine S. Fletcher. Cranberry, N.J.: Associated University Press, 1977.

Wetherill, Marietta. *Marietta Wetherill: Reflections on Life with the Navajos in Chaco Canyon.* Edited by Kathryn Gabriel. Boulder, Colo.: Johnson Books, 1992.

Wetherill, Richard. "The Cliff Dwellings of the Mesa Verde." *Mancos Times,* August 1895.

Williams, Terry Tempest. *Pieces of White Shell: A Journey to Navojoland.* New York: Scribners, 1983.

————. *Coyote's Canyon.* Salt Lake City: Gibbs M. Smith, 1989.

Yava, Albert. *Big Falling Snow: A Tewa-Hopi Indian's Life and Times and the History and Traditions of His People.* Edited by Harold Courlander. Albuquerque: University of New Mexico Press, 1978.

Zwinger, Ann. *Wind in the Rock: The Canyonlands of Southeastern Utah.* Tuscon: University of Arizona Press, 1978.

Credits

The Days of Our Ancients: *Imagining the Lives of the Anasazi*

N. Scott Momaday, from "The Native Voice" in *Columbia Literary History of the United States*, Emory Elliott, ed. (New York: Columbia University Press, 1988). Copyright © 1988 by Columbia University Press. Reprinted by permission of the publisher.

Adolf Bandelier, from the conclusion in *The Delight Makers* (San Diego: Harcourt Brace, 1971), 485–90. Originally published in 1890.

Charles F. Lummis, from "Wanderings of Cochiti" in *The Land of Poco Tiempo* (Albuquerque: University of New Mexico Press, 1966), 137–47. Originally published in 1928. Reprinted by permission.

Mary Austin, from "The Days of Our Ancients" in *Survey* 53 (1924): 37–39. © School of American Research, Santa Fe. Reprinted by permission.

D'Arcy McNickle, from "Disaster in the Canyon" in *Runner in the Sun* (Albuquerque: University of New Mexico Press, 1987), 96–109. Originally published in 1954. Reprinted by permission.

Gary Snyder, "Anasazi" in *Turtle Island*, copyright © 1974 by Gary Snyder. Used by permission of New Directions Publishing Corp.

Franklin Barnett, from chapter 13 in *Crooked Arrow: A Novel of Southwestern Prehistoric Indians of the 13th Century* (Tempe, Ariz.: Beaumaris Books, 1977). Reprinted by permission.

Robert Frost, "A Missive Missile" in *The Poetry of Robert Frost*, Edward Connery Lathem, ed. Copyright © 1936 by Robert Frost, © 1964 by Lesley Frost Ballantine, © 1969 by Henry Holt and Co., Inc. Reprinted by permission of Henry Holt and Company, LLC.

Seven Cities of Gold: *The Findings of the Early Explorers*

Pedro de Castaneda, from *The Coronado Expedition, 1540–1542*, George Parker Winship, trans. (Chicago: Rio Grande, 1964).

Hernando de Alvarado, from "Relacion de lo que Hernando de Alvarado y Fray Joan de Padilla descubrieron en demanda de la Mar del Sur, agosto de 1540" (The Report of Hernando de Alvarado), George Parker Winship, trans., in *Coronado: Knight of Pueblos and Plains*, by Herbert E. Bolton (Albuquerque: University of New Mexico Press, 1949). Used by permission.

Eusebio Francisco Kino, from *Kino's Historical Memoir of Pimeria Alta*, 2 vols., Herbert E. Bolton, ed. and trans. (Cleveland: Arthur H. Clark, 1919).

Josiah Gregg, from chapter XV in *The Commerce of the Prairies*, Max L. Moorehead, ed. (Norman: University of Oklahoma Press, 1954). Copyright © 1954 by the University of Oklahoma Press. Used by permission.

John Wesley Powell, from "To the Foot of the Grand Canyon" in *The Exploration of the Colorado River and Its Tributaries* (New York: Dover, 1961), 259–60. Originally published in 1895.
Ernest Ingersoll, from *The Crest of the Continent* (Chicago: R. R. Donnelley, 1885), 160–63.
Frederick H. Chapin, from chapter XVI, "The Mesa Verde," in *The Land of the Cliff Dwellers* (Tucson: The University of Arizona Press, 1988). Originally published in 1892.

Digging into Antiquity: *Archaeology, Excavation, and Discovery*

Frank McNitt, from *Richard Wetherill—Anasazi: Pioneer Explorer of Southwestern Ruins* (Albuquerque: University of New Mexico Press, 1957), 21–27. Reprinted by permission.
Richard Wetherill, from a letter to F. W. Putnam, April 7, 1890. Reprinted courtesy of the Harvard University Archives.
Frank Hamilton Cushing, from "Life at Zuni," Frank Hamilton Cushing Manuscript Collection, folder #MS.6.BAE.4.4 (Los Angeles: Southwest Museum, Braun Research Library).
Gustaf Nordenskiöld, Letter No. 24 to his father in *Letters of Gustaf Nordenskiöld*, Irving L. Diamond, ed., Daniel M. Olson, trans. (Mesa Verde, Colo.: Mesa Verde Museum Association, 1991). Reprinted by permission.
Ann Axtell Morris, from "An Airplane" in *Digging in the Southwest* (New York: Doubleday Doran, 1940), 224–30.
Neil M. Judd, from "Betatakin and the Clay Hills" in *Men Met Along the Trail: Adventures in Archaeology.* Copyright © 1968, University of Oklahoma Press. Reprinted by permission.
Marietta Wetherill, from "The Princess Mummy and Other Burials" in *Marietta Wetherill: Reflections on Life with the Navajos in Chaco Canyon,* Kathryn Gabriel, ed. (Boulder: Johnson Books, 1992). Copyright © 1992 Kathryn Gabriel. Reprinted by permission.
Clyde Edgerton, from "The Trail" in *Redeye: A Western* (Chapel Hill, N.C.: Algonquin Books, 1995). Copyright © 1995 by Clyde Edgerton.
Barry Holstun Lopez, "The Blue Mound People" in *Desert Notes: Reflections in the Eye of a Raven* (New York: Avon, 1976). Copyright © 1976 by Barry Holstun Lopez. Reprinted by permission of Sterling Lord Literistic, Inc.
Tony Hillerman, from *A Thief of Time* (New York: HarperCollins Publishers, 1988), 1–16. Copyright © 1988 by Tony Hillerman. Reprinted by permission of HarperCollins Publishers, Inc.

The Places They Lived: *Spending Time in the Ruins*

Harry Noyes Pratt, "The Seventh City of Cibola" in *Literary Digest* 106 (July 1930): 34.
Willa Cather, from *The Song of the Lark* (Boston: Houghton Mifflin, 1983), 367–83. Originally published in 1915.
Colin Fletcher, from *The Man Who Walked through Time,* copyright © 1967 by Colin Fletcher. Used by permission of Alfred A. Knopf, a division of Random House, Inc.
Jimmy Santiago Baca, from "Martin VII" in *Martin and Meditations on the South Valley,* copyright © 1987 by Jimmy Santiago Baca. Used by permission of New Directions Publishing Corp.
Richard F. Fleck, "Anasazi Depths," copyright © 1995 by Richard F. Fleck. All rights reserved. Printed by permission of Richard F. Fleck.

Newer Stories: *Antiquity in the Twentieth Century*

Among the Ancients: *Dwelling Within the Puebloan Homeland*